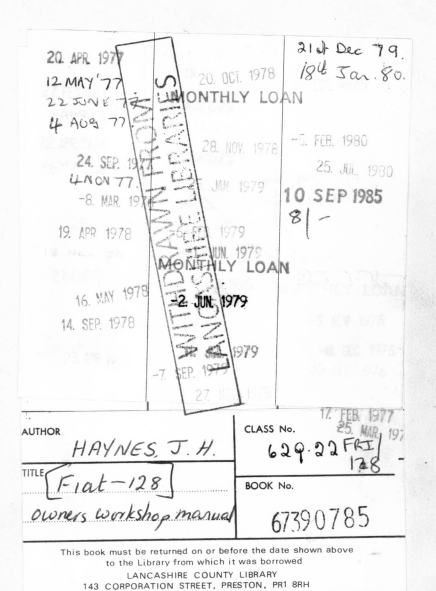

FIAT 128

Owner's Workshop Manual

by J.H.HAYNES

Associate member of the Guild of Motoring Writers

and J.C.LARMINIE

Models covered

1116 cc Saloon (Berlina)	1969 on
1116 cc Estate (Familiare)	1970 on
1290 cc Rally	1971 on
1116 cc 1100 Coupe	1972 on
1290 cc 1300 Coupe	1972 on

SBN 900550 87 2

© J H Haynes and Company Limited 1973

Sparkford, Yeovil, Somerset
Telephone North Cadbury 562

Price £2 (UK only)

Acknowledgements

The greatest help possible has been given by FIAT. Many of the drawings in this book are theirs. Their London publicity agents, Woolf, Laing, Christie and Partners, and FIAT (England) at Brentford have been most helpful.

Brian Horsfall stripped our own car, with Les Brazier taking the photographs.

Tim Parker edited the text.

About this manual

This book has been written to help an enthusiastic owner keep his car in first class condition. Even should you not want to do the work yourself, but get it done by a garage, it will give you guidance in what you need to tell them to do, and help you to understand problems that must be discussed with them. To the practical owner who works on his car himself, the book gives great detail of servicing, repairs, and fault diagnosis. Doing the job yourself can give great satisfaction, and can save the costs a garge must charge to cover their labour and overheads. It will often save time too. This book can be a great help to you because it is written after studying all the available literature, and also actually working on the car.

The book has drawings and descriptions to show the function of the various components so that their layout can be understood. Then the work is described and photographed in a step by step sequence so that even a novice can cope with complicated work.

The jobs are described assuming only normal spanners are available, and not special tools. But a good outfit of tools will be a worthwhile investment. Many special workshops tools produced by the makers merely speed the work, and in these cases we show how we did the work without them. But on a few occasions the special tool is essential to prevent damage to components. Though it might be possible to borrow the tool, such jobs will probably have to be entrusted to the official agent.

To avoid labour costs, a garage will often give a cheaper repair by fitting a reconditioned assembly. The home mechanic can be helped by this book to diagnose the fault and make a repair using only a minor spare part. The classic case is repairing a non charging dynamo by fitting new brushes.

The manufacturer's official workshop manuals are written for their trained staff, and so assuming special knowledge, detail is left out. This book is written for the owner, and so goes into detail.

The book is divided into twelve chapters. Each chapter is subdivided into numbered sections which are headed in bold type between horizontal lines. Each section consists of serially numbered paragraphs.

There are two types of illustration. There are figures numbered according to chapter and sequence of occurrence in that chapter. These figures are mainly to show how some component works or where it is. Then there are series of photographs supporting the text to make some job more easy to understand. Such photographs have a reference number, which is the revelant section and paragraphs in that chapter.

Procedures once described in the text are not normally repeated. If a cross reference is necessary it is given by chapter and section number: Thus: Chapter 1/16. A particular paragraph could be referred to by putting Chapter 1/16:3. A cross reference without the word 'Chapter' applies to the same chapter.

When the left or right side of the car is mentioned it is as if looking forward.

Great trouble has been taken to ensure that this book is complete and up to date. The manufacturers continually modify their cars. Whilst every care is taken to ensure that the information in this manual is correct no liability can be accepted by the authors or publishers for loss damage or injury caused by any errors in or omissions from the information given.

Contents

Introduction to the Fiat 128

The FIAT 128 was introduced in 1969. It has been able to benefit by lessons learned from earlier front wheel drive transverse engine cars, and has plenty of space, lively performance, good handling and comfortable suspension. So good is its performance it is easy to forget it is a cheap small family car. The ordinary Saloon (Sedan), or Berlina in Italy, is attractive to the enthusiast who might not be able to buy the more expensive Rally or Coupe versions. Another measure of this excellence is that these latter special performance models are so little altered from the standard car. The estate car (station wagon), or Familiare in Italy, provides a useful dual purpose vehicle.

The Rally and 1300 Coupe have the power increased by using an engine of enlarged cylinder bore to give 1290 cc instead of the normal 1116 cc. They also have a different camshaft, carburettor, and manifold. The Coupe has a shorter wheelbase. It does not have a front anti-roll bar.

The car is quite straight forward to work on. Accessibility is poor at the right hand side of the engine, particularly on right hand drive models prior to the move of the brake master cylinder to the left, and on cars in North Amercia fitted with the fuel vapour control system needed with other additions to meet the emissions regulations of the USA. It is a sign of the efficiency of the engine that so few modifications are needed for the USA.

General Data

	Saloon/Sedan	Estate car	Rally	Coupe (1300)
Car type	128 A	128 AF	128 AR	*128AC
Length	151.8 in (3856 mm)	As saloon	153 in (3886 mm)	150 in (3808 mm)
Width	62.6 in (1590 mm)	As saloon	62.6 in (1590 mm)	61.4 in (1560 mm)
Height (unladen) ...	55.9 in (1420 mm)	As saloon	54.7 in (1390 mm)	51.6 in (1310 mm)
Wheelbase	96.4 in (2448 mm)	As saloon	96.4 in (2448 mm)	87.5 in (2223 mrn)
Track (front)	51.49 in (1308 mm)	As saloon	51.49 in (1308 mm)	52.1 in (1325 mm)
(rear)	51.69 in (1313 mm)	As saloon	51.69 in (1313 mm)	52.5 in (1333 mm)
Ground clearance (unladen) ...	5.75 in (157 mm)	As saloon	5.7 in (145 mm)	4.5 in (115 mm)
Turning circle	33.79 ft (10.3 m)	As saloon	33.79 ft (10.3 m)	32 ft (9.75 m)
Weights: Kerb	1775 lb (805 kg)	1819 lb (825 kg)	1807 lb (820 kg)	1798 lb (816 kg)
Laden	2657 lb (1205 kg)	2766 lb (1255 kg)	2688 lb (1220 kg)	
Towable	1500 lb (680 kg)	1500 lb (680 kg)	1500 lb (680 kg)	1500 lb (680 kg)
Approximate maximum speeds:				
1st gear	28 mph (45 km/h)	25 mph (40 km/h)	28 mph (45 km/h)	28 mph (45 km/h)
2nd gear	47 mph (75 km/h)	44 mph (70 km/h)	47 mph (75 km/h)	47 mph (75 km/h)
3rd gear	71 mph (115 km/h)	65 mph (105 km/h)	74 mph (120 km/h)	74 mph (120 km/h)
4th gear	over 87 mph (140 km/h)	87 mph (140 km/h)	93 mph (150 km/h)	100 mph (160 km/h)
Maximum gradients:				
1st gear	30%	As saloon	34%	34%
4th gear	6%	As saloon	6.5%	6.5%
Acceleration:				
30 to 50 mph in top (3rd) ...	12½ secs (8 secs)	As saloon	11¾ secs (7 secs)	11 secs (6¾ secs)
50 to 70 mph in top (3rd) ...	18 secs (14 secs)	As saloon	13½ secs (9 secs)	12 secs (8½ secs)
Typical fuel consumption ...	29 mpg	29 mpg	28 mpg	29 mpg

*128AC5 for 1100 coupé

1973 4 door saloon (European specification) Inset: 1972 2 door saloon (North American specification) Note change in grill pattern and difference in lighting.

1973 2 door saloon (North American specification)

1973 Familiare — Estate/Station Wagon (European specification)

1973 Rally (European specification)

1973 1300 SL Coupe (European specification)

1973 1300 SL Coupe (North American specification)

Ordering spare parts

Parts should always be obtained from the official FIAT agent. Then they will be to the correct specification, and incorporate the appropriate modifications. It is important to give the agent the car numbers. Many modifications have been introduced in the life of the car. There are also variations in the specifications for different countries.

There is a data plate giving the type approval numbers, chassis, engine, and spare numbers. This plate is in the engine compartment, near the regulator. Nearby, closer to the mounting for the right hand suspension strut, the chassis number is stamped in the metal. The engine number is on the engine, on the left end of the cylinder block, just below the cylinder head joint, behind the thermostat.

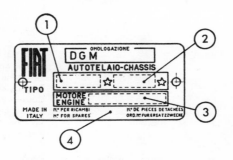

Orders for spares must give the car type, eg estate, 2 door saloon, coupe, and the details from the plate on the car:
1   Type number
2   Car number
3   Engine type
4   Number for spares

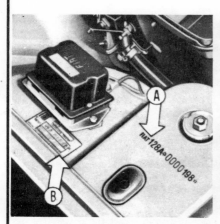

The car number is on the right mudguard

The engine number is on the left end of the block.

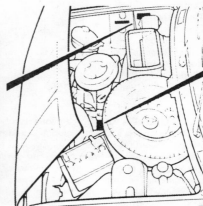

Placing of the numbers.

As this book has been written in the United Kingdom it uses the appropriate English component names. Some of these differ from those used in America. Normally this causes no difficulty. But to make sure, a glossary is printed below.

Glossary

English	American
Anti-roll bar	Stabiliser or sway bar
Bonnet (engine cover)	Hood
Boot (luggage compartment)	Trunk
Bottom gear	1st gear
Bulkhead	Firewall
Clearance	Lash
Crownwheel	Ring gear (of differential)
Catch	Latch
Camfollower or tappet	Valve lifter or tappet
Cat's eye	Road reflecting lane marker
Circlip	Snap ring
Drop arm	Pitman arm
Drop head coupe	Convertible
Dynamo	Generator (DC)
Earth (electrical)	Ground
Estate car	Station wagon
Exhaust manifold	Header
Fault finding	Trouble shooting
Free play	Lash
Free wheel	Coast
Gudgeon pin	Piston pin or wrist pin
Gearchange	Shift
Gearbox	Transmission
Hood	Soft top
Hard top	Hard top
Half shaft	Axle shaft
Hot spot	Heat riser
Leading shoe (of brake)	Primary shoe
Layshaft (of gearbox)	Counter shaft
Mudguard or wing	Fender
Motorway	Freeway, turnpike etc
Paraffin	Kerosene
Petrol	Gas
Reverse	Back-up
Saloon	Sedan
Split cotter (for valve spring cap)	Lock (for valve spring retainer)
Split pin	Cotter pin
Sump	Oil pan
Silencer	Muffler
Steering arm	Spindle arm
Side light	Parking light
Side marker light	Cat's eye
Spanner	Wrench
Tappet	Valve lifter
Tab washer	Tank; lock
Top gear	High
Transmission	Whole drive line from clutch to axle shaft
Trailing shoe (of brake)	Secondary shoe
Track rod (of steering)	Tie rod (or connecting rod)
Windscreen	Windshield

Miscellaneous points

An 'Oil seal' is fitted to components lubricated by grease!

A 'Damper' is a 'Shock absorber': it damps out bouncing, and absorbs shocks of bump impact. Both names are correct, and both are used haphazardly.

Note that British drum brakes are different from the Bendix type that is common in America, so different descriptive names result. The shoe end furthest from the hydraulic wheel cylinder is on a pivot; interconnection between the shoes as on Bendix brakes is most uncommon. Therefore the phrase 'Primary' or 'Secondary' shoe does not apply. A shoe is said to be Leading or Trailing. A 'Leading' shoe is one on which a point on the drum, as it rotates forward, reaches the shoe at the end worked by the hydraulic cylinder before the anchor end. The opposite is a trailing shoe, and this one has no self servo from the wrapping effect of the rotating drum.

The word 'Tuning' has a narrower meaning than in America, and applies to that engine servicing to ensure full power. The words 'Service' or 'Maintenance' are used where an American would say 'Tune-up'

Routine maintenance

Introduction

1 In the paragraphs that follow are detailed the routine servicing that should be done on the car. This work has the prime aim of doing adjustments and lubrication to ensure the least wear and most efficient function. But there is another important gain. By looking the car over, on top and underneath, you have the opportunity to check that all is in order.

2 Every component should be looked at, your gaze working systematically over the whole car. Dirt cracking near a nut or a flange can indicate something loose. Leaks will show. Electric cables rubbing, or rust appearing through the underneath paint will all be found before they bring on a failure on the road, or if not tackled quickly, a more expensive repair. Also it prevents the car becoming a danger to yourself or others because of an undetected defect.

3 The tasks to be done are in general those recommended by the maker. But we have also put in some additional ones which will help to keep your car in good order. For someone getting his service done at a garage it may be more cost effective to accept component replacement after a somewhat short life in order to avoid labour costs. For the home mechanic this tends not so.

4 When you are checking the car, and find something that looks wrong, look it up in the appropriate chapter. If something seems to be working badly, look in the fault-finding section.

5 Always drive the car on a road test after a repair, and then inspect the repair is holding up all right, and check nuts or hose connections for tightness. Check again after about another 150 miles.

Routine maintenance tasks

1 Every 300 miles (500 km) or weekly, if sooner

1.1 Check the engine oil level. This should be done with the car standing on level ground. Never let the oil level fall below the low mark. It should not be overfilled. Only replenish with the same type of oil as is in the sump. Use a top quality multi-grade oil.

1.2 Check the engine coolant level. The normal level can be seen in the plastics expansion tank. The rise as the engine warms up, and contraction on cooling can be seen. The radiator cap should be removed when the engine is cold. The radiator should always be found to be full. Should a suspected leak require the radiator cap to be removed when the engine is hot, it should be allowed to stand first for ten minutes to cool down. Then pressure should be released by gradually turning the filler cap, holding it down, preferably with some rag to protect the hand. Topping up should be done with the water and anti-freeze mix. It should not be necessary often. A need to do it frequently indicates the expansion tank system is not working, or there is a leak. See Chapter 2 for details of the cooling system.

1.3 Check the tyre pressures. This should be done when they are cold. After running only a few miles the pressure rises due to

the heat generated by their flexing. At highway cruising speeds this can be as much as 3 or 4 lbf/in^2. The tyre pressures cold should be:

Saloons:
Front	26 lbf/in^2	(1.8 kg/cm^2)
Rear	24 lbf/in^2	(1 7 kg/cm^2)

Estate:
Front	27 lbf/in^2	(1.9 kg/cm^2)
Rear	28 lbf/in^2	(2.0 kg/cm^2)

The rear tyres of the saloon should be inflated a further 4 lbf/in^2(0.3 kg/cm^2) if heavily laden or towing a trailer.

1.4 Check the level of the brake fluid in the hydraulic reservoir. This can be seen through the plastics. There should be no need for regular topping up: if it is needed check for leaks. See Chapter 8. Use only brake fluid to the specification SAE J 1703 or MVSS 116 DOT 3 or 4. Do not mix makes of fluid. Always use new clean fluid.

1.5 Top up the battery. Use pure water such as distilled. Top up to ½ inch above the plates, or for easy-fill batteries, the set level.

1.6 Check the engine compartment for leaks.

1.7 Check all lights are working. The brake lights can be checked by backing up close to a wall.

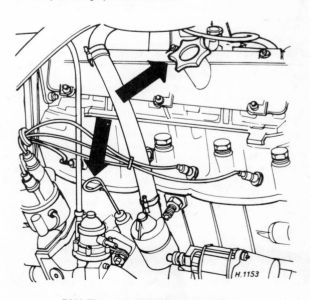

RM1 The engine oil filler and dipstick

2   Every 3,000 miles (5,000 km)

2.1   Check the tension of the 'V' belt driving the generator. The belt should be tightened so that the longest run of the belt can be pushed down ½ inch (12 mm), pressing hard with one finger. To tighten the belt slacken the pivot bolts underneath the generator. Slacken the bolt working in the slot on top, and move the generator away from the engine to tension the belt. Hold it whilst the bolt is tightened. Finally retighten the pivot underneath. A slack belt wears due to slip. Overtightening overloads the generator bearings. New belts stretch, so need checking after 100 miles.

2.2   Change the engine oil if in a cold climate, or the car is used in town for stop-start driving. When the oil is hot from a journey park the car on level ground and put a container safe for 1 gallon (9 pints in USA) under the engine. Clean around and then remove the drain plug in the centre of the sump (oil pan). A 12 mm hexagon allen key is needed. One can be made by filing the jaw of a large adjustable spanner. Allow the oil to drain for ten minutes, then clean and replace the plug. Refill with 7½ Imp pints (4¼ litres) 9 US pints of top quality multi-grade oil, normally of 20/50 viscosity. See the table of Recommended Lubricants at the end of the Routine Maintenance chapter. Do not use other additives.

2.3   Check the front brake pad thickness (see Chapter 8). Check the brake flexible pipes for rubbing, cracks or leaks. Check the condition of the rubber boots on the drive shaft inner and outer joints, and on the steering knuckle and the track rod ball joints. If they are not in perfect condition replace them at once before dirt gets in and ruins the component. Check also the condition of the component in case it is already damaged.

2.4   Check the car underneath. Jack the car up high, or run it up on blocks, if you cannot get it on a hoist. Make sure it is secure. Then crawl underneath. Check the whole car thoroughly for leaks, things damaged, or items loose. If there are seepages of oil from the engine or transmission, watch them at future checks for increase, and check their oil level as required. Items that are loose will be shown by the way dirt around them flakes. Look for signs of paint coming off, or rust, on the body, particularly where the wheels throw up dirt. If renovation is necessary refer to Chapter 12.

2.5   Check the tyres for damage. The inner side can be looked at when under the car. Look for cracks or bulges in the sides.

2.6   Top up the windscreen washer reservoir. Use a mild household detergent (washing up liquid) with the water.

2.7   In dusty conditions change the air cleaner element. See Chapter 3/6.

3   Every 6,000 miles (10,000 km) or six months if sooner

Do all the 3,000 miles tasks and in addition:-

3.1   Change the engine oil. See the preceding task 2.2.

3.2   Change the engine oil filter. Whilst the engine oil is draining, remove the front shield under the car. Put a second drain pan under the filter. Unscrew the filter. If it is tight try a chain wrench. One can be made out of a length of bicycle chain, with a screwdriver pushed through the links. If this cannot be done, hammer a steel bar through the side of the filter element and out the other, to form a 'T' handle. It is quite thin, and easily punctured. Wipe the filter seat clean. Check the new element's sealing washer is in order. Smear some engine oil on it. Then screw it in, hand tight only. When the engine has been refilled with oil, and before refitting the shield, start up, running the engine gently till the pump has filled up the new filter and got up pressure. Then check for leaks.

3.3   Change the air cleaner element. Clean the outside of the cleaner. Take off the top by undoing the three wing nuts. Lift out the old element, and throw it away. Wipe out the inside of the cleaner, but make absolutely sure no trace of dirt or piece of rag goes down the carburettor air intake. Wipe the hands clean: then fit the new element. Check the air cleaner is drawing air

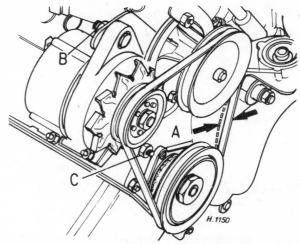

RM 2 The generator 'V' belt should yield ½ inch (12 mm). (A). Adjust at (B) after slackening pivot (C)

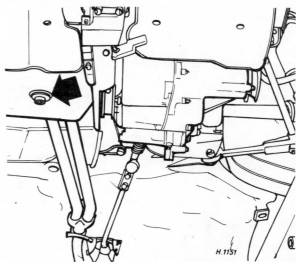

RM 3 The engine sump drain

RM4 The front sheild gives access to the oil filter

from the intake, hot or cold, appropriate to the season, then replace the top. For cars with oil bath air cleaners, see Chapter 3/6:3.

3.4   Clean and reset the contact breaker gap, to 0.014 - 0.017 in (0.37 - 0.43 mm). Lubricate the distributor. See Chapter 4/2 and 4/3.

3.5   Reset the ignition timing. See Chapter 4/4.
Europe: Set static, to 10°BTDC (1st marker on belt cover).
USA: Set by stroboscope, to TDC at 850 rpm (3rd marker on belt cover).

3.6   Clean and reset the gaps of the sparking plugs. Plugs should be cleaned using a sand blaster machine. Hand cleaning is not thorough enough. Plugs can be cleaned once, giving a total life of 12,000 miles (10,000 km). Then new ones should be fitted. The gap should be 0.020 - 0.024 in (0.5 - 0.6 mm). Adjust by bending the side contact, never the centre one. Plugs should be Champion N9Y. Bosch W200 T30, or Marelli CW240 LP.

3.7   Check the tappets. Clearance should be checked cold. Inlet 0.012 in (0.30 mm). Exhaust 0.016 in (0.40 mm). See Chapter 1/36. Adjusting the tappets is difficult, so if found wrong it could be best to get your FIAT agent to correct them.

3.8   Clean the carburettor inlet filter. See Chapter 3/3. Clean the carburettor itself if necessary: see Chapter 3/5.

3.9   Check the clutch pedal free travel. It should be 1 inch (25 mm). Adjust by undoing the locknut and moving the adjuster nut on the end of the cable on the clutch withdrawal lever on the top of the transmission. See Chapter 5/6.

3.10   Check the transmission oil level. Clean around and remove the level plug on the front. Fill to overflowing with the same make and type of oil as already in it.

3.11   Remove the rear brake drums. Blow the dust out and check the lining wear and general state of the brakes. See Chapter 8/7.

3.12   Check the handbrake adjustment. If the lever comes up more than four clicks of its ratchet, refer to Chapter 8/10.

3.13   Measure the amount of tread remaining on the tyres. The depth must be within the legal and safety limits. (1 mm in the United Kingdom). If the wear is uneven refer to Chapter 11/15.

3.14   Check the alignment of the wheels.
Front: Unladen, toe-out 3/16 in (5 mm) See Chapter 10/9.
Rear: Unladen, toe-in 1/8 - 1/4 in (3 - 6.5 mm) See Chapter 11/11.

3.15   Check the steering for wear. See Chapter 10/2 and 10/7:4.

3.16   Check the suspension for wear and the shock absorbers for proper damping. See Chapter 11/2 and 11/13.

3.17   Check the battery for security and corrosion. If there is corrosion, deal with it as described in Chapter 10/5.

3.18   Check the head lamp aim. Verify that the quick adjustment levers are in the appropriate position, laden or unladen. See Chapter 9/25.

3.19   Check the engine. Listen to it at idle. Check for leaks of fuel, oil, coolant, or exhaust. Odd noises can be traced either by using some plastic tubing as a listening aid, or a heavy screwdriver with a large wooden handle as sounding rod, put to the ear. Get to know the noises the car makes, so the onset of a new one will be noticed. Try to compare the noise of other FIAT 128s.. If the engine is not idling smoothly and at the correct speed refer to Chapter 3/8. For Europe the correct speed is 750 rpm. For North America, on cars with emissions control equipment that meets the 1973 regulations of the USA the speed should be 850 rpm. On saloon or estate cars it is difficult to guess idle speed, as they have no tachometers. On cars with dynamos the idle speed can be judged by the no charge warning light just coming on. Otherwise learn to judge idle speed by listening and watching four cylinder cars with tachometers.

3.20   Lubricate all controls, door and bonnet hinges and locks etc with an oil can filled with engine oil.

In spring and autumn:

3.21   Wash underneath and check for rust.

3.22   Shift the air cleaner intake to the seasonal setting.

RM 5 The oil filter is on the front of the engine

RM 6 The filter is just screwed on by hand

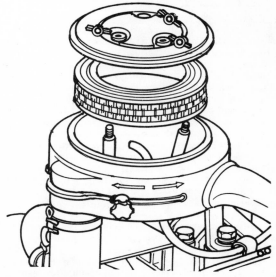

RM 7 The air cleaner element, and hot and cold weather settings

4 Every 12,000 miles (20,000 km) or annually if sooner

Do the 6,000 and 3,000 miles tasks, and in addition:

4.1   Change the transmission oil. After a journey, so the oil is warm and thin, park the car on level ground. Put a container that will hold ¾ gallon under the transmission and remove the drain plug on the left flank of the final drive part of the casing. This needs a 12 mm hexagon allen key, the same as the engine sump. If none is available, the jaw of a large adjustable spanner can be filed to suit. Clean around the plug, remove it, and allow the oil 10 minutes to drain. Clean the plug and replace it. Clean the filler plug on the front of the transmission casing, and remove it. Fill to overflowing with an oil to the specification. This is normally SAE 90, though an oil without the EP quality. FIAT England recommend the use of engine oil. Use oil in a plastic dispenser, so the tube can be put straight in to the filler hole.

4.2   Clean out the carburettor. See Chapter 3/5.

4.3   Clean the crankcase ventilation system. See Chapter 3/14.

4.4   Reset the camshaft timing belt tension. See Chapter 1/37:14.

4.5   Check for tightness all body bolts, engine mountings, door locks and hinges etc.

5 Every 18,000 miles (30,000 km)

Do all shorter mileage tasks, and also:

5.1   Change the generator 'V' belt. See Chapter 1/40. See also task 5.3 or 6.2.

5.2   Remove the starter motor. Clean the commutator, renew the brushes, and relubricate the bearings and drive. See Chapter 9/19 and 9/20.

5.3   If the generator is a dynamo, remove it, and clean the commutator, renew the brushes, and relubricate the bearings. See Chapter 9/9 and 9/10.

5.4   If fitted with fuel vapour control, replace the absorption canister filter. See Chapter 3/12.

5.5   Clean the fuel pump filter on cars with mechanical pumps. On cars so equipped change the fuel line filter. (In the supply pipe just short of the carburettor). See Chapter 3/4.

6 Every 36,000 miles (60,000 km)

Do all shorter mileage tasks, and also:

6.1   Change the camshaft cogged timing belt. See Chapter 1/9 for removing the old one and 1/37 for fitting the new one. Never turn the engine over with the belt removed unless the camshaft is at its Top Dead Centre position, with the camshaft pulley timing dot aligned with the pointer on the bearing bracket just past 6 o'clock. Otherwise the pistons may hit the valves. Turn the engine over by putting the car in top gear, jacking up the front right wheel, and turn that. Before putting the belt cover back turn the engine forwards four revolutions. Then recheck that the belt is fitted so the marks on crankshaft and camshaft come into line at the same time, with the belt's cogs seated well into the pulley. Allow the tensioner spring to reassert itself, and then tighten its pulley lock nut.

6.2   If the generator is an alternator, remove it, clean the slip rings and renew the brushes. See Chapter 9/12.

6.3   Change the brake fluid. Do this by extended bleeding. See Chapter 8/20. But first get rid of all the old fluid in the reservoir by detaching its pipes to the master cylinder. Take care no fluid gets on the car's paint, as it will spoil it. Road test the car, and check for leaks.

6.4   Change the engine coolant. Drain and flush the system as described in Chapter 2/4. Refill with coolant of a water and anti-freeze mix, or water with inhibitor. See Chapter 2/3.

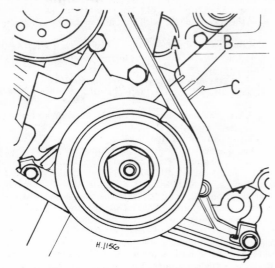

RM 8 The ignition timing marks. A = 10º BTDC. B = 5º BTDC. C = TDC.

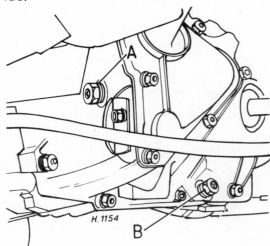

RM 9 The transmission filler/level and drain plugs

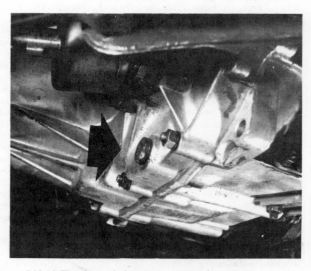

RM 10 The transmission drain needs a 12 mm Allen key

RM 11 The absorption canister (white arrow). In the nest of pipes by the emissions control valve (black arrow) is the fuel line filter; cars for USA emissions control only

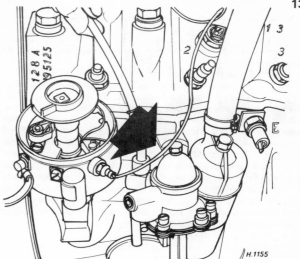

RM 12 The mechanical pump filter is under the bowl

Tools

1   The most useful type of spanner is a "combination spanner". This has one end open jaw, the other a ring of the same size. You can then use whichever end is the most convenient type. The usual double ended open jaw spanners are not very satisfactory anyway in metric sizes, as they are usually only available with the next millimetre size up at the other end: and you do not need all of them. You need two spanners of each size, so that one can hold the bolt whilst the other is on the nut. The second spanners should be the cranked ring spanners.

2   The sizes you need are:-

8,	10,	12,	13,	14,	17,	22,
which fit:- M5	M6		M8		M10	M14

24, & 27 mm. AF (across flats)
M16 M18   diameter bolts

Those used most frequently are underlined.

If you already have some inch spanners there is in several cases a good match.

2 BA	for	8 mm
½ AF	for	13 mm, though too tight in some cases.
¼ Whit	for	13 mm, but very loose, (not applicable in USA).
9/16 AF	for	14 mm, but very loose.
11/16 AF	for	17 mm, but a bit loose.
¾ AF	for	19 mm, but a bit loose.
7/8 AF	for	22 mm, but a bit loose.
1 1/16 AF	for	27 mm, good fit.

3   You will need a set of feeler gauges. Preferably these should be metric. In most cases the inch equivalent of dimensions is given, and conversion tables are at the back of the book. But the car is metric, and errors will be avoided by working metric. In the long term metric equipment will be a good investment as Britian will very soon be standardising on it, and the USA has just taken the first steps within the Automobile Industry to do so.

4   Tightening torques are specified for nuts and bolts. This needs an expensive torque wrench. Many people get on well without them. Contrariwise many others are plagued by things falling off, or leaking, from being too loose. Others suffer broken bolts, stripped threads, or warped cylinder heads, because of overtightening.

5   Torque wrenches use the socket of normal socket spanner sets. Sockets, with extensions and rachet handles, are a boon. In the meantime you will need box spanners for such things as cylinder head nuts, and the spark plugs. They are thinner than sockets in the small sizes, and will go where the latter cannot, so will always be useful even if later you plan to get sockets.

6   Screwdrivers should have large handles for a good grip. You need a large ordinary one, a little electrical one, and a medium cross headed one. Do not buy one handle with interchangeable heads. You will spend all your time changing heads. The large screwdriver must have a tough handle that will take hitting with a hammer when you misuse it as a chizel.

7   You should blush when you use an adjustable spanner, as they wear nuts badly, since they do not fit very well. But they are very useful. So also are self grip or pipe wrenches of the "Mole" or "Stillsons" type.

8   Major jobs require a drift. This is a steel rod or "tommybar" of about 3/8 in diameter, and made of tough steel to stand hammering. Do not use a brass drift lest little chips are cut off and get into some component and ruin it. You will need a "ball/pane" hammer, fairly heavy too, because it is easier to use gently than a light one hard.

9   Files are soon needed. Four make a good selection:
   6 inch half round smooth.
   8 inch flat, second cut.
   8 inch round second cut.
   10 inch half round bastard.

10 You need a good, firm, hydraulic jack. Whilst a trolley type is useful, the small sort i into place more easily. The car's own jack raises one side, and tilts the car to such an angles that it is insecure, and not suitable for much of the work.

11 For the FIAT 128's engine and transmission drain plugs you need an Allen key size 12 mm. FIAT have this as special tool A 50113. You should also try to get their special tappet holding tool, A 60421. See Chapter 1/36.

Use of Tools

1 Throughout this book various phrases describing techniques are used, such as:-
   "Drive out the bearing".
   "Undo the flange bolts evenly and diagonally".

2 When two parts are held together by a number of bolts round their edge, these must be tightened to draw the parts down together flat. They must be slackened evenly to prevent the component warping. Initially the bolts should be put in finger tight only. Then they should be tightened gradually, at first only a turn each; and diagonally, doing second the one opposite that tightened first, then one to a side, followed by another opposite that, and so on. The second time each bolt is tightened only half turn should be given. The third time round, only a quarter of a turn is given each, and this is kept up till tight. The reverse sequence is used to slacken them.

3 If any part has to be "driven", such as a ball bearing out of its housing, without a proper press, it can be done with a hammer provided a few rules for use of a hammer are remembered. Always keep the component being driven straight so it will not jam. Shield whatever is being hit from damage by the hammer. Soft headed hammers are available. A drift can be used, or if the item being hit is soft wood. Aluminium is very easily damaged. Steel is a bit better. Hard steel, such as a bearing race, is very strong. Something threaded at the end must be protected by fitting a nut. But do not hammer the nut: the threads will tear.

4 If levering items with makeshift arrangements, such as screwdrivers, irretrievable damage can be done. Be sure the lever rests either on something that does not matter, or put in padding. Burrs can be filed off afterwards. But indentations are there for good, and can cause leaks.

5 When holding something in a vice, the jaws must go on a part that is strong. If the indentation from the jaw teeth will matter, then lead or fibre jaw protectors must be used. Hollow sections are liable to be crushed.

6 Nuts that will not undo will sometimes move if the spanner handle is extended with another. But only extend a ring spanner, not an open jaw one. A hammer blow either to the spanner, or the bolt, may jump it out of its contact: the bolt locally welds itself in place. In extreme cases the nut will undo if driven off with drift and hammer. When reassembling such bolts, tighten them normally, not by the method needed to undo them.

7 For pressing things, such as a sleeve bearing into its housing, a vice, or an electric drill stand, make good presses. Pressing tools to hold each component can be arranged by using such things as socket spanners, or short lengths of steel water pipe. Long bolts with washers can be used to draw things into place rather than pressing them.

8 There are often several ways of doing something. If stuck, stop and think. Special tools can readily be made out of odd bits of scrap. Accordingly, at the same time as building up a tool kit, collect useful bits of steel.

9 Normally all nuts or bolts have some locking arrangement. The most common is a spring washer. There are tab washers that are bent up. Castellated nuts have split pins. FIAT use special collared nuts on the suspension stub axles that are staked to the axle. Sometimes a second nut locks the first. Self-locking nuts have special crowns that resist shaking loose. Self-locking nuts should not be reused, as the self-locking action is weakened as soon as they have been loosened at all. Tab washers should only be reused when they can be bent over in a new place. If you find a nut without any locking arrangement, check what it is meant to have.

Other aspects of routine maintenance

1 **Jacking up.** Always chock a wheel on the opposite side, in front and behind. The car's own jack has to be able to work when the car is very low with a flat tyre, so it goes in a socket on the side, taking up both wheels on that side. Using a small jack at one wheel is more secure when work has to be done. There are jacking points reinforced in the centre of the car at front and rear for a trolley jack. Never put a jack under the body work or the thin sheet steel will buckle.

2 **Wheel bolts.** These should be cleaned and lightly smeared with grease as necessary during work, to keep them moving easily. If the bolts are stubborn to undo due to dirt and over-tighening, it may be necessary to hold them by lowering the jack till the wheel rubs on the ground. Normally if the wheel brace is used across the hub centre, a foot held against the tyre will prevent the wheel from turning, and so save the wheels and bolts from the wear when they are slackened with weight on the wheel. After replacing a wheel make a point later of rechecking again for tightness.

3 **Safety.** Whenever working, even partially, under the car, put an additional strong support such as a baulk of timber onto which the car will fall rather than onto you.

4 **Cleanliness.** Keep the mechanical parts of the car clean. It is much more pleasant to work on a clean car. Whenever doing any work, allow time for cleaning. When something is in pieces, components removed improve access to other areas and give an opportunity for a thorough clean. This cleanliness will allow you to cope with a crisis on the road without getting yourself dirty. During bigger jobs when you expect a bit of dirt it is less extreme. When something is taken to pieces there is less risk of ruinous grit getting inside. The act of cleaning focusses your attention on parts, and you are then more likely to spot trouble. Dirt on the ignition parts in a common cause of poor starting. Large areas such as the bulkheads of the engine compartment, should be brushed throughly with a detergent like GUNK, allowed to soak for about ¼ hour, then carefully hose with water. Water in the wrong places, particularly the carburettor or electrical components will do more harm than dirt. Detailed cleaning can be done with paraffin (kerosene) and an old paint brush. Petrol cleans better, but remember the hazard of fire, and if used in a confined space, of fumes. Use a barrier cream on the hands.

5 **Waste disposal.** Old oil and cleaning parafin must be destroyed. It makes a good base for a bonfire, but is dangerous. Never have an open container near a naked flame. Pour the old oil where it cannot run uncontrolled, BEFORE you light it. Light it by making a "fuse" of newspaper. By buying your oil in one gallon cans you have these for storage of the old oil. The old oil is not household rubbish, so should not be put in the dust bin (trash). Most councils have collection points.

6 **Long journeys.** Before taking the car on a long journey, particularly a long holiday trip, do in advance many of the maintenance tasks that would not normally be due before going. In the first instance do jobs that would be due soon anyway. Then also do those that would not come up until well into the trip. Also do the other tasks that are just checks, as a form of insurance against trouble. For emergencies carry on the car some copper wire, plastic insulation tape, plastic petrol pipe, gasket compound such as Hermatite Golden, and repair material of the plastics resin type, such as "Plastic padding". Carry a spare 'V' belt, and some spare bulbs. About 3 ft of electric cable, and some odd metric nuts and bolts should complete your car's first aid kit. Also carry a human first aid kit: some plasters, germolene ointment, etc, in case you get minor cuts.

7 **On purchase.** If you have bought your 128 brand new you will have the maker's instructions for the early special checks on a new car. If you have just bought a second hand car then our advice is to reckon it has not been looked after properly, and so do all the checks, lubrication and other tasks on that basis, assuming all mileage and time tasks are overdue.

Lubrication Chart

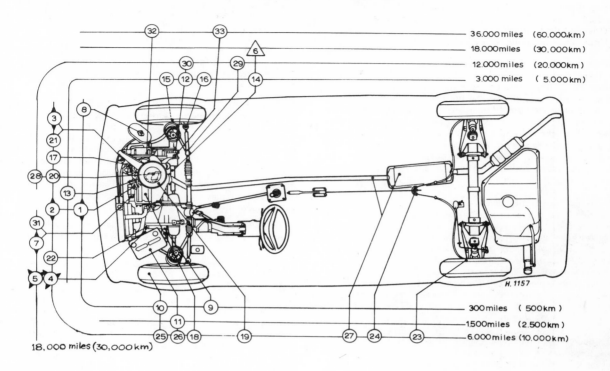

H. 1157

	36,000 miles (60,000 km)
	18,000 miles (30,000 km)
	12,000 miles (20,000 km)
	3,000 miles (5,000 km)

18,000 miles (30,000 km)

300 miles (500 km)
1,500 miles (2,500 km)
6,000 miles (10,000 km)

◯ Engine oil   △ Gear oil   △ Grease
1.   2.   3.

Every 300 miles (500 km) or weekly

1	Engine	Check oil level

Every 6,000 miles (10,000 km)

2	Engine	Change oil
3	Distributor	Lubricate
4	Gearbox and axle	Check oil level
—	Body	Lubricate

Every 18,000 miles (30,000 km)

5	Gearbox and axle	Change oil
6	Constant velocity joints	Check
7	Starter	Lubricate

Every 300 miles (500 km)

8	Cooling system	Check level
9	Brake fluid reservoir	Check level
10	Tyres	Check inflation pressures

Every 1,500 miles (2,500 km) or monthly

11	Battery	Check electrolyte level

Every 3,000 miles (5,000 km)

12	Alternator/water pump belt	Check tension
13	Spark plugs	Clean, check gap
14	Constant velocity joints	Check boots
15	Front brakes	Check for wear
16	Ball joints	Check
—	Screen washer	Clean nozzles, check level

Every 6,000 miles (10,000 km)

17	Oil filter	Renew
18	Valves	Check clearance
19	Air cleaner	Renew element
20	Carburettor	Clean jets and filter, adjust slow running

21	Distributor	Check point gap
—	Ignition timing	Check
22	Clutch	Check free travel
23	Rear brakes	Check for wear
24	Handbrake	Check
25	Tyres	Check for wear and rotate
26	Battery	Check terminals
—	Headlamps	Check alignment
27	Exhaust system	Check for looseness
—	Seals, sleeves, connectors, plugs	Check for leakage

Every 12,000 miles (20,000 km)

28	Carburettor	Clean
—	P.C.V. system	Clean
29	Wheel alignment	Check
—	Mechanical units	Check for looseness

Every 18,000 miles (30,000 km)

30	Alternator/water pump belt	Renew
31	Starter	Clean commutator, renew brushes

Every 36,000 miles (60,000 km)

32	Timing belt	Renew
33	Alternator	Clean slip rings and renew brushes

NON-PERIODIC MAINTENANCE

Valve timing	Check
Distributor	Renew contact points
Brakes	Check
Shock absorbers	Check

Recommended lubricants

Component	FIAT Designation	International Designation	CASTROL Product	Capacity Imp. Pints	Capacity Metric Litres	Capacity U.S. Pints
Oils Engine		MS type MIL-L-2104B		7½	4¼	9
Below − 15°C	VS 10 W	SAE 10 W or 10 W/30 etc.	CASTROLITE or CR1 10			
− 15°C − 0°C (5°F − 32°F)	10 W/30 or VS 20 W	10 W/30 or 20 W/40 or SAE 20 W	CASTROLITE or GTX or CR1 20			
0°C − 35°C (32°F − 95°F)	20 W/40 or VS 30	20 W/40, 20 W/50 etc or SAE 30	GTX			
Over 35°C (95°F)	20 W/40 or VS 40	20 W/40, 20 W/50 SAE 40	GTX			
Transmission	ZC 90	SAE 90 (Not EP)	ST 90 but GTX in Great Britain and temperate climates.	5½	3.15	6 2/3
Steering rack	W 90/M	SAE 90 EP	Castrol Hypoy B (90 EP)			
Greases Constant velocity joints	MRM 2	Lithium plus Molybdenum disulphide to NLG 2	Castrol MS3 Grease			
Wheel bearings	MR 3	Lithium NLG 3	Castrol LM Grease			
Brake calipers etc. ...	SP 349	Castrol oil/sodium base rubber and brake fluid compatible				
Hydraulic Fluid	Azzura (Blue)	SAE J1703 FMVSS 116 DOT 3	Castrol Girling Universal Clutch and Brake Fluid	½	1/3	2/3

Chapter 1 Engine

Contents

Specifications

"1100" engine:

Type	128 A.000	
Cubic capacity	1116 cc	68.10 in^3
Bore	80 mm	3.149 in
Stroke	55.5 mm	2.185 in
Compression ratio	8.8 : 1	
Firing order	1 3 4 2	
Ignition timing: European spec.	Static 10º BTDC	
American spec.	At 850 rpm, TDC	

(See Chapter 4 for other ignition specifications)

Power ... ...   DIN net
European specification 55 hp at 6,000 rpm

Torque ... ...   DIN rating
European specification 57 lb f. ft (7.9 kg m) at 3,600 rpm

Power ... ...   SAE net
American specification 49 hp

Cylinder block

	in	mm
Cylinder bore diameter	3.1496 to 3.1516	80.00 to 80.50
in grades: intervals	0.0004	0.01
Maximum permissible wear/out of round	0.006	0.15
Rebore sizes	0.008, 0.016, 0.024	0.2, 0.4, 0.6
Maximum rebore	0.024	0.6
Liners external diameter	3.3070 to 3.3078	84.0 to 84.02
Cylinder diameter for liners	3.3043 to 3.3051	83.93 to 83.95
Bore liners after fitting		
Auxiliary shaft bushing seats, diameters:		
— drive end	1.5236 to 1.5248	38.700 to 38.730
— inside end	1.3794 to 1.3806	35.036 to 35.066
Crankshaft bearing saddle bore diameter	2.1459 to 2.1465	54.507 to 54.520
Length of rear main bearing bore between thrust ring seats ...	.8716 to .8740	22.140 to 22.200

Connecting rods

	in	mm
Big-end bearing housing diameter	1.9146 to 1.9152	48.630 to 48.646
Small-end bore diameter	.8638 to .8646	21.940 to 21.960
Thickness of standard big-end bearings	.0603 to .0606	1.531 to 1.538
Range of undersize big-end bearings for service	.010 - .020 - .030 - .040	0.254 - 0.508 - 0.762 - 1.016
Gudgeon pin connecting rod fit:		
— interference	.0004 to .0017	0.010 to 0.042
— con rod temperature for fitting - 15 minutes at	464°F	240°C
Big end bearings:		
— fit clearance	.0014 to .0034	0.036 to 0.086
— wear limit	.004	0.10
Maximum misalignment between C/Ls of connecting rod small-end and big-end:		
— measured at 4.92 in (125 mm) from the shank	± .0039	± 0.10

Crankshaft and main bearings

	in	mm
Main bearing journal standard diameter	1.9990 to 1.9998	50.775 to 50.795
Main bearing seat bore	2.1459 to 2.1465	54.507 to 54.520
Standard main bearing insert thickness	.0718 to .0721	1.825 to 1.831
Main bearing inserts for service	Std., .01 - .02 - .03 - .04 US.	Std. 0.254 - 0.508 - 0.762 - 1.016 US.
Crankpin standard diameter	1.7913 to 1.7920	45.498 to 45.518
Main bearing-to-journal fit:		
— clearance of new parts	.0020 to .0037	0.050 to 0.095
— wear limit	.006	0.15
Length of rear main bearing journal, shoulder-to-shoulder ...	1.0620 to 1.0639	26.975 to 27.025
Width of rear main bearing seat, between thrust ring seats ...	.8716 to .8740	22.140 to 22.200
Rear main bearing seat thrust ring thickness	.0909 to .0929	2.310 to 2.360
Oversize thrust ring thickness	.0959 to .0979	2.437 to 2.487
Oversize is	.005	0.127
Crankshaft end float, thrust rings installed:		
— clearance of new parts	.0021 to .0104	0.055 to 0.265
— wear limit	.0137	0.35
Maximum misalignment of main bearing journals	.0012	0.03
Maximum misalignment of crankpins to main bearing journals ...	± .014	± 0.35
Maximum out-of-round of crankpins and main bearing journals, after grinding	.0002	0.005
Maximum taper of crankpins and main bearing journals, after grinding	.0002	0.005
Squareness of flywheel resting face to crankshaft centerline:		
— max. out-of-true with dial indicator plunger set laterally some 1 11/32 in (34 mm) apart from crankshaft rotation axis	.0010	0.025
Flywheel:		
— parallel relationship of driven plate face to crankshaft mounting face: max. out-of-true	.0030	0.1
— squareness of above faces to rotation axis: max. out-of-true	.0039	0.1

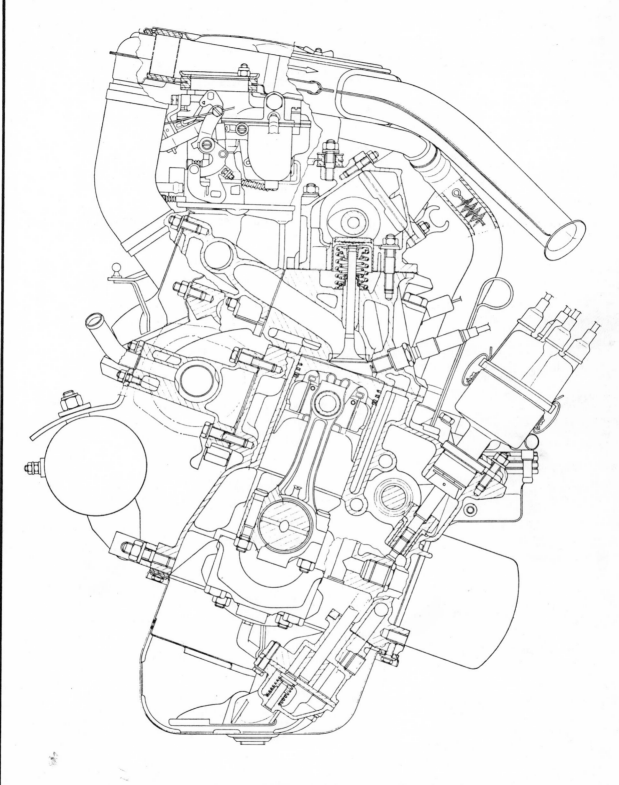

Fig 1.1. The FIAT 128's overhead camshaft engine is mounted across the car, and sloped forward 20°

Pistons and gudgeon pins

		in	mm
Diameter of standard replacement pistons, measured at right angles to C/L of piston pin:			
— at 2.008 in ± .001 in (51 ± 0.25 mm) from piston head	(Class A	3.1472 to 3.1476	79.940 to 79.950
	(Class C	3.1480 to 3.1484	79.960 to 79.970
	(Class E	3.1488 to 3.1492	79.980 to 79.990
Piston weight variation permissible		± .088 oz	± 2.5 g
Oversize pistons range		.0079 - .0157 - .0236	0.2 - 0.4 - 0.6
	(Grade 1	.8654 to .8656	21.982 to 21.986
Piston small end boss bore diameter	(Grade 2	.8656 to .8657	21.986 to 21.990
	(Grade 3	.8657 to .8659	21.990 to 21.994
	(Top groove	.0604 to .0612	1.535 to 1.555
Piston ring groove width	(Center groove	.0793 to .0801	2.015 to .2035
	(Bottom groove	.1558 to .1566	3.957 to 3.977
	(Grade 1	.8650 to .8651	21.970 to 21.974
Standard piston pin diameter	(Grade 2	.8651 to .8653	21.974 to 21.978
	(Grade 3	.8653 to .8654	21.978 to 21.982
Oversize gudgeon pin		.0079	0.2
Piston ring thickness:			
— first: compression ring		.0582 to .0587	1.478 to 1.490
— second: oil ring		.0779 to .0787	1.980 to 2.000
— third: oil ring with oilways and expander		.1544 to .1549	3.925 to 3.937
Piston fit in bore (at right angles to pin, 2.008 in ± .001 in (51 ± 0.25 mm) from piston crown			
— clearance of new parts		.0020 to .0028	0.050 to 0.070
— maximum permissible due to wear		.006	0.15
Gudgeon pin in boss: clearance of new parts		.0003 to .0006	0.008 to 0.016
wear limit		.002	0.05
Piston ring fit (side clearance):			
— first compression ring: clearance of new parts		.0018 to .0030	0.045 to 0.077
— second oil ring: clearance of new parts		.0006 to .0022	0.015 to 0.055
— third oil ring: clearance of new parts		.008 to .0020	0.020 to 0.052
— wear limit (all three)		.006	0.15
Ring end gap in bore:			
— first compression ring: clearance of new parts		.0118 to .0176	0.30 to 0.45
— second oil ring: clearance of new parts		.0079 to .0138	0.20 to 0.35
— third oil ring: clearance of new parts		.0079 to .0138	0.30 to 0.35
Oversize piston rings range:			
— compression and oil rings		.0079 - .0157 - .0236	0.2 - 0.4 - 0.6

Cylinder head

		in	mm
Valve guide seat bore		.5886 to .5896	14.950 to 14.977
Outside diameter of valve guide		.5913 to .5920	15.018 to 15.036
Inside diameter of valve guides, fitted in cylinder head ...		.3158 to .3165	8.022 to 8.040
Fit between valve guide and seat in head: interference		.0016 to .0034	0.041 to 0.086
Diameter of valve stems	(intake	.3140 to .3146	7.975 to 7.990
	(exhaust	.3142 to .3148	7.980 to 7.995
Fit between valve stem and guide: inlet and exhaust			
New fit clearance		.0012 to .0026	0.030
Wear limit		.006	0.15
Angle of inclination of valve seats in cylinder head		45° ± 5'	
Angle of inclination of valve head face		45° 30' ± 5'	
Diameter of valve head	(intake	1.4173	36
	(exhaust	1.2008	30.5
Max. eccentricity of valve head in one complete turn guided by stem, with indicator plunger set on center of contact face		.0012	0.03
Width of valve seat in cylinder head (contact face), abt ...		.080	2.1
Inside diameter of valve seats in cylinder head	(intake ...	1.1811	30
	(exhaust ...	1.0433	26.5
Lift on C/L of valve (without play)		.3583	9.1
Diameter of tappet bores in camshaft housing		1.4566 to 1.4576	37.000 to 37.025
Outside diameter of tappets		1.4557 to 1.4565	36.975 to 36.995
Fit clearance between tappets and bores in head		.002 to .0020	0.005 to 0.050

Thickness of cap plate: basic dimension ...   .   .1575 ± .0004   4 ± 0.01
Tappet cap plates are supplied in thirty thicknesses: **at** intervals of 0.020 in (0.05 mm) from 0.1279 in (3.25 mm) to
    0.1850 in (4.70 mm)

Valve springs

	in	mm
Inner: Free length	1.64	41.8
: Under load of 32.7 lbs (14.9 kg)	1.22	31
Outer : Free length	2.12	53.9
: Under load of 75.5 lbs (38.9 kg)	1.42	36

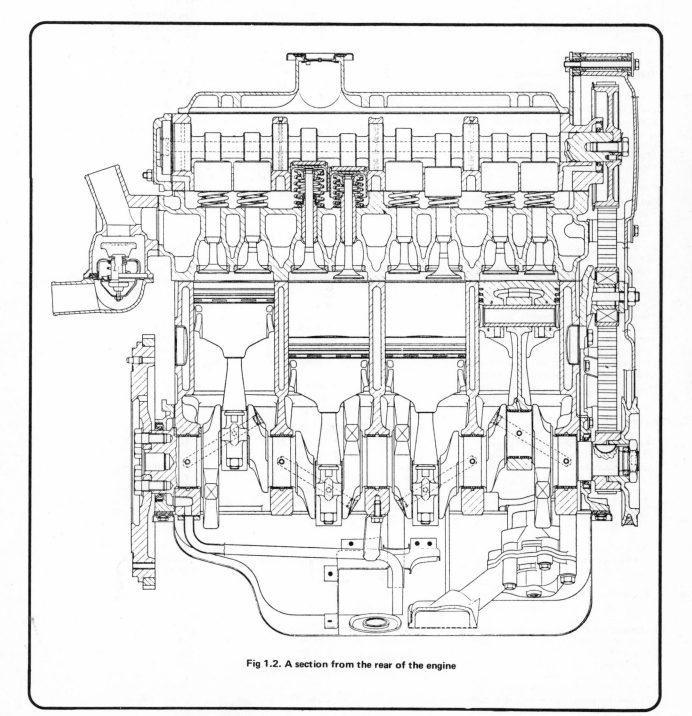

Fig 1.2. A section from the rear of the engine

Valve clearance

							in	mm
Tappet clearance cold:	Inlet	...	...	...	...	...	0.012	0.30
	Exhaust	...	...	...	...	...	0.016	0.40

Camshaft

							in	mm
Diameter of bores in camshaft housing:								
— drive end	...	...	...	...	...	...	1.1806 to 1.1816	29.989 to 30.014
— intermediate, drive side	...	...	...	...	...	...	1.8890 to 1.8899	47.980 to 48.005
— middle	...	...	...	...	...	...	1.8968 to 1.8978	48.180 to 48.205
— intermediate, flywheel side	...	...	...	...	...	...	1.9047 to 1.9057	48.380 to 48.405
— flywheel end	...	...	...	...	...	...	1.9126 to 1.9136	48.580 to 48.605
Diameter of camshaft journals:								
— drive end	...	...	...	...	...	...	1.1789 to 1.1795	29.944 to 29.960
— intermediate, drive side	...	...	...	...	...	...	1.8872 to 1.8878	47.935 to 47.950
— middle	...	...	...	...	...	...	1.8951 to 1.8957	48.135 to 48.150
— intermediate, flywheel side	...	...	...	...	...	...	1.9030 to 1.9035	48.335 to 48.350
— flywheel end	...	...	...	...	...	...	1.9108 to 1.9114	48.535 to 48.550

Fit between bores in camshaft housing and camshaft journals:

						in	mm
	(drive end	...	...	...	...	.0011 to .0027	0.029 to 0.070
	(intermediate, drive side	...	...	...	.0012 to .0027	0.030 to 0.070
— fit clearance:	(middle	...	...	...	...	.0012 to .0027	0.030 to 0.070
	(intermediate, flywheel side	...	...	...	.0012 to .0027	0.030 to 0.070
	(flywheel end	...	...	...	...	.0012 to .0027	0.030 to 0.070

									in	mm
Cam height	...	...	...	...	...	...	...	...	.3583	9.1
Valve timing:	Inlet	...	...	...	...	...	...	Opens 12º BTDC closes 52º ABDC	
	Exhaust	...	...	...	...	...	...	Opens 52 BBDC closes 12º ATDC	

Auxiliary shaft

							in	mm
Diameter of bushing bores in crankcase:								
— drive end	...	...	...	...	...	...	1.5236 to 1.5248	38.700 to 38.730
— inside end	...	...	...	...	...	...	1.3794 to 1.3805	35.036 to 35.066
Inside diameter of bushings finished in bores:								
— drive end	...	...	...	...	...	...	1.4041 to 1.4049	35.664 to 35.684
— inside end	...	...	...	...	...	...	1.2598 to 1.2606	32.000 to 32.020
Diameter of shaft journals:								
— drive end	...	...	...	...	...	...	1.4013 to 1.4023	35.593 to 35.618
— inside end	...	...	...	...	...	...	1.2575 to 1.2583	31.940 to 31.960

					in	mm
Fit between bushings and bores in crankcase	...	...	...	interference fit at all times	
Fit between bushings and shaft journals:						
— fit clearance	(drive end	...	...	...	.0018 to .0036	0.046 to 0.091
	(inside end	...	...	...	.0016 to .0031	0.040 to 0.080

Oil pump

							in	mm
End clearance, gears to cover:	new	...	...	...	...	...	.0008 to .0041	0.020 to 0.105
	wear limit	...	...	...	...	...	.006	0.15
Side clearance, gears to wall:	new	...	...	...	...	...	.0043 to .0071	0.11 to 0.18
	wear limit	...	...	...	...	...	.01	0.25
Length of new gear	...	...	...	...	...	...	1.101 to 1.102	27.967 to 28.0
Driven gear shaft to housing	...	...	...	...	...	Interference fit	
Driven gear fit on shaft :	new	...	...	...	...	...	.0006 to .0022	0.017 to 0.057
	: wear limit	...	...	...	...	...	.004	0.10
Pump drive shaft to housing:								
— new clearance	...	...	...	...	...	...	.0006 to .0023	0.016 to 0.060
— wear limit	...	...	...	...	...	...	.004	0.10
Backlash of gears :	new	...	...	...	...	...	.006	0.15
	: wear limit	...	...	...	...	...	.010	0.25

Oil pressure relief valve

								in	mm
Spring free length	...	...	...	...	...	...	...	1.583	40.2
Seated length	...	...	...	...	...	...	...	0.886	22.5
Load seated :	normal	...	...	...	...	...	...	10.16 lb f.	4.61 kg
	: minimum	...	...	...	...	...	...	9.48 lb f.	4.3 kg
Oil pressure warning light switches on	...	...	...	...	5.7 to 11.4 lbf/in^2	0.4 to 0.8 kg/cm^2
Normal oil pressures with oil at temperatures 212ºF (100ºC) ...					50 to 70 lbf/in^2	3.5 to 5 kg/cm^2

"1300" Engine variations

The Rally spec. engine differs from the 1116′ in the following respects

Type ... ...   128 AR

Cubic capacity	1290 cc	78.7 in^3
Bore	86 mm	3.385 in
Compression ratio	8.9 : 1	

Power. DIN net: European spec. ... ...   67 hp at 6400 rpm

Torque. DIN net: Eurpean spec. ... ...   65 lbf ft (9 kgm) at 4,000 rpm

Valve tappet clearance cold

Inlet	0.016 in	0.40 mm
Exhaust	0.018 in	0.45 mm

Valve timing

Inlet	Opens 24° BTDC	Closes 68° ABDC
Exhaust	Opens 64° BBDC	Closes 28° ATDC

Piston fit in bore (at right angles to pin, 2.008 in. (51 mm) from crown

	Inch	mm
New	.0028 to .0035	0.070 to 0.090
Wear limit	.007	0.175

Connecting rod small end is bushed

Bush interference fit	.0017 to .004	0.044 to 0.102
Grooves in pistons for second and third rings are wider by ...	.0004	.010
Wear limit is the same		

Gudgeon pin diameter

Grade 1	21.991 — 21.994 mm
Grade 2	21.994 — 21.997 mm

Piston small end

Grade 1	21.996 — 21.999 mm
Grade 2	21.999 — 21.002 mm

Con rod bush inner diameter

Grade 1	22.004 — 22.007 mm
Grade 2	22.007 — 22.010 mm

Gudgeon pins are fully floating and retained by circlips.

The undermentioned variations affect the 1300 Coupe and differ from those for the Rally.

Compression ratio

Europe	8.9 : 1
America	8.5 : 1

Power

DIN net, European spec.	75 hp at 6,600 rpm
SAE net, American spec.	51 hp at 5,600 rpm

Torque

DIN net, European spec.	68 lbf ft (9.4 kgm) at 3,600 rpm
SAE net, American spec.	62 lbf ft (8.6 kgm) at 3,000 rpm

Engine dimensions as Rally (128 AR)

Tightening torques

	lbf ft	kg m
Flywheel to crankshaft	65	9
Main bearing caps	58	8
Big end caps	36	5
Clutch to flywheel	11	1.5
Camshaft sprocket	61	8.5
Crankshaft sprocket and pulley	101	14
Cylinder head 1st pass	29	4
final	61	8.5
Camshaft housing nuts	14	2
Tensioner of camshaft belt	33	4.5
Manifolds to cylinder head	22	3
Water pump upper bracket	18	2.5
Generator mountings	36	5
Spark plugs	29	4
Transmission to engine	58	8
Bolts, engine mounting bracket beam to body	18	2.5
Bolt/nut engine mounting, right end	25	3.5

1 General description

1 The engine has four cylinders and an overhead camshaft driven by a rubber, cogged, belt. It is water cooled. The cylinder block is cast iron, the head aluminium. The camshaft runs in bearings in a housing that is an extension of the head, and works the tappets direct, the latter being large buckets.

2 The engine is mounted across the car, and sloped forward at 15°. The transmission is to the left and below the engine. Though it is integral, the transmission has separate lubricant.

3 There are five main bearings. The combination of massive crankshaft, short stroke, and overhead camshaft make the engine willing to run fast, therefore its performance is good for its size.

4 The spare wheel is mounted on top of the left side of the engine compartment. Once this is removed, there is good access from the left. When working on a component on the right of the car, it will often be easier to attack from the left for instance the generator can be reached this way.

5 The underneath of the engine has shields to keep off dirt. These have to be removed for many jobs.

6 One special problem is posed by the method of tappet adjustment. To adjust the tappets a special tool is needed. Also a selection of shims is wanted. The tool is unlikely to be in stock at your agent, so should be ordered as soon as the car is bought. Also the shims might be hard to get, and this should be discussed with the agent. See Section 36.

7 On cars to the North American specification the fuel vapour control system's absorption cannister impedes accessibility to the right of the engine. This is described in Chapter 3. It will often pay to dismantle it partially to get better access.

PART A – DISMANTLING PROCEDURES

2 The necessity for engine removal

1 In this chapter much of the work on the engine is described as if it has been removed. However, only a small proportion of readers will need to take out an engine. Such obvious jobs as removing the cylinder head will be done with the engine in place. Indeed it is possible to do many fundamental repairs without removing the engine.

2 However, on an engine that has done high mileage, if one component is worn out, others are likely to be in the same state. It then becomes worthwhile to take it out.

3 Another factor that will influence the decision is the availability of the necessary lifting tackle.

4 Each situation must be judged on its own merits. In this chapter some comment is made in sections where we removed the engine on how some of the work could be done with the engine in place. But the main sequence of paragraphs is assuming complete dismantling. If only doing a partial repair, the particular component should be followed through Parts A, B, and C for dismantling, overhaul and reassembly.

3 Removing the cylinder head (engine in place)

1 The need for this will be shown by the symptoms and response to tests discussed in Part D of this Chapter. It is assumed the valves need attention, or the cylinder head gasket

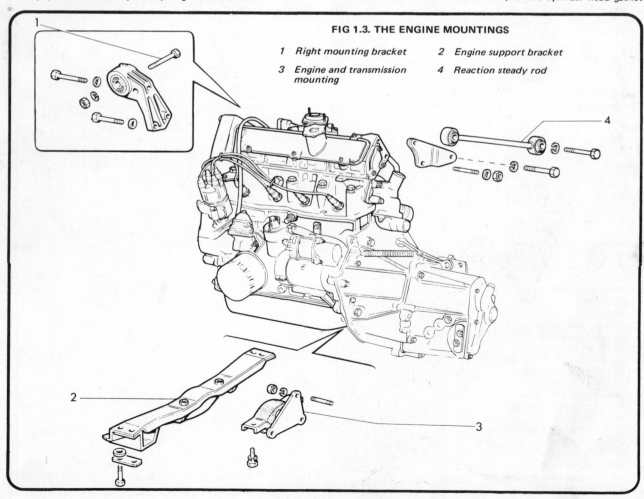

FIG 1.3. THE ENGINE MOUNTINGS

1 *Right mounting bracket*   2 *Engine support bracket*

3 *Engine and transmission*   4 *Reaction steady rod*
   mounting

has failed, or the cylinders and pistons need examination to decide if the engine has got to come out, due to inability to make a proper diagnosis without seeing inside.

2 With the engine warm, drain the coolant from the tap at the bottom of the radiator, and the other on the rear side of the cylinder block.

3 Whilst under the car remove the right hand shield. One bolt must be undone from above. The centre shield too can be removed to assist cleaning.

4 Remove the spare wheel.

5 Remove the air cleaner. Undo the support bracket to the cylinder head. Take out the element and remove the two nuts holding the body to the carburettor. Pull off the breather hose at the front. As the cleaner is pulled upwards, pull the cold weather inlet out of the flexible pipe from the manifold shield.

6 Slacken the hose clips for the top and bottom hoses for the radiator at the thermostat. Pull these hoses off.

7 Remove the bonnet. See Chapter 12 for the different methods applicable to saloon/estate and coupes. FIAT mechanics do not remove the bonnet, but it will be worth doing it for someone who does not work on the engine so often, and does not have the special tools.

8 Undo the hose clip and take off, at the thermostat, the hose from the water pump.

9 Unclip the ignition leads from the plugs, and the king lead from the centre of the coil. Take off the distributor cap.

10 Unplug the wire at the thermometer sender unit on the front of the cylinder head.

11 On cars with fuel vapour control systems note the run of the pipes. Then disconnect and remove the absorption cannister, the fast idle system pipe, and the fuel pipe with line filter. (photos).

12 On other cars remove the pipe from the mechanical fuel pump at the carburettor.

13 Disconnect the heater feed pipe from the right end of the cylinder head. (photo).

14 Unclip the throttle linkage at the carburettor. Unclip the throttle cross shaft from its mountings, and tuck it up out of the way. These links just pull off their pivot ball mountings. (photos).

15 Undo the clamps for the choke inner and outer cables at the carburettor.

16 Disconnect the exhaustpipe at the manifold, by undoing the clamp, (photo).

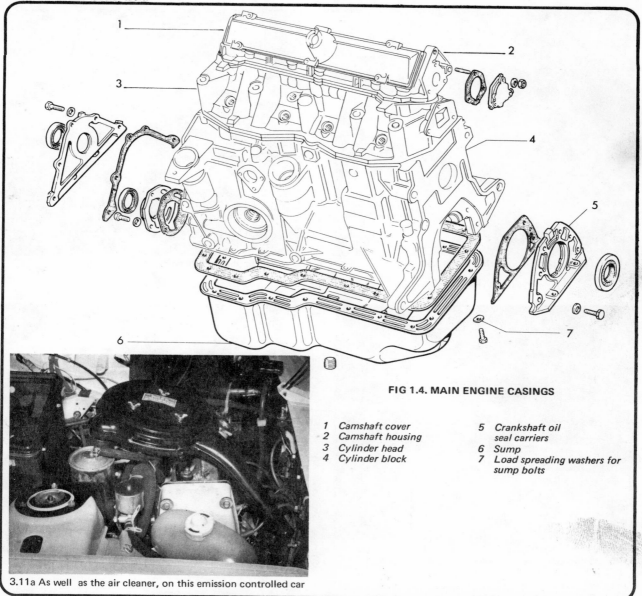

FIG 1.4. MAIN ENGINE CASINGS

1 Camshaft cover
2 Camshaft housing
3 Cylinder head
4 Cylinder block
5 Crankshaft oil seal carriers
6 Sump
7 Load spreading washers for sump bolts

3.11a As well as the air cleaner, on this emission controlled car

3.11b the absorption canister and other pipes must come off to give room to work

3.13a Take off the heater hose from the head,

3.13b and all the hoses off the thermostat housing.

3.14a Unclip the throttle linkage from the carburettor,

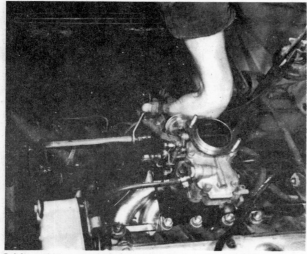

3.14b and its cross shaft from the pivot on the manifold.

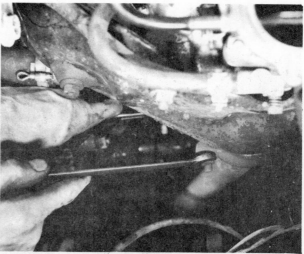

3.16a Unclamp the exhaust pipe from its manifold.

3.16b On Rally and Coupe the joint has a bolted flange.

17 Remove the camshaft belt cover. One bolt must be reached from underneath, and it is for this that the shield was previously removed.
18 The tension must now be taken off the camshaft belt prior to its removal. Slacken the nut in the centre of the tensioner pulley. Lever the pulley against its spring away from the belt with a long screwdriver, and retighten the nut. See photos with Section 9.
19 Slip the belt off the camshaft, leaving it round the crankshaft pulley. But if it is thought the belt is nearly due for changing, it is suggested the new one is fitted now. In this case slacken the 'V' belt at the alternator, and get it out of the way, to let the camshaft belt come off.
20 Remove the flat guard for the camshaft belt that runs up the right end of the engine. One bolt is just below the tensioner pulley. The others are behind the camshaft pulley. See photos with Section 15.
21 Take off the manifold shield, by removing the four nuts holding it to the manifold, and on cars with brake servos, pull the vacuum pipe off the inlet manifold.

22 Remove the bolt through the engine end of the reaction rod, at the bracket on the left end of the cylinder head. Slacken the bolt at the other end, and swing the rod up out of the way.
23 If the special "crow's foot" spanners are available, the cylinder head can now be removed. But it is assumed these are not, so proceed as follows.
24 Take off the two water pipes to the carburettor, at the thermostat, and at the manifold. Remove the carburettor by undoing the two nuts holding it to the manifold. Unclamp the drip tray pipe at the left end of the exhaust manifold: take off the tray.
25 Remove the camshaft housing cover.
26 Remove the camshaft housing from the cylinder head. Slacken all the nuts evenly and gradually. The valve springs will push the whole assembly upwards. One row of nuts is on the outside of the housing, to the rear, whilst the front ones are inside it.
27 Lift off the camshaft housing carefully, as the tappets and the tappet adjustment shims will be loose. Keep each in its proper place: turn the housing upside down as quickly as possible to keep them in, by tilting the top towards the front of the car.
28 Slacken the cylinder head nuts and bolts gradually, and in reverse order to the tightening sequence given in Fig.1.18 in Part B: start at the outer ends and slacken inwards.
29 Now break the joint between the cylinder head and the block. Do not prise at the joint. Turning the engine on the starter might blow it off. Also rock it by pulling up on the manifolds and thermostat.
30 Lift off the cylinder head. Put it where the carbon will not get wet or knocked off, so that you can have a change to look at it for signs that will show the engine condition.
31 Peel off the old cylinder head gasket. Take care no carbon falls into the cylinders.
32 If the "crow's foot" spanners were available, the head should be removed with the camshaft still in place on the head, and the carburettor on the manifold, and these removed more easily later on the bench.
33 Remove the manifolds from the head, by removing the nuts and large thick washers.
34 For the decarbonising of the engine, and work on the valves, refer to the later sections in Part B of this Chapter.

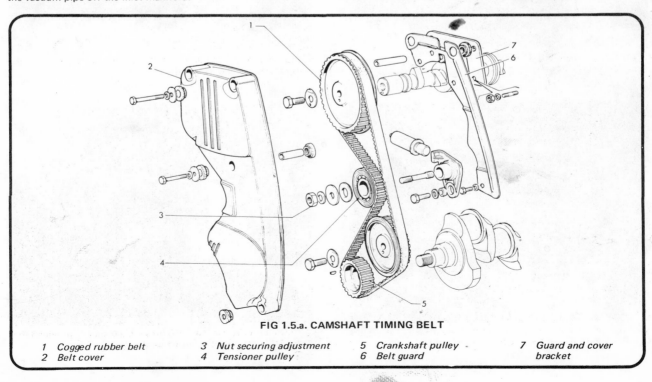

FIG 1.5.a. CAMSHAFT TIMING BELT

| 1 Cogged rubber belt | 3 Nut securing adjustment | 5 Crankshaft pulley | 7 Guard and cover |
| 2 Belt cover | 4 Tensioner pulley | 6 Belt guard | bracket |

4 Engine removal: preliminary work

1   Before starting work, decide how the engine is to be lifted. The engine is lowered out of its mountings, and removed under the car. Also the drive shafts have to be disconnected. If a decent tackle is available to lift the engine, the car can be blocked up, and then the engine lowered out, and dragged from underneath. Without such a tackle, the car must be jacked up from the preliminary work, then lowered as far as possible. Blocks are then put under the engine, the mountings disconnected, and the car then jacked up again to allow the engine to be pulled clear. This latter method is not recommended, because it will be difficult to reach the supporting bracket under the left end of the engine, and it is probably also less safe. A tackle can be slung from a strong beam, or rigged over the front of the car using stout timber as shearlegs. If using ropes, get enough pulley blocks to make a tackle with a purchase of 8 to 1.

2   Drain the engine oil, and the transmission oil too if that is going to be dismantled.

3   Under the car remove the bracket from the transmission to the exhaust, (photos).

4   Remove the shields under the car. The front one is straightforward. The left hand one has two inaccessible bolts above the drive shaft. For the right hand one two bolts must be reached from above.

5   Disconnect the gear change linkage at the single bolt just before the rod goes inside the transmission casing. Tie the rod to the gear lever up to the car with some string. Undo the earthing strip from power unit to body, at the rear of the transmission.

6   Take out the spare wheel.

7   Disconnect the battery leads, and remove its clamp. Lift out the battery.

8   Drain the radiator at the tap at the bottom, and the engine at the tap on the rear of the crankcase, directly below the carburettor.

9   Slacken the clips on the radiator top and bottom hoses, at the radiator and thermostat, and take the hoses off.

10 It is now recommended the bonnet is removed. See Chapter 12 for the appropriate methods for saloon/estate, and the coupe. In the case of the saloon/estate it is suggested the method calling for the removal of the radiator is best for such a job as this, as the radiator is in the way.

11 Remove the air cleaner. Undo and support bracket on the cylinder head. Pull off the engine oil breather pipe at the front. Take off the lid, and remove the element. Undo the two nuts holding the body to the carburettor. Pull the aircleaner off, pulling the cold weather inlet out of the flexible pipe from the manifold.

12 Unplug the ignition leads from the spark plugs, and the king lead from the centre of the coil. Unclip the distributor cap, and remove the harness. Disconnect the low tension wire at the distributor.

3.24a Get the manifold shield out of the way

3.24b Remove the carburettor and drip tray, to allow the camshaft-housing to come off.

3.27 Catch all the tappets as the camshaft comes off. Taking this off allows the cylinder head bolts to be reached

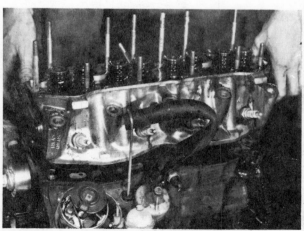

3.30 Do not prise the head off; hit with a mallet or provided the camshaft is off, turn the engine on the starter

13 Unplug the thermometer sender unit's wire on the front of the cylinder head.

14 Unplug the wire to the oil pressure warning light on the front of the crankcase.

15 Unplug the red lead to the starter solenoid. Undo the heavy cable to the starter by taking off the nut on the terminal.

16 Disconnect the generator. If a dynamo, undo the two terminal nuts. These are different sizes, so cannot be muddled. On alternators there is a simple plug.

17 Disconnect the throttle by unclipping the link at the carburettor itself. Then take the cross shaft off its pivot and tuck it up out of the way near the heater intake.

18 Unclamp the choke inner and outer cables from the carburettor.

19 Disconnect the heater hoses from the cylinder head and the water pump.

20 Undo the hose clip on the fuel pump inlet (on cars with engine mounted mechanical pumps) on the front of the engine, and pull the pipe off the pump.

21 On cars with fuel vapour emissions control disconnect the absorption cannister after noting where all the pipes go, and marking them as necessary. Disconnect the pipes to the emissions control fast idle system. Disconnect the fuel pipe at the carburettor.

22 Take out the bolt though the engine end of the reaction rod at its mounting on the left end of the cylinder head. Slacken the other end on the bulkhead, and pull the rod up out of the way. Put the bolt back in the bracket on the cylinder head as it makes a handy lifting point for the engine on the bench, (photo).

23 Tie a piece of string round the exhaust pipe, and to the steering rack, to hold the pipe up. Then remove the clamp securing the pipe to the exhaust manifold.

24 On cars with brake servos take the vacuum pipe off the inlet manifold, and coil it up round the master cylinder.

5 Engine removal: disconnecting the transmission

1 Whilst it is possible to remove the transmission without taking out the engine, the converse is not practicable. Therefore the drive shafts must be disconnected, which is the greatest task in engine removal apart from the actual engine lift.

2 Undo the nut and lock nut on the end of the clutch cable, and disconnect it from the clutch withdrawal lever. Tuck the cable up out of the way.

3 Remove the shield on top of the transmission. (This one is not fitted to some cars).

4 Disconnect the speedometer from the transmission casing.

4.3 Under the car remove the exhaust bracket,

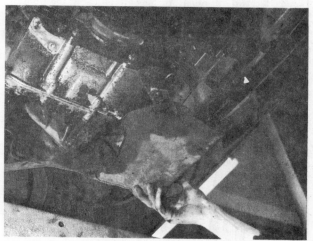

4.4a Take off the shields,

4.4b on both sides and the front.

4.5 Disconnect the gear lever linkage

5 Disconnect the wires to the various switches on the transmission casing. These vary on versions for various markets. For America there are two on the front not fitted for Europe. These work such things as the seat belt warning system, and the emissions control 3rd/4th gear switch. There is another behind and underneath. Note the colours of the wires going to each.

6 Now the drive shafts must be disconnected. The various methods are given in Chapter 7. If deciding to do it by taking out the complete shaft as an assembly, by withdrawing the constant velocity joint from the hub, first remove the hub cap from the wheel, and whilst the car is still on the ground, undo the nuts on the outer end of the drive shafts.

7 Jack the car up until the wheels, hanging free on the suspension, are 1 foot (30 cm) clear of the ground. Put the firm supports under the strong points of the body just behind the wheel arches. Put extra blocks in case the car should shift. There will now be room to work underneath, and pull the power unit clear after it has been lowered to the ground, (photos).

8 Clean the area around the inner end of the drive shafts, so when the rubber boots are removed, no dirt will get in.

9 Remove the drive shafts, as described in Chapter 7.

10 It is then convenient, as it gives more room, to take the suspension completely out of the way. Undo the pivot bolts at the inner end of the suspension arms. Take out the two bolts through the two mountings for the anti-roll bar at the front of the car. The whole assembly is now free, and can be put out of the way whilst the engine is being lowered out.

4.22 Slacken the other end of the reaction steady rod as well as taking out the bolt at the engine.

6 Engine removal: lowering out the power unit

1 The power unit of engine and transmission should now be disconnected after doing the work in the preceding sections, only the actual mountings being left in place. Check that nothing has been forgotten.

2 Connect the lifting tackle to the engine. One eye is on the water pump, and the other just in front of the thermostat. Arrange the sling so that the power unit will hang horizontally. If using ordinary rope, put shackles on the lifting eyes as they are sharp, and would cut the rope.

3 Take the weight of the power unit on the tackle.

4 Bend back the tab washers and take out the two bolts at each end of the bracket under the transmission. Remove the bracket, (photo).

5 Take out the bolt through the mounting bracket at the right end of the engine. Adjust the tackle to ease the load on the bolt so it is free to be pulled out.

6 Recheck nothing is now still connecting the power unit to the car.

7 Lay some planks on the ground onto which the power unit can be lowered, to make it easier to slide it away from under the car.

8 Lower the power unit down onto the planks on the ground.

9 Undo the sling. Drag the power unit from underneath. If it will not fit at the front, it might come out through the wheel arch. But if the car could not originally be jacked up to the recommended height, now transfer the tackle to the front, and lift up the car to allow the engine to be pulled clear.

5.2 Take off the locknut and the adjusting nut from the clutch cable

7 Separating the engine and transmission

1 Clean the outside of the power unit once it has been pulled clear of the car.

2 Remove the starter motor (3 x 13 mm bolts).

3 Undo the 3 bolts holding the bracket to the transmission that pass through the engine end plate.

4 Remove the shield below the engine to transmission joint.

5 Support the transmission so its weight does not hang on the shaft through the clutch.

6 Remove the remaining nuts on the studs holding the transmission to the engine.

7 Pull the transmission off the engine, keeping it straight so the shaft comes out of the clutch without putting any weight on it.

5.3 If the car has one, take off the top shield

5.7 Jack up till the wheels are 1 ft (30 cm) off the ground. Make the car secure

6.4 Support the engine with the lifting tackle, and then undo the bracket underneath

6.5 Take the bolt out of the right bearer mounting

6.8 As the engine is lowered, check nothing is catching

6.9 Once on the ground, it can be pulled from underneath the car

8 Engine replacements: exchange and 'Short' engines

1 Having removed the engine it must be further dismantled, either in preparation for exchange for an official replacement unit. or stripped so overhaul work can be done on it.

2 Exchange units come without all the external components, such as generator, water pump, manifolds, etc. 'Short' engines are also available without other things, such as cylinder head, flywheel, and oil pump.

3 In the sections that follow the removal of these items is covered as for a major overhaul, thhough with comment as to how a particular component can be removed in isolation.

9 Removing the camshaft cogged timing bolt

1 Slacken the 'V' belt at the alternator, and remove it. (See Section 40).
2 Remove the camshaft belt cover. When in the car, the shield under the right end of the engine must be removed, and the belt cover's lower bolt taken off from underneath. If the new belt is being put on without further dismantling, turn the engine over before removing the cover, so that the crankshaft and camshaft pulleys are aligned with their marks. Once the belt is off, do not turn the engine over unless the camshaft is aligned with its mark, or the pistons may hit the valves.
3 Take the load off the belt tensioner. To do this, slacken the nut at the centre of the tensioner pulley. Push the pulley against its spring away from the belt, with a long screwdriver as a lever, and clamp it there by retightening the pulley nut.
4 Slide the belt off the pulleys (photos).
5 Fitting the new belt is described in Section 37.

10 Removal of carburettor and manifolds

1 If the engine is in the car, remove the complete air cleaner, throttle and choke controls, and heat shield as described in sections 3:5 and 3:14.
2 Disconnect the fuel pipe at the carburettor.
3 Take off the water pipes to the carburettor throat from thermostat and inlet manifold, and the brake servo vacuum pipe at the inlet manifold.
4 Unclamp the pipe from the drip tray under the carburettor at the left end of the exhaust manifold.
5 Remove the two nuts holding the carburettor to the inlet manifold. Lift off the carburettor and drip tray.
6 Take off the nuts and large washers that hold both inlet and exhaust manifolds to the engine by their shared studs.
7 Pull off the manifolds, the inlet coming first.

11 Removing the water pump

1 If the engine is still in the car, drain the coolant. Remove the spare wheel and the air cleaner. Slacken the 'V' belt at the generator by easing the pivot bolts underneath, and the adjustment nut at the bracket slot on top. Remove the belt from the pump pulley. Disconnect the carburettor and remove the shield and both exhaust and inlet manifolds complete. Disconnect the heater hoses from the pump and the cylinder head.
2 Remove the adjuster nut from the generator, where it works in the bracket on the pump, so that the bracket will lift clear when the pump is taken off.
3 Undo the hose connections at the thermostat on the end of the pipe running back behind the engine from the pump, and take off the hose.
4 Remove the four large bolts holding the pump to the rear of the cylinder block. (See photos in Chapter 3).
5 Overhaul of the water pump is described in Chapter 2/9.

12 Removing the generator

1 If the engine is in the car, remove the spare wheel and air cleaner. Disconnect the battery lead. Uncouple the throttle linkage. Remove the manifold shield.
2 Disconnect the leads to the generator. Dynamos have two screwed terminals of different sizes, which cannot be muddled. Alternators have a plug.
3 Slacken the two pivot bolts underneath, and the adjuster nut on top of the generator, where it works in the slot in the bracket from the water pump.
4 Take off the 'V' belt.
5 Remove the adjuster nut completely now.
6 Take out the two pivot bolts, holding the generator by hand.

7 Lower the generator clear of the adjuster bracket, and thread it up to the left.

13 Removing the flywheel

1 Take the clutch off the flywheel. Before slackening the bolts mark the position of the clutch. Then slacken the bolts round the edge of the clutch cover gradually and diagonally. This is easing the load on the clutch spring, so must be done carefully.
2 Take the clutch cover assembly off the dowels on the flywheel, catching the friction plate, now loose inside.
3 Slacken the bolts holding the flywheel to the end of the crankshaft, and pull the flywheel off. If the sump is also being removed, a convenient way to prevent the crankshaft turning is to wedge a block of wood between a crank throw and the crank case wall.

14 Auxiliary drive, and minor components

1 If the cylinder block is to be overhauled, the minor components must all be removed to get them out of the way, and to allow cleaning.
2 Remove the crankcase breather fitting on the front of the engine.
3 Take off the distributor. It is held in by a small finger plate secured by a nut. Pull the distributor up out of the engine. Its drive gear may get left behind. This can be retrieved later.
4 Remove the petrol pump, by undoing the two nuts. Pull off the pump bringing with it the plastic distance piece, and take out the rod that actuates the pump from the eccentric on the auxiliary shaft.
5 Remove the right engine mounting bracket from the end of the cylinder block, taking with it the spring loaded plunger of the camshaft drive belt tensioner.
6 Undo the nut on the tensioner pulley, and the bolts through the pulley mounting plate into the cylinder block, and remove the tensioner pulley assembly.
7 Remove the oil pressure warning sender.
8 Take off the oil filter element, and throw it away.
9 Remove the auxiliary shaft. Take out the three bolts holding its end plate to the cylinder block. It can be taken out with the pulley still attached, and if necessary later, this can be taken off when held in a vice. The shaft and end plate draws fowards out of its bearings, and its journals can pass the distributor and oil pump gear still in place.
10 Lift out the distributor drive gear. With long enough fingers, one of these can be wedged inside it. Otherwise, sharpen a wooden stick to a suitable taper, and jam it in the gear. Then pull it up out of the block.

15 Removing the camshaft

1 To remove the camshaft from its housing, the latter must be removed from the cylinder head. But before doing that, or removing the head from the engine, remove the camshaft drive pulley. It is easier to undo the pulley bolt when all is securely mounted. It is assumed the drive belt and the carburettor have already been removed from the engine.
2 To undo the pulley bolt, first bend back its tab washer. Then hammer the end of the spanner hammer, to shift the bolt by using the inertia of the camshaft.
3 Remove the flat shield down the right side of the engine. One bolt is low down. The others by the camshaft pulley, and these can be reached more easily if the pulley is taken off the camshaft.
4 Take the access cover off the camshaft housing.
5 Remove the nuts inside the housing, and these outside, along the rear side, that hold the camshaft housing down on the cylinder head. Ease them all evenly and gradually, as the valve springs will push the housing up.

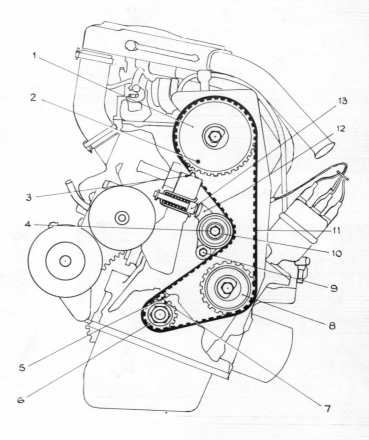

FIG 1.5.b. CAMSHAFT DRIVE

1   Camshaft sprocket
2   Camshaft sprocket timing mark
3   Camshaft mark
4   Adjustment nut
5   Mark on cylinder block
6   Crankshaft cogged pulley
7   Mark on crankshaft cogged pulley, normally concealed by 'V' belt pulley :so the latter's used with belt cover on
8   Auxiliary shaft for oil and fuel pumps, and distributor
9   Tensioner bracket bolt (this can be left tight)
10 Tensioner pulley
11 Cogged belt
12 Lug on tensioner bracket
13 Tensioner spring

9.2 Start dismantling the engine by taking off the belt cover

9.3 After taking off the 'V' belt slacken the camshaft belt by pushing back against the tensioner

9.4 If a new belt is to be put straight back on, turn the engine over till the timing marks align

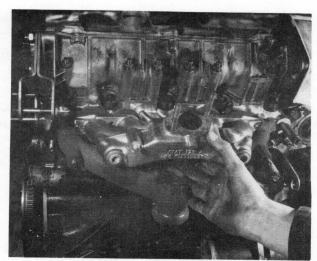

10.7a The manifolds are more easily taken off

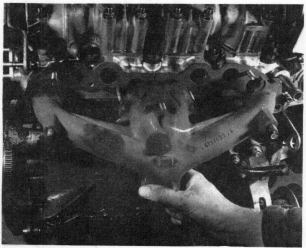

10.7b on the bench.

15.3a Before the camshaft housing can come off the belt guard

15.3b must be unbolted

15.3c There is no need to remove the pulley to get at these three studs, but it is easier

6 Lift off the camshaft housing, taking care the tappets do not fall out. Retrieve them with their shim discs, and keep them all in their respective positions, till they are carried to the bench. (photos).

7 Put all the tappets in some place such as a cardboard box, so they cannot get muddled. Note that No. 1 cylinder is the drive belt end.

8 If not already removed, pull the pulley off the camshaft.

9 Take off the end cap at the other end of the housing.

10 Withdraw the camshaft from the housing.

16 Removing the pistons, rods and big ends

1 The camshaft housing having been removed as described in the previous section, now remove the cylinder head. Slacken the bolts and nuts in reverse order to the tightening sequence shown in Fig.1.18. Jolt the head to break the joint, but do not prise, or the surface will be damaged. Remove the old cylinder head gasket.

2 Note that the pistons are installed so that the cut-out portions for the valves are on the rear side of the engine, away from the auxiliary shaft. Note the amount of carbon on each piston, as this will help give an indication of the state of wear. Such a small engine is usually driven hard. The amount of carbon should be small, and it should be dry. Near the exhaust valve it will be very pale, getting progressively darker nearer the exhaust valve, at which it should be very dark grey. Large amounts of black carbon indicate the engine has been burning oil.

3 Turn the engine onto its side.

4 Remove the sump. Slacken all the bolts gradually and evenly, and take them out with their spring and load spreading washers. Break the joint carefully, so as not to distort the sump face.

5 Remove the oil drain pipe from No 5 main bearing (flywheel end). Remove the breather return drain from beside No. 3 main bearing.

6 If dismantling the main bearings too, take off the oil pump by undoing the three large bolts on its base, (photos).

7 Undo the big end bolts, slackening each in turn slightly first.

8 Take off the big end caps. The caps and the rods are both numbered on the flanks, on the rear side, away from the auxiliary shaft. Keep each bearing shell with its own cap.

9 Push each connecting rod away from the crankshaft, to send the pistons up to the tops of the cylinders. They will not go out of the end easily, as the rings will foul the ridge left on the unworn part. They can finally be pushed out more easily after the crankshaft has been removed.

10 This work can be done with the engine in the car. To remove the sump, the weight of the engine at the left must be taken by a block of wood held up by a jack under the transmission. Then the support bracket is removed.

17 Removing the main bearings and crankshaft

1 Remove the oil pump by undoing the three large bolts on its base.

2 Take the distributor and oil pump drive gear out of its bearing in the block.

3 Remove the flywheel at this stage. The crankshaft can be prevented from turning by wedging a piece of wood between a crank throw and the crankcase wall.

4 Remove the 'V' belt and camshaft pulleys from the crankshaft. Again hold the crankshaft from turning whilst the nut is undone by wedging the crankshaft with wood between throw and wall. A socket or box spanner 38 mm or 1½ in AF will be needed.

5 Take off the oil seal carriers from both ends of the crankshaft, (photos).

6 Mark the main bearing caps with a punch to show the bearing number and which way round each goes.

7 Undo the main bearing cap bolts. Remove the caps, keeping each shell with its cap.

15.6a After lifting up the camshaft housing,

15.6b secure the tappets that fall out and put them in order in their holes

15.9a The pulley must come off if the camshaft is to be taken out of its housing

15.9b Then take off the end cover,

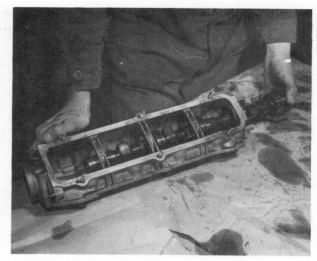

15.10 and simply pull the camshaft out of its bearings

16.4 To take out the pistons, first remove the sump. It is easier on the bench, but possible in the car.

16.5a Clear out of the way

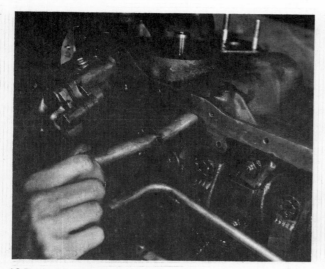

16.5b the oil drip pipes.

16.6 The oil pump must come off anyway if the main bearings have to be taken off.

16.8 But it makes it easier removing the big ends too.

16.9 Push the connecting rod up from the crankshaft, to get the piston over the unworn lip at the top of the cylinder.

17.3a The flywheel is most easily undone when the shaft can be wedged in the crankcase with a block of wood.

17.3b The flywheel cannot go back on the wrong way as the holes are offset

17.5 Take off the oil seal carriers from both ends of the crankshaft

17.7 Before taking off the mains, mark them with a punch to show where and which way round they go.

8 Lift out the crankshaft. Check that the other halves of the bearing shells are not adhering to it. Secure the two semicircular thrust bearings from No. 5 main bearing.

9 If the main bearing shells are being replaced with the engine in place the top half of the shells can be extracted by pushing them round the shaft with a thin screwdriver, turning the shaft at the same time. They must of course go the way the locating groove will allow. Whilst this is being done the crankshaft is supported at the left by the gearbox and on the right by the metal lips of the crankshaft oil seal carrier. When refitting the oil pump, its freedom of rotation must be checked as described in Part C.

PART B — COMPONENT OVERHAUL

18 Renovation: general remarks

1 With the components stripped they can be thoroughly cleaned and then examined. If the car has been run on cheap oil it will be covered internally by sludge. All this must be washed off, and out of hollow sections and oil ways. If the engine is clean having been run on high quality detergent oil do not immerse components in dirty baths of solvents, less dirt is washed in. Scrape off all remnants of gaskets from all joint surface. Use a paint scraper, or a blunt screwdriver.

2 A decision must be taken on what must be replaced. This could be due to cracks, scoring, or just wear. If things you can measure or see are bad, then this will be indicative that other components less easily assessed are in the same state. However, if things are not too bad the engine could be given an extension of life by replacing the components subject to the highest wear; the pistons with rings, and the main and big end bearing shells. The valves will certainly need regrinding. However, such a partial refit will not last long if things like the crankshaft and cylinders are badly worn, as they will be worn oval, and the new components will suffer quickly.

3 Some measurements need micrometers, dial gauges, and the like. On others where clearance is the vital factor, feeler gauges can achieve a lot. If the feeler set is taken apart individual blades can be inserted in things on their own, to see how great a thickness can be put in before the components becomes stiff to move.

19 Work on the cylinder head: decarbonising: valve jobs

1 The overhaul of the cylinder head is much the same whether it has been taken off with the engine in place for a "top overhaul", or if part of a more general engine rebuild. But if doing only a "top overhaul" then it is likely that the soundness of the camshaft, tappets, and valve guides can be taken for granted.

2 Clean off the general dirt and oil from the cylinder head. Remove the thermostat housing from the end.

3 Prepare a box for the valves and their retainers. The lid of a cardboard box can have eight holes punched in it to hold the valves. All must be labelled so they go back where they came from.

4 Place a valve spring clamp round the head and compress the spring enough to fish out the two parts of the split cotter with a small screwdriver. Release the clamp. Take off the cap, the outer and inner valve springs, the two parts of the spring seats, the rubber sealing ring. Early cars only have these on the inlet valves, (photos).

5 Examine the valve seats for signs of bad pitting, and in the case of the exhausts, burning. Check the mating surface of the head to the cylinder block for signs of gasket blowing. With the carbon still on the head the washing marks of leaks and blows should be apparent. Such a engine is usually worked hard. The carbon should be dry and fairly thin, and look "hot"; maybe white, but anyway greyish. If thick, damp, and soft it indicates too much oil getting into the cylinders, either up past the pistons, or down the inlet valve guides.

17.8 If any bearings are reused, they must go back where they came from.

19.4a Place the valve spring clamp so it can span from valve head to spring, and tighten till

19.4b the spring cap has moved far enough to allow the split cotters to be fished out.

19.4c Ease the clamp and remove the valve, storing it so it cannot be muddled up .

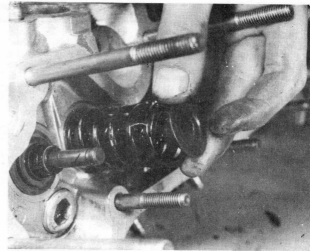

19.4d Take off the spring cap

19.4e and inner and outer springs.

19.4f Then the small

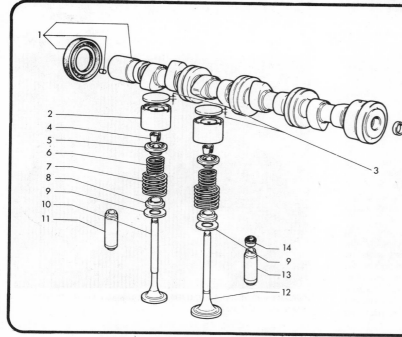

FIG 1.6. THE VALVE GEAR

1 Camshaft
2 Tappet
3 Tappet adjustment shims (in 30 thicknesses at 0.05 mm intervals)
4 Split cotters
5 Spring caps
6 Inner valve springs
7 Outer valve springs
8 Spring seats
9 Spring seats
10 Exhaust valve
11 Exhaust valve guide
12 Inlet valve
13 Inlet valve guide
14 Valve stem oil seal

6 If the cylinder head gasket has been blowing then the head will need refacing. Either your FIAT agent or a local engineering works will get this done for you. The minimum amount necessary to get a clean flat surface should be removed.

7 If the valve seats are badly pitted or burned they will need refacing. Again your FIAT garage, or any large repairer will have the cutters. If you try to do it by lengthy valve grinding then the valve will get badly worn, and the seating contact area will be too wide. The refacing operation includes narrowing of the seat with cutters at 20° and 75°. (See Fig.1.8).

8 If the valve seats are being faced then the valves could be refaced too by the same firm at the same time. However, if the head is all right but the exhaust valves bad, then the most convenient and economical thing to do is to buy new exhaust valves. The inlet valves are usually in quite good condition.

9 The valve guides will be worn. It is very difficult to measure the wear. A useful yardstick is that if you need the crankshaft regrinding you will need new valve guides. It is tricky pressing the old ones out and the new in. It is recommended you get the FIAT agent to do it. He also will have the experience on which to judge the wear. The guides wear more than the valve stems so fitting new valves will not help this much.

10 Having decided what work must be done by a professional, now clean up the head. Scrape off all the carbon. Be careful not to scratch the valve seats. These are hard inserts, but a small scratch will be difficult to grind out. The head is made of aluminium, so soft, and easily cut when scraping. The combustion chambers, and inlet and exhaust ports, must be cleaned. A blunt screwdriver and flat paint scraper are useful. If using a wire brush on an electric drill wear goggles.

11 It is after this that the head should be taken for any machining. Also during the cleaning any cracks will be found. Should this unlikely event occur the solution must be another head.

12 Clean all carbon off the valves. It is convenient to do their head tops by putting them (unfixed) in their seat in the cylinder head. Scrape off all deposits under the head, and down the valve stem. The rubbing surface where the stem runs in the guide should be highly polished by wear; do not touch this, but the part of the stem nearer the head may have lacquered deposits that can be removed with fine emery paper. At this stage do not touch the valve's seating surface.

13 Now grind in the valves. Even new ones will need grinding in to bed them to their actual seat. If the seats and valves or just the one, have been recut, the hand grinding must still be done.

14 The idea is to rub the valve to and fro, to mate valve and seat, and give a smooth flat perfectly circular sealing surface. The end product should be matt grey, without any rings or shine worn on it. The seating surface should be about midway up the valves 45°

surface, not at the top, which happens if a valve is refaced so often it becomes small, and sits too deep in the seat.

15 The best tool is a rubber sucker on the end of a stick. Unless the sucker is good, and the valve absolutely oil free it keeps coming off. Handles that clamp to the stem overcome this, but they are clumsy to hold. On no account use an electric drill; a to-and-fro motion is essential.

16 If the valves and seats have been refaced you will only need fine grinding paste. If cleaning up worn seats start with coarse.

17 Smear a little of the paste all round the seat, being very careful to get none on the valve stem. Insert the valve in its place. Put the valve grinding handle on the valve, and pushing it lightly down onto its seat rotate one way then the other. Every now and then lift the valve clear of the seat, turn it about half a turn, and then carry on. By altering the position the grinding paste is redistributed, and also the valve will work all round the seat and make it circular.

18 If coarse paste is used try and judge the change to fine just before all marks have disappeared so that they and the large grain of the coarse paste are ground out at the same time; the least metal rubbed off the better, otherwise the seat will get too broad.

19 The seat should be a uniform pale grey. Rings are a sign that the valve has not been lifted and turned enough. If a long grind is needed the paste will get blunt, so wipe off the old and smear on some new. A spring under the valve head can help in the lifting, but it is difficult to find a suitable light one.

20 Clean off all traces of valve grinding paste very thoroughly. Wipe out the valve guides by pushing clean rag through a number of times. Engine oil makes a good detergent for this, particularly if squirted through hard with a good oil can such as a Wesco. Leave everything oily to prevent rust.

21 The valve springs may need replacing. Measure their height as they stand free. If they have shortened by 1/16 in or 1.5 mm they should be renewed.

22 Reassemble the valves to the head. Make sure the valve goes into the correct seat, into which it was ground. Oil the guides, and the valves all over, before assembly.

23 Insert the valve in its seat. In the case of inlet valves, (all valves on the 1290cc engine) then fit the new oil seal, and push it down into place on the valve guide. Put the spring seats over the stem, followed by the springs. If the springs used have a varying spiral, put the end which has the spring coils closest together next to the head.

24 Put the cap on the spring.

25 Put the valve spring compressing clamp round the head and compress the spring. It needs to go just so far that the groove in the end of the stem is about half clear of the cap.

26 Put in the two split cotters. Undo the clamp gradually, if

19.4g and large seat washers

19.4h Throw away the oil seals, and use new ones.

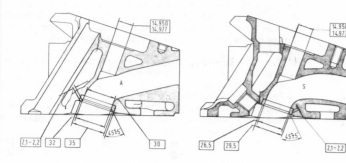

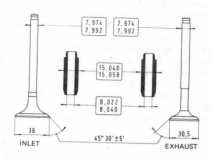

Fig 1.7. Inlet valve seat (left)
Exhaust valve seat (right)

Fig.1.8 Dimensions of inlet and exhaust valves and their guides. If refaced, there must be a margin of 0.02 in (0.5 mm) between crown and seat

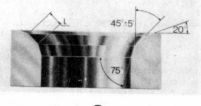

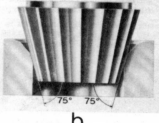

a   b   c

FIG 1.9 a VALVE SEATS SHOULD BE NARROWED TO L= .083 TO .087 in (2.1 TO 2.2 mm) AFTER REFACING

b   The seat bottom is narrowed with a 75º cutter
c   The top is narrowed with a 20º cutter

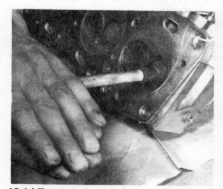

19.14 To ensure a smooth, matt seat, grind the valve to and fro,

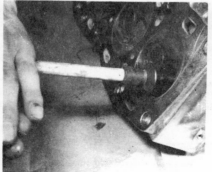

19.17 occasionally lifting and turning it to respread the grinding paste, and change position. There must not be rings on the seat surface.

20.4 The pistons have letter A to E giving their size grade, and numbers 1, 2, 3, for the small end bearing size. This one is a faint C2.

necessary moving the spring cap about to let it slide up the cotters to settle into position and clamp them properly.

27 When all the valves are assembled, fit the camshaft in its housing, with the tappets, to the head whilst the latter is still on the bench, even though it will later have to be removed if the head is being fitted without the special spanners. Do not bother which shim goes to which tappet. Indeed use eight of the thinnest at this stage.

28 Now check the tappet clearances.

29 At the first try there may be no clearance on some valves, particularly if the seats or the valves have been refaced, and so allowed the valve to move a long way into its seat. If so, remove the camshaft housing again. If the thinnest made shim was already in use, the tip of the valve stem will have to be ground away. To do this, remove the valve from the head. On a fine grind stone, holding the valve very straight, grind a little metal off. Put the camshaft housing back on the head, and try the valve without springs, and using in the tappet a shim about a third of the way up the range from the thinnest. Keep trying the valve and grinding a little off at a time till it is a suitable length.

30 For other valves having some clearance at the trial assembly, write down the tappet clearances found. Then remove the camshaft, read off or measure the thickness of the shims in use, and change them for ones that will correct the tappet clearance. Put these shims with the tappets, ready for final assembly after the head is back on the engine. Note that the side with the number on it should be towards the tappet, away from the camshaft, so the correct side will take the wear.

31 After final assembly it may be necessary to alter some of the tappet clearances, so do not ignore later checks.

32 If you removed the cylinder head just for a top overhaul the cleaning of the head must be matched by removing the carbon from the piston crowns. Turn the engine over, to get two pistons to top dead centre. Scrape, using a flat blunt paint scraper or wide screwdriver, all the carbon and odd bits of gasket off the piston crown and the cylinder top face. When all is clean debris between the cylinders must be removed, and not allowed to fall into the neighbouring cylinder, or the water passages. Then turn the engine over to lower the piston about an inch. Carefully wipe away carbon sticking to the walls, rubbing gently so as not to knock off the carbon on the top, unworn bits, of the wall. This reputedly should be left as it helps the piston seal at TDC. Now squirt engine oil over the piston to flood the edge. Work the piston up and down several times to was delvis to the top, where it can be wiped away.

33 If the cylinder head face was remachined, it will bring the valves down nearer the pistons. If the machining was done by a FIAT agent he should have checked the height with the FIAT gauge A 96216. If the gap between the head and the measuring edge of this gauge is more than .01 in (0.25 mm) the head is too thin and must be replaced. If this gauge is not available then the head must be reassembled temporarily using tappet shims to reduce the clearance to .001 in (0.02 mm), and without a cylinder head gasket. Then turn the engine over very gently by hand to check there is no foul of piston and valve. If there is a foul, it is essential that the head is measured using the proper FIAT gauge. Though with normal tappet clearance and using a gasket, the valves might not foul when the engine is running slowly, at speed the pistons fly up to the top of their bearing clearance, and valves can deviate from close contact with the cam, so such a crude method of checking clearance as detailed earlier can only be used to a limited extent. See Fig.1.10.

20 Cylinder, Piston, Small end Overhaul

1 The oil consumption and exhaust oil smoke will have given some indication as to the wear of the bores and pistons. Once the cylinder head has been removed they can be measured properly.

2 Scrape the carbon off the unworn lip at the top of the bore so that its original size can be compared with the worn.

3 Measure the bore diameters. They will be worn more, near the top than the bottom, and more across than fore and aft. If the difference between the largest and smallest dimension exceeds .006 in (.15 mm) then the ovality is excessive and a rebore is necessary. If the bores have any scores they should be rebored.

4 Even if the cylinders may not need reboring it is possible the pistons and rings will need replacing. They will have worn on their outer circumferential surfaces, and where the ring contacts the piston land in its groove.

5 Slide an appropriate feeler sideways into the piston groove to measure the clearance between each ring and its neighbouring land (and write down the result to think about later).

6 Carefully expand the rings and lift them off the piston. Insert the piston into the cylinder at its correct axis (valve cut outs away from the auxiliary shaft). Find the fattest feeler gauge that will pass between piston and bore with the piston halfway down its stroke to get the widest part of the bore. Also measure opposite the ridge at the top. You have now got the actual clearance at the worn bit, and by comparing it with the clearance at the top, the cylinder wear. Take out the pistons. Insert a piston ring. Push it halfway down the cylinder with a piston, so that it is square. Measure the gap in the ring.

7 If the clearance between cylinder and piston or piston and ring is excessive then the pistons must be replaced, and new rings fitted to them. New rings can be fitted to old pistons by specialist firms who will machine out the grooves, which will be worn conical, and supply suitable fat rings. But this is not really economic. The wear limits are listed separately in the specification.

8 Note that it is most important if fitting new pistons in the existing bores that the top ring has a step cut out of its top so that it will not hit the ridge left at the top of the bore This will have been left by a worn piston ring. Should normal new rings be fitted, they will foul, which would anyway cause a knock, but probably also break the rings. Note also that the second and third rings have a special scraping bottom edge. The bores have three sizes, and the piston matching size is marked on it.

9 FIAT supply new pistons (and oversize ones) complete with rings and gudgeon pin; but not ones with the stepped top ring necessary if not reboring. This may persuade you to have the cylinders rebored, which would make a thorough job anyway.

10 Unless the pistons are to be replaced, on the 1116 cc engine do not try to remove the gudgeon pins. They are a shrink fit in the connecting rods.

11 On the 1290 cc engine of the Rally and Coupe the gudgeon pins are fully floating, and can be removed after taking out one of the circlips.

12 The small ends should last the life of the pistons. If new pistons are being fitted, then new gudgeon pins should be used too. On the 1290 cc engine this also involves a replacement bush for the connecting rod. There should be no discernible free movement in the small ends at all.

13 To get out the gudgeon pin on the 1116 cc engine it must be pressed. Without the special tools, it is likely the piston will be crushed but this does not matter if they are being renewed.

14 To fit the new gudgeon pin, first check its fit in the piston. It should go in by hand pressure, but be such a good fit it will not fall out due to its own weight.

15 Also before fitting the pistons to their connecting rods, weigh all the pistons, and check their weights are all within specifications. If not, see paragraph 20.

16 Turn on a kitchen oven, and allow it to heat to 464°F (240°C). Once it is up to the set temperature put one connecting rod in. Do not do all at the same time, or some will be held at the high temperature too long. Leave the rod to heat for 15 minutes. Get the piston and gudgeon pin ready so that they can be fitted to the rod with the valve cuts in the crown on the same side as the number stamped at the big end. Then remove the rod from the oven and fit the gudgeon pin quickly, giving no time for the rod to cool, or the pin to expand when it starts to get hot from the rod. Get the pin symetrically placed, equally in each boss of the piston.

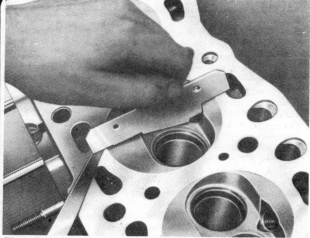

Fig.1.10 Checking the depth of the combustion chamber with FIAT gauge A.96216, to ensure the valves will not hit the pistons. There must be clearance of at least 0.01 in (0.25 mm) between gauge and head face. If not the head must be scrapped.

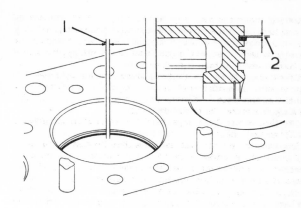

Fig.1.11 Measure the piston ring gap in the bore, (1). Measure the gap between ring and piston land, (2).

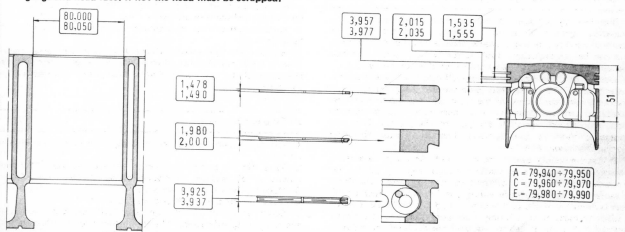

Fig.1.12a Cylinder bore, piston, and piston ring dimensions. If fitting new rings in a worn bore, the top ring must have a step cut out of its top face.

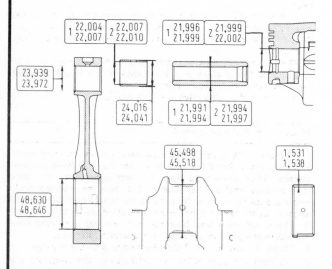

Fig.1.12b Dimensions of big and small ends

Fig.1.13 Piston and connecting rod markings

1 Gudgeon pin bore class number (1 to 3)
2 Piston grade letter (A to E)
3 Cylinder number for big end on rod and cap

17 Before fitting the new rings to the pistons check the size of the ring gap. Insert the ring into its cylinder, and push it halfway down the bore, using a piston so that it is square. Measure the gap with feeler gauges. If the gap is too small file it with a fine file, being careful, as the rings are brittle.

18 Check when fitting that all the rings are the right way up. They must be expanded only the minimum amount to get them over the piston lands. It is useful to cut a guide out of an old tin, and wrap this round the top of the piston.

19 The gaps in the three rings should all be equally spaced out, at 120° to each other.

20 The pistons' weights must all be within 2.5 grams, the same. If the spread is wider than this, the heavier ones must be lightened by milling metal off the underside of the small end bosses. If a proper milling machine is not available, then a disc of diameter 70 mm should be put on the sander of an electric drill. Use 'wet or dry' paper of grade 180. On no account reduce the piston height more than the minimum 52.20 mm (2.055 in), or the small end will be too weak, (See Fig.1.14).

21 Crankshaft, mains, big ends, overhaul

1 The bearing surfaces of the crankshaft journals and pins should be bright and smooth. If there are scratches or scoring they will need regrinding. Measure the diameters of the bearings in a number of directions, looking for ovality, (photo). If the ovality exceeds 0.001 in (0.03 mm) then this is excessive purely as ovality, but also implies that overall wear will be too much. Take it to a FIAT agent, who can arrange the regrinding simultaneously with the supply of the main and big end shells to the suitable undersize. Otherwise you must take it to a machine shop, who could regrind it for you to the journal sizes, less undersize, given in specifications. Then you order the new bearing shells from FIAT.

2 If the crankshaft ovality seems all right you may be able to measure the clearance to confirm overall wear is within the condemnation limit. It is difficult to measure, and difficult to measure the shaft accurately enough, to know how much of the wear is from the shaft, and how much off the shells. But ovality is easier to measure as it is only a comparison. No ovality means neglible shaft wear. It can be assumed the shells will have worn. One way to measure the clearance is to use 'Plastigage' a crushable plastics strip. The bearings are reassembled with the gauge inside, and the amount it is squashed is measured.

3 Unless the engine has done a very low mileage, and the shells appear of an even, matt colour, they should be replaced anyway, if events have made the engine require dismantling. Remove the shells from their caps. If they are stubborn, just slide them round by pressure at the end. Confirm that the crankshaft is standard by looking at the markings on the backs of the shells. Because the shells are so easily fitted, are relatively cheap, it is false economy to try and make do with the old ones. The converse is true. New shells to the big ends and mains without otherwise dismantling the engine is a useful way of giving an engine renewed soundness.

4 If the white metal of the old shells is badly broken up, and if the engine had been knocking badly, and for a long time, then this will be confirmation that the crankshaft needs regrinding as well as the shells renewing.

5 The connecting rods need to be straight. It is difficult to check them without proper instruments and blocks on the surface plate. If the engine is just suffering "fair wear and tear" then straightness can be assumed. But they should be checked if there has been any catastrophy such as seizure. If you have not the experience or equipment, take the connecting rods to your local engineering works. They can be bent straight if faulty.

22 Flywheel overhaul

1 There are two things to check; the clutch pressure surface, and the starter ring.

2 If the clutch has been badly worn, or badly overheated by slipping the surface on which the clutch presses may be scored or cracked. This would wear a new clutch plate rapidly. The flywheel should not be skimmed to remove these, but replaced.

3 Wear on the starter gear ring should not be bad, as the starter is the pre-engaged type. Check that there are no broken teeth, or burrs. Minor blemishes can be filed off. If there is a bad defect a new starter ring is required, though it may prove cheaper in the long run, and will certainly be easier, to buy a complete new flywheel.

4 To remove the old ring, it must be split by cutting with a cold chisel. Take care not to damage the flywheel, though again, minor burrs can be filed off.

5 To fit a new ring gear, it will be necessary to heat it gently and evenly with an oxy-acetylene flame until a temperature of approximately 350°C is reached. (This is indicated by a grey/brown surface colour). With the ring gear at this temperature, fit it to the flywheel with the front of the teeth facing the clutch fitting end of the flywheel. The ring gear should be either pressed or lightly tapped onto its register and left to cool naturally when the contraction of the metal on cooling will ensure that it is a secure and permanent fit. Great care must be taken not to overheat the ring gear, for if this happens the temperature of the ring gear will be lost.

6 An alternative method is to use a high temperature oven to heat the ring.

7 Because of the need of oxy-acetylene equipment or a special oven it is not practical for refitment to take place at home. Take the flywheel and new starter ring to an engineering works willing to do the job.

23 Oil pump overhaul

1 Carefully clamp the pump housing in a vice, shaft downwards.

2 Take off the pump cover, with the suction pipe. This will release the oil pressure relief valve inside. Also inside is a filter.

3 Remove the internal cover plate.

4 Take out the drive shaft and the gears.

5 Clean and examine all the parts. Measure the clearances against the specification. The end clearnace is measured by putting a straight edge across the cover face.

6 The oil pump should only need replacements after very long mileage, when the rest of the engine is showing great signs of wear.

7 The length of a new gear is given in specification, so that the effect of just replacing that can be judged, to see if it will restore the end clearance to specification. Otherwise the housing must be changed.

8 The driven gear shaft is mounted in the housing with an interference fit. If there is any slackness a new housing, which will come with shaft fitted, must be used.

9 The pump shares its drive with the distributor.

24 Camshaft and tappet checks

1 The camshaft journals and cams should be smooth and shiny.

2 Any tappet shims that are to be reused must have a mirror surface. After some time their size gets rubbed off, and they must be measured by micrometer. It is recommended the thicknesses are measured, and tappet clearances adjusted using metric measure, as all the parts lists and orders are done by this.

3 Check the camshaft bearings and the tappets, and their corresponding parts in the housing are within tolerance.

4 Check the cam height. This is best done with a dial gauge.

5 Provided the cam height is satisfactory, the camshaft will probably be serviceable, and bearing wear will be confined to the housing. If the housing is worn, either at the tappets or the camshaft bearings, it should be replaced. Worn bearings will allow too much oil to escape. Worn tappet bores allow the tappets to get crooked, then wear becomes faster.

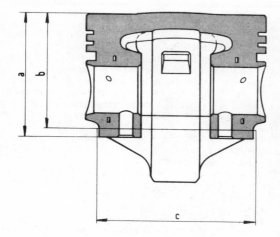

Fig.1.14 Milling dimensions when balancing piston weights

a = Nominal piston height, =
2.232 in (56.70 mm)
b = Minimum height after mill-

ing = 2.055 in (56.20 mm)
c = Maximum milling diameter
= 2.756 in (70 mm)

Note that on the 1290 cc pistons, the milling will not go to the
outer part of the small end boss.

21.1 Measure the crank journals and pins in two directions to
gauge ovality, which is just as important as the actual size.

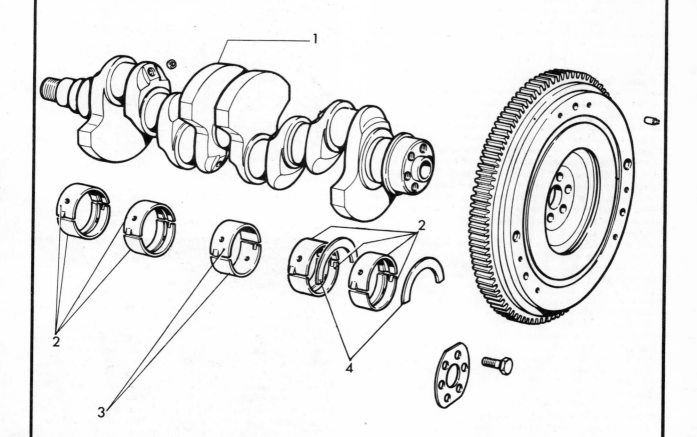

FIG 1.15. CRANKSHAFT AND MAIN BEARINGS

1 Crankshaft	2 Main bearing shells	3 Centre (no 3) main bearing shells without oil groove	4 Thrust bearings in no 5 main bearing

25 Auxiliary shaft and drives: examination

1   The shaft journals, the fuel pump eccentric, and the drive gear for the distributor and oil pump should be smooth and shiny. If not, the shaft will have to be replaced.
2   The bushes should still be tight in the cylinder block, their oil holes lined up with those in the block.
3   Measure the bearing clearance. If excessive the bushes will have to be replaced. They are a press fit, and require reaming with a special reamer after fitting. This is a job best done by a FIAT agent with the special tools. See Fig.1.16.
4   Ensure the new bushes are fitted with the oil holes lined up.
5   Also check the driven gear and its bush.
6   It is recommended a new oil seal is fitted in the end plate. Hold the shaft in a vice, and remove the pulley. Fit the new oil seal in the end plate, lips inwards.

26 Drive belt tensioner checks

1   Check the bearing revolves smoothly and freely, and has no play. Do not immerse it in cleaning fluid, as it is partially sealed. But wipe the outside, and then smear in some new general purpose grease, such as Castrol LM Grease.
2   The action of the spring will have been felt when the belt was taken off. It should be cleaned, and oiled, to prevent seizure by dirt and rust.

27 Engine mounting condition

Check the rubber of the mountings. If these are deformed, or soft from oil, or badly perished, they should be replaced.

PART C – REASSEMBLY PROCEDURES

28 Reassembly: General remarks

1   Cleanliness is vital. Particles of grit in components, particularly when starting up, will score them, the situation being aggravated by the good new tight fit, and the time taken for the oil pump to circulate oil to wash them clean.
2   All parts must be liberally oiled, with engine oil. This oil must serve the component till the oil ways are all filled by the pump, after which proper circulation will start. The oiling is also a final protection against dirt, as it washes as well as lubricating.
3   All parts must be tightened evenly and gradually. New gaskets and oil seals must be used to ensure an oil-tight engine, and they must only be fitted to clean surfaces, with the remains of old gaskets removed.
4   Lay out the parts in order, checking you know where everything goes before starting. Sheets of clean newspaper should be laid out on the working surface. The garage should not be liable to wind blowing dust over the parts.

29 Refitting the crankshaft with main bearings

1   Fit the main bearing shells to their seats in the crankcase, and to the caps. The seatings, and the rear of the shells, must be spotlessly clean, and dry, or they will not seat properly. (photos)
2   Put the semicircular thrust bearings in No. 5 main bearing.
3   Oil the bearings in the crankcase, and the journals on the crankshaft.
4   Lift the shaft into place.
5   Fit the main bearing caps to the correct bearing positions, the right way round, using the marks made before dismantling.
6   Tighten the caps evenly to the set torque of 58 lb ft (8 kg m).
7   Check the shaft rotates smoothly.
8   Fit the new oil seals to the carriers: lips inwards: Note the arrow for the direction of rotation. Using new gaskets fit the carriers to the ends of the crankcase. Keep the bottom edge straight and level with that of the crankcase, using a rule. Do not let any gasket stick out, or else trim off the excess with a knife. (photos).

29.1 The bearings, especially their backs, must be scrupulously clean.

29.3 Everything must be oiled as it goes together

29.8 Fit the oil seals lips inwards, and take care the sharp sealing edge does not get damaged.

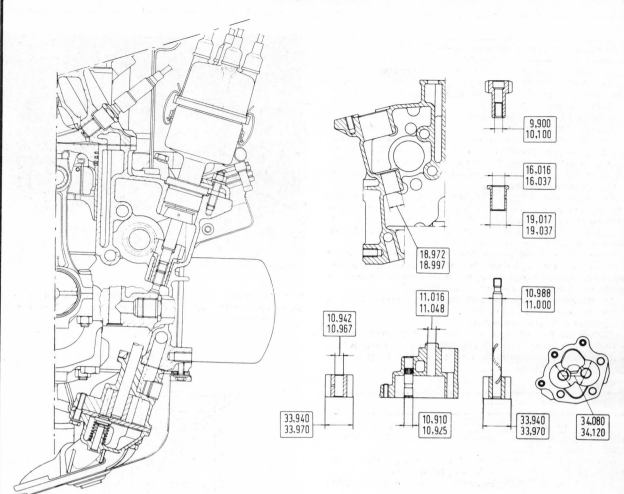

Fig 1.16.a. Oil pump and its drive dimensions

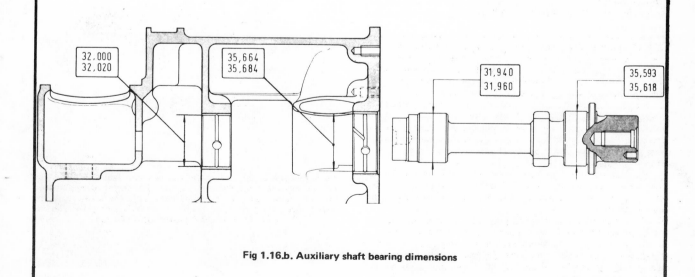

Fig 1.16.b. Auxiliary shaft bearing dimensions

30 Refitting pistons, connecting rods, and big ends

1 Fit the new shells into the rods and caps, ensuring the surfaces on which the shells sit are clean and dry. The pistons will already have been fitted to the connecting rods, as described in Section 20:14.

2 Arrange the piston rings so that their gaps are evenly spaced, at 120°. Oil them liberally.

3 Fit a clamp round the rings of No. 1 piston. Though they can be eased in by fingers, they are brittle, and easily broken, and replacements are unlikely to be available. A large hose clip of the Jubilee or Cheney type will do as a clamp, but do not screw it up so tight the piston is nipped.

4 Oil the cylinder bores. Insert the connecting rod down the bore, checking the cylinder number is correct. The number stamped on the rod's big end should be to the rear of the engine, away from the auxiliary shaft, and the same for the cuts for the valves in the piston crown. (Photo and Fig.1.17).

5 Lower the rod and piston down till the clamp round the rings is on the top of the cylinder block. Then tap the crown of the piston softly to push it out of the clamp into the bore. Be careful the rings do not catch and break, (photo).

6 Oil the crankpin, and then pull the big end down into place.

7 Fit the big end cap, and the nuts.

8 Repeat for the other cylinders.

9 Tighten the big end nuts evenly, and to the torque of 36 lb ft (5 kg m). The correct torque is very important for these, as they have no locking arrangements. Check the shaft rotates freely after tightening each one.

31 Refitting the auxiliary shaft

1 Oil and fit the distributor/oil pump drive gear into the cylinder block, lowering it stuck on a finger, or if too short, a length of wood, (photo).

2 Oil and fit the auxiliary shaft into the right end of the cylinder block. Check it turns the distributor gear easily.

3 Fit a new oil seal to the end plate, and put this on the end of the engine.

4 Fit the pulley, and its nut, tightening it as much as convenient for now, and doing so fully when the camshaft belt has been fitted.

5 Refit the right hand engine bearer bracket, with the belt tensioner in its hole, and the new engine rubber mounting if being replaced.

6 Fit the belt tensioner pulley (photo).

32 Refitting the flywheel, clutch, and the crankshaft pulleys

1 Put the flywheel in place on the end of the crankshaft. Make sure the flange for the flywheel is clean, so it seats down true. The bolt holes are offset, so it can only go on one way.

2 Fit the bolt bearing plate, then the bolts, and tighten them evenly to 61 lb ft (8.5 kg m). If the sump is still off, the engine can be stopped from turning by wedging a block between crank throw and case, provided the block is absolutely clean. Otherwise prevent the engine from turning by using a screwdriver on the starter ring.

3 Fit the cogged belt pulley to the crankshaft, the timing dot mark outwards, (photo). Fit the 'V' belt pulley. Put the large nut on the end of the crankshaft, and holding the shaft as before, tighten the nut.

4 Hold the clutch driven plate up against the flywheel. The disc holding the cushion springs must be away from the flywheel.

5 Put the clutch cover assembly over the driven plate, lining up the dowel holes, and fit the bolts. Tighten the bolts finger tight, just enough to take the weight of the driven plate between the pressure plate and the flywheel.

6 Now centralise the clutch plate. The splines in the plate must be accurately lined up with the end of the crankshaft, otherwise

30.4 The piston must be on the rod so the big end numbers on cap and rod, and the valve cuts in the piston are all the same side.

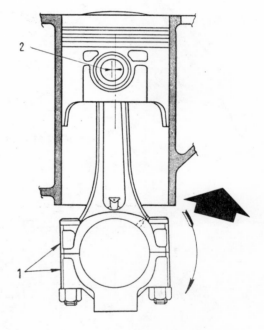

Fig.1.17 Pistons and connecting rods are installed so that the Big end numbers (1) and the cuts for the valves in the piston crown, and the piston off-set (2) are all away from the auxiliary shaft (Broad arrow) which is in the front of the engine. This view is from the camshaft-belt-end of the engine.

30.5a They go into the engine AWAY from the auxiliary shaft

30.5b Use a piston ring clamp, loose enough to allow the rings to slide out and into the cylinder

30.9 Of all things, the correct torque is vital for the big end nuts. They have no other locking arrangement

31.1 Poke in the distributor drive gear with long fingers or a wooden stick

31.2 Engage the auxiliary shaft with the distributor gear

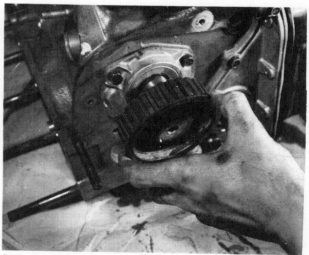

31.3a After fitting the oil seal and pulley

31.3b and the oil pump, turn the auxiliary shaft to check it drives the pump freely. If there is binding, slacken and reposition the oil pump. Then fit the sump.

31.6 The belt tensioner has this stepped washer and supporting washers so it can move on its stud, for adjustment.

32.2 The crankshaft can be held whilst tightening nuts by a screw driver in the starter ring

32.3a Though normally hidden, there is a timing mark on the crankshaft belt pulley.

32.3b The 'V' belt pulley goes timing notch outside. Then tighten the pulley nut to the correct torque, using a 38 mm (or 1½ in) AF socket

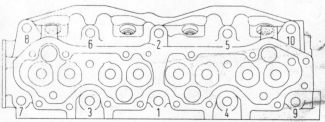

Fig.1.18 Tightening sequence for the cylinder head nuts and bolts. They must be done gradually, working round and round in the order shown.

when the clutch is clamped up tight, and the friction plate cannot be moved, the shaft will not fit through, and reassembly of transmission to engine will be impossible. FIAT use a special mandrel that fits into the end of the crankshaft. The transmission could be lifted temporarily into place, though usually then the plate is inadvertently shifted as it is taken off again. The alignment can be done satisfactorily using a metal or wooden bar, and checking carefully by eye.

7 Tighten the bolts round the edge of the clutch cover carefully and diagonally, gradually compressing the clutch spring.

33 Refitting the oil pump and sump

1 Refit the oil drip pipe for the breather by No. 3 main bearing.
2 Refit the oil drain pipe to No. 5 main bearing.
3 Put back the oil pump, using a new gasket between it and the crankcase, and tighten the 3 large bolts.
4 Temporarily insert the distributor into the block.
5 Rotate the auxiliary shaft, to check the oil pump turns without binding. If there is any binding, release the oil pump bolts, shift it slightly and try again: try tightening the pump whilst rotating the auxiliary shaft.
6 Remove the distributor for now.
7 Grease the new sump gasket to stick it in place, and fit the sump. Put the load spreading washers on each bolt, and fit them.
8 Tighten the sump bolts evenly.

34 Putting the camshaft into its housing

1 Oil the housing and the shaft.
2 Hold the housing on end, and lower the camshaft into it.
3 Fit a new gasket, and then put the end plate on the left end of the housing.
4 Fit the pulley to the camshaft after the head is back on and the guard fitted.

35 Refitting the cylinder head

1 The cylinder head will have been cleaned up as described in Section 19. The camshaft housing will have been removed again from the head after setting the valve clearance, so that the cylinder head nuts can be tightened without the special spanners. The tappets were set before fitting the head as part of the valve grinding operation, because the valves will be sitting deeper in the seats after grinding. If the grinding had taken any valve beyond the range of shims, then the valve stem will have had to be ground down, and this must be done with the valve removed from the head.
2 Make sure all dirt has been wiped off the cylinder bores, then turn the engine over till all the pistons are half way down their cylinders. Then there can be no risk of valves fouling pistons whilst the timing is being set prior to fitting the camshaft belt.
3 Fit the two dowels to the cylinder block.
4 Fit the cylinder head gasket, with the word 'ALTO' upwards, (photo).
5 Lower the cylinder head into position.
6 Using the large thick washers to spread the load on the soft aluminium head, fit the nuts and studs, and tighten them finger tight. Then using a torque spanner, tighten them gradually and in the sequence in the diagram. First bring them to a tightness of 29 lb ft (4 kg m). Then finally tighten them to 61 lb ft (8.5 kg m). See Fig. 1.18.
7 Fit the camshaft, in its housing, with all the tappets in their numbered places, and the correct adjustment shims in their seats. If for any reason the tappets have not been set, then use thin shims for now. Or if the valves have not been touched, then keep the existing shims in their original places. Use a new gasket between the head and the camshaft housing.
8 Before tightening down the camshaft housing, check the

pistons are still halfway down the bores. This is shown by the timing notch in the 'V' belt pulley being at 3 or 9 o'clock, 90° away from the TDC position. Then there is no risk of a valve fouling a piston before the timing has been set or the tappets adjusted.
9 Fit the washers and nuts to the camshaft housing studs, and tighten them gradually, so the housing is pulled down level, keeping parallel to the top of the cylinder head, despite places in the head.
10 Fit the two parts of the guard to the right end of the engine, stretching down from the head to the engine cylinder block.
11 If the pulley has been removed from the camshaft, fit it now, but only tighten its bolt as much as is convenient at this stage, as this is easier done when the belt has been fitted.
12 Recheck the tappet clearances, ensuring the engine is still with the pistons half way down their bores, and turning the camshaft over by the bolt through the pulley.
13 Reset any tappet clearances that are wrong. See the next Section.
14 Once the tappets have been adjusted, turn the camshaft until its timing dot on the pulley is aligned with the pointer on the right end of the engine.
15 Now turn the engine to TDC. There are marks on the flywheel that are used with pointers on the transmission casing, through a hole just below the thermostat. Otherwise, temporarily put the camshaft belt cover in place, and align the notch in the 'V' belt pulley with the right hand line on the cover.
16 It is important that the camshaft is put to the TDC position before the crankshaft is moved, otherwise valves may foul the pistons as they come to the top of their stroke with valves fully open.
17 Now fit a timing belt. It is kinder to the new belt if the old one is temporarily fitted. With this to hold the pulleys, tighten the bolts on the camshaft and auxiliary shafts. Bend over the lock tabs on both the shafts.
18 Now fit the new camshaft drive belt, and adjust it. See Section 37.
19 Fit the thermostat into its housing, and the housing to the left end of the cylinder head, using new gaskets.
20 If the head was removed with the engine in the car, now fit the manifolds, and carburettor, as described in Section 41. Reconnect all the controls. Fit and adjust the 'V' belt as described in Section 40. Refit all the hose connections, and the radiator and bonnet if these were removed. Fill up with water. Refer to Chapter 2, the later part of Section 4, regarding swilling out the cooling system to remove carbon. See Section 45 regarding precautions to be taken when first starting up.

36 Tappet adjustment

1 The valve clearance at the tappets is item 3.7 of the 6,000 miles (10,000 km) task. The tappets should also be checked if the camshaft housing is removed from the cylinder head for any reason, and particularly if a new gasket has been fitted which would upset the height of the camshaft above the head. Adjustment will be essential if the valves have been reground into the head. If the clearance is too large, the engine will be noisy, timing and valve lift will be wrong, and the valves will be opened with an excessive blow. If too small, timing is wrong, and lift may be excessive enough for a valve to hit a piston. If there is no clearance at all, then compression is lost, and the valve and seat will soon burn. The tappets should be set with the engine cold.
2 Remove the camshaft housing cover. Jack up a front wheel, and engage top gear, to use the wheel to turn the engine over.
3 Each tappet must be checked when its cam is 'On its back', (photo) that is the lobe is upwards, 180° away from the valve. Work along the engine doing the cylinders in the firing order, 1 (the right hand cylinder), then 3, 4, 2, doing the exhaust of one cylinder and the inlet of the one after at the same time to minimise the amount the engine must be turned over.
4 Insert the feeler for the appropriate valve Inlet 0.012 in (0.30 mm); Exhaust 0.016 in (0.40 mm). The feeler should slide

35.4 Fit the cylinder head gasket with the word 'ALTO' uppermost

35.5 Before fitting the cylinder head, turn the engine over till the pistons are all half way down their stroke.

35.11 With the pistons out of the way the camshaft can be turned over independantly without fear of the valves fouling a piston

FIG 1.19.a. CHECKING TAPPET CLEARANCE

1 Cam lobe
2 Tappet shim
3 Tappet
4 Feeler gauge

Fig.1.19b Inserting FIAT tool A. 60421 to adjust the clearance

Fig.1.19c The shim (1) of the tappet being adjusted can now be extracted. The tool is holding down the two adjacnet tappets (2).

in readily, but with slight friction. Try one of size larger and smaller. The large should not fit at all, the smaller go in loosely. If wrong, try different feelers to measure what the clearance actually is. Write down the result. When all results are known, change the tappet shims to correct the clearances.

5 To change a shim, with the cam on its back again, turn the tappet in its housing till the slot in the rim is towards you.

6 Depress the tappet with the special tool.

7 If you have not got a special tool, push the tappet down with one screwdriver placed centrally. Then wedge it down with another on edge at the side. This is very tricky. It might be quicker possibly to remove the camshaft housing. (See Section 15 and 3:26). Best of all is to get the job done by the FIAT agent. As well as the tool, they will have a stock of shims from which to choose the necessary ones to correct the clearance It is expensive to buy a stock.

8 Prise out the shim with a thin screwdriver in the tappet slot. The FIAT way is to blow them out with compressed air, which is effective if an air line is available. They are held in quite strongly by the oil film. They must lift up square, or else they jam, (photos).

9 Check the thickness of the skim removed, and substitute one of an appropriate thickness to correct the clearance. When new, shims have the thickness marked on the bottom, but this wears off, so they must be measured by micrometer. It is best to work in millimetres, as the new shims are marked, and listed in the parts list, under millimetre sizes.

10 Insert the new shim, numbered side down, towards the tappet and valve.

37 Fitting a new camshaft cogged timing bolt

1 Fitting a new camshaft cogged timing belt is item 6.1 of the 36,000 mile (60,000 km) task. When reassembling the engine after overhaul the old belt should only be put back on if it has run a very short distance and is apparently in excellent condition. The strength of the belt depends on the cords embedded in the rubber. In time these break, though not necessarily showing any frayed ends on the outside. Should the belt break, the valves will stop, but the engine run on for some time, particularly if in

gear. It is then likely that the pistons will hit the valves, and damage the engine.

2 Removal of the belt was described in the dismantling procedures, at Section 9.

3 If the new belt is being fitted after engine dismantling, so the timing has been lost, turn the camshaft to the TDC position, by lining up the dot mark on its pulley with the timing pointer on the engine mounting on the right end of the engine.

4 Turn the engine over till the notch on the 'V' belt pulley is aligned with the TDC mark. This is on the belt cover, so this will have to be put back in place temporarily. Note that the engine must only be turned over without a belt on when the camshaft is at the TDC position, otherwise valves may hit pistons. Turn the engine over by jacking up the right front wheel engaging top gear, and turning the wheel, (photos).

5 Slip the new belt over the pulleys.

6 Keep the belt clean, and do not let it get kinked in a tight loop, or the cords may be strained.

7 Get the cogs of the belt fitted into the grooves of the pulleys. The pulleys will have to be in a slightly different position from what they were with the old belt, as that will have stretched. The engine may need to be turned slightly to engage the teeth.

8 Once the teeth are in mesh, release the nut on the spindle of the tensioner, to allow the spring to reassert itself. Then re-tighten the nut.

9 Turn the engine over twice to allow the belt to settle, and get the slack at the right place, then bring the camshaft pulley timing mark back to the pointer again. If the marks are overshot, turn the engine on forwards two more turns. Never turn the engine backwards, or the slack will appear in the wrong place and give misleading results.

10 Slacken the tensioner nut again, to let the spring reset the tension correctly.

11 Put the belt cover in place again, and check that the crankshaft pulley timing mark is lined up. Check all the pulleys have their teeth properly slotted in the belt. If the camshaft is one tooth out, this will show most definitely on the marks.

12 Refasten the camshaft belt cover.

13 Fit and adjust the 'V' belt at the generator, as described in Section 40.

36.3 Check the tappet clearance with the cam away from the valve.

36.6 If you have not got the special tappet tool, it is best to go to a FIAT agent. But by prising down with one screwdriver

36.7 and wedging the tappet down with another one on edge at the rim,

36.8a the tappet can be freed, prised up,

36.8b and lifted out.

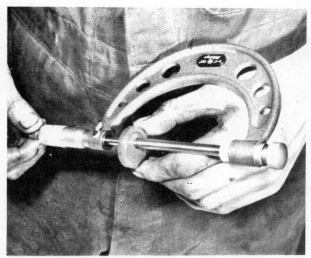

36.9 If the tappet shim is not new, the thickness marking will have worn off, so measure it to choose what new size to put it.

37.4a Before taking off the old camshaft belt, line up the timing marks. The camshaft turns at half crankshaft speed. This also times ignition for number 4 cylinder.

14 To check the tension of the belt it is only necessary to remove the cover, release the nut on the spindle of the tensioner pulley, allow its spring to reassert itself to take up the slack at the correct tension, then retighten the nut. If the pulley does not seem to move under spring tension, the spring action may be checked by prising the pulley back with a screwdriver. The spring in its case can be removed by taking the tensioner off the cylinder block. Resetting the belt tension is a 12,000 mile (20,000 km) task.

38 Refitting the water pump

1 Refitting is the reversal of dismantling. Use a new gasket between pump and cylinder block. Refit the manifolds as described in Section 41.
2 Check the condition of the hose to the thermostat, and if in any doubt use a new one.
3 If the ends of the heater hoses are splayed out, trim a little off: not too much or they will be too short.
4 Refer to Chapter 2/4 when refilling with coolant.
5 Refit and adjust the belt as described in Section 41 of this Chapter.

39 Refitting the generator

1 Fit the generator to the engine with the two pivot bolts underneath, checking the adjuster bolt is in the slot.
2 Refit the belt and adjust it as described in the next Section.
3 Tighten the adjuster and pivot bolts.
4 Reconnect the wiring, and the battery.
5 Refit the manifold shield, and the throttle linkage.

40 Fitting and tensioning the 'V' belt

1 The 'V' belt driving the generator and water pump should be checked for the correct tension every 3,000 miles (5,000 km), item 2.1 of Routine Maintenance. The belt is replaced every 18,000 miles (30,000 km). Fitting a belt is a messy and troublesome job, particularly on cars with emissions control equipment. So the belt should not be left on longer than recommended, so that it need not be fitted as an emergency at the road side. An old belt should only be put back on the engine if the mileage done is small.
2 To fit a new belt, slacken the pivot bolts under the generator, and the adjuster nut at the slot on top in the bracket sticking out from the water pump. Pull the generator up, so it is as close as possible to the water pump.
3 Slip the old belt off the generator pulley, and then the other pulleys.
4 Lower the new belt into position, down past the water pump pulley, and then forward till it can loop under the crankshaft pulley. Then pull it up again to engage the pulley. If your hands are large it may be easier to lower the belt with a length of string round it to pull it up again, (photos).
5 Pull the belt up, and over the water pump pulley.
6 Then with an arm round from the left of the engine, below the manifold shield, prise the belt over the generator pulley. Make sure the belt is well into the other two pulleys first, otherwise it will be a tight fit: if too tight the belt may be nicked as it goes over the edge of the generator pulley.
7 For cars with emissions control equipment, the absorption cannister, fuel filter, and associated pipes are in the way. It will prove easier to remove the shield under the right of the engine, and work from underneath. If no pit is available, remove the front right wheel.
8 With the belt on, pull the generator out from the water pump to tension the belt, and tighten the adjuster nut.
9 The correct tension is a sag of ½ in (12 mm) when pushed with a force of 10 kg, which is the firm pressure of one finger, at the mid-point of the run of belt between crankshaft and water pump pulley.
10 Clamp up the pivot bolts underneath.
11 Do not overtighten the belt, or the generator bearings will be overloaded. If the belt is too slack, it will wear from slippage.

37.4b When putting on the new belt, the camshaft pulley may need a small turn to line up the teeth, as the old belt will have stretched. But keep it by the mark: not one tooth out.

40.4a Lower the new 'V' belt down from the top

40.4b On cars with emissions absorption canisters it is probably worth removing the shield, to get this access from below.

41 Refitting the manifolds and carburettor

1 Put the pair of new manifold gaskets on the studs on the head.
2 Fit the exhaust manifold onto the studs, followed by the inlet.
3 Put on their communal studs the large washers, and then the nuts, and tighten them evenly.
4 Connect the exhaust pipe to the manifold using a new gasket in the case of the flanged joint on the Rally or Coupe, and hard setting exhaust compound such as white 'Fire gum' for the cupped joint on normal engines.
5 Put one gasket on the carburettor flange, then fit the drip tray.
6 Follow with the second gasket and the carburettor itself. Fit and tighten the carburettor nuts.
7 Then fit the manifold nuts so that only those that hold the shield remain to be fitted, clamping the drip tray drain pipe at the left end of the engine.
8 Connect up the carburettor throat water pipes to manifold and thermostat.
9 Refit the manifold shield.
10 If the engine is already in the car, reconnect the brake vacuum pipe.
11 Refit the throttle cross link, taking off the spring clip on the end, and sliding it back on once the rod is in position.
12 Refit the link to the throttle.
13 Reconnect the heater pipes if these have been undone.
14 Reconnect the emissions control connections to the absorption canister and fast idle system. See Chapter 3 for additional detail.
15 Refit the fuel pipe to the carburettor.
16 Put back into the clamps the choke inner and outer cables, and adjust the inner so that the dash board control can push the lever on the carburettor fully home.
17 After the engine has been started up, the idle will need re-adjusting. See Chapter 3/8.

42 Refitting the distributor, petrol pump, and minor components

1 Using new gaskets, fit the fuel pump spacer to the engine, and then check the protrusion of its actuating rod as described in Chapter 3/9:7.
2 Fit the pump, and connect up its pipes.
3 Time the engine in accordance with Chapter 4/5, and fit the distributor.
4 Refit the oil pressure warning sender to the front of the cylinder block, and the thermometer sender to the head.
5 Put the breather fitting on the front of the engine.
6 Fit a new oil filter element, oiling its sealing ring first, and screwing it up hand tight.

43 Preparation for replacing the engine

1 With the engine reassemble on the bench, it must have the transmission fitted so that it is ready as a power-unit to go back in the car.
2 The clutch must have been centralised as described in Section 32:6. Wipe clean and dry the splines on the end of the transmission input shaft, and in the clutch friction plate. Lubricant would, in time, get sticky, and give clutch drag.
3 Offer up the transmission to the engine, holding it square. Slide the stud on the rear into the tubular dowel, and the shaft through the clutch. An assistant can help by turning the engine over slightly by a spanner on the crankshaft pulley nut, to allow the splines to line up and engage.
4 As the transmission goes into place, keep the weight supported, so it does not hang on the clutch.
5 Fit the bolts and the nut holding the engine and transmission together. Tighten the top one first so that it takes the weight of

the transmission.
6 Fit the shield to the bottom of the flywheel housing, and then the bearer bracket.
7 Fit the starter motor.

44 Refitting the engine to the car

1 With the engine and transmission joined, move them into position under the car. The support bracket should already be on, so that the power unit can be bolted into place as soon as it has been lifted. Connect up the lifting tackle. If this is not very maneouvrable, make sure the power unit is precisely below its proper position, and the tackle lifting vertically.
2 Lift the engine straight up until the hole in the right bearer is lined up. As the engine comes up check nothing is fouling.
3 Fit the right bearer bolt. To get the hole lined up accurately put a screwdriver through, and use this to pull it straight. The bolt can then push out the screwdriver.
4 Get the support bracket up into place. A jack under the transmission supplementing the lifting tackle will help to control the movement accurately.
5 Fit the bolts to secure the support bracket to the car. Put all four in loosely first, then tighten them all, then lock them with the tab washer.
6 Reconnect the steady rod from the bulkhead to the cylinder head.
7 Remove the lifting tackle.
8 Connect the exhaust pipe to the manifold. On saloons and estates use some hard setting exhaust compound, such as white 'Fire gum'. On the Rally or Coupe use a new gasket at the flange.
9 Under the car, refit the exhaust bracket to the transmission, reconnect the gear linkage, and the earthing strip.
10 On top reconnect the throttle linkage and choke cable. Adjust the latter so it pushes the choke fully open.
11 Fit the heater hoses to the cylinder head and water pump.
12 Reconnect the clutch cable, and adjust it to give 1 inch (12 mm) free play at the pedal, ensuring the grommet at the end of the outer cable is fitted properly into its seat.
13 Reconnect the speedometer cable.
14 Connect the leads to the gearbox switches for 'Fasten seat belts', 3rd/4th emissions control, and the reverse light.
15 Connect the heavy cable to the starter, and its red solenoid wire.
16 Reconnect the wires to the thermometer and oil pressure senders.
17 Connect up the generator.
18 Refit the fuel pipe to the mechanical pump, or on cars with electric pumps, the pipe to the carburettor.
19 On emissions controlled cars reconnect the absorption canister and fast idle device.
20 Refit and reconnect the front drive shafts as described in Chapter 7.
21 Refit the wheels, and lower the car to the ground.
22 Refit the water hoses, and the bonnet and radiator if these were removed.
23 Fill the cooling system with water.
24 Fill the engine sump and the transmission with oil.
25 After testing the car as described in the next section, fit all the shields to the engine and transmission.

45 Starting up sequence

1 Check no parts have been left off!
2 Inspect the engine under the bonnet, and the car underneath, and inside the car, that all pipes, wires etc seem correctly in place.
3 Confirm coolant and all oil levels are correct.
4 Check the ignition leads are on the correct plugs.
5 Switch on the ignition. On cars with electric petrol pumps, check the system for leaks.
6 Check all warning lights come on properly.

7 Start up the engine.

8 Watch the oil pressure warning light, and see if the generator is charging. If there is no charge, or if the oil pressure warning light does not go out after a few seconds, having had time to refill the new filter, switch off and recheck.

9 If the lights go out correctly, set the engine to run on the fast idle, and check the engine for leaks, particularly the lubricating system.

10 Check the coolant level: in the first few moments it is likely to go down as air locks are filled.

11 If the carburettor has been dismantled, temporarily adjust the idle.

12 Drive gently. All new parts will have to be allowed to settle in. Only do about 3 miles.

13 Recheck for leaks. Listen for knocks.

14 Now that the engine is warm, adjusts the carburettor idle again. (See Chapter 3/8).

15 Switch off. Drain the coolant, and refill with the anti-freeze or inhibitor (See Chapter 2).

16 Check the engine oil level, and that of the gearbox too if that was drained.

17 Start up warm up again, and make a final check of the coolant level.

18 After 500 miles change the engine oil.

PART D — DIAGNOSIS AND FAULT FINDING

46 Scope

1 Though nominally part of the engine chapter, Diagnosis and Fault-Finding cannot be dissassociated from the problems of components the subject of other chapters. The matter is therefore covered most fully here, and only narrowly in the other chapters.

2 The word 'diagnosis' is used to refer to the consideration of symptoms of major mechanical problems, such as noises implying expensive repair or overhaul is needed.

3 'Fault-finding' implies the tracing of a defect preventing some component from functioning.

4 Defects can often be cured by luck. At other times there is no defect, merely a foolish mistake has been made. For example the engine may not start because the rotor arm has been left out. But proper diagnosis or fault finding requires knowledge as to how the thing works, and its construction. Experience helps a lot, as then symptoms can be recognised better. Symptoms must be considered and tests made in an orderly and logical way, step by step, to eliminate possibilities. Beware the dogmatic reputed expert. The true expert is usually non-committal until proved correct by actually finding the faulty component or effecting a cure. You need patience.

5 Many obtuse defects defy diagnosis by garages as they cure themselves temporarily when the car gets there. The owner who cures his own has a great advantage over the garage mechanic as he lives with the symptoms. He knows how everything has been functioning in the past; and may have some item on his conscience, such as plugs overdue cleaning.

6 The subject is dealt with as follows:-
Fault-finding: Engine will not run.
Fault-finding: Engine runs erratically.
Diagnosis of knocks and noises.

47 Fault-finding: Engine will not run at all

1 Problems in this class will occur under two main circumstances: either when you come to start up the engine initially; or when previously running satisfactorily.

2 Under these circumstances there are many possibilities, so the elimination system in the Chart should be followed.

3 Stoppages on the road have been found from large samples of breakdowns to be most often an ignition defect. The system therefore at an early stage aims to eliminate the fuel system.

4 Failure to start from cold is usually a combination of damp with dirt, weak spark because of overdue maintenance of the ignition system, and a weak battery.

5 Therefore in deciding to treat the car's temperament as a 'Defect' may be misleading. On a cold damp day it is often best to try a push start before going into the fault-finding sequence. The slightest lack of verve in the way the starter spins the engine should therefore be interpreted in the chart as 'Starter cranks sluggishly .

6 The fault-finding chart now follows.

The fault finding chart appears overleaf

Engine will

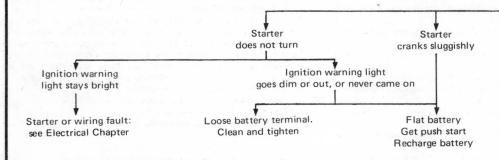

Starter
does not turn

Starter
cranks sluggishly

Ignition warning
light stays bright

Ignition warning light
goes dim or out, or never came on

Starter or wiring fault:
see Electrical Chapter

Loose battery terminal.
Clean and tighten

Flat battery
Get push start
Recharge battery

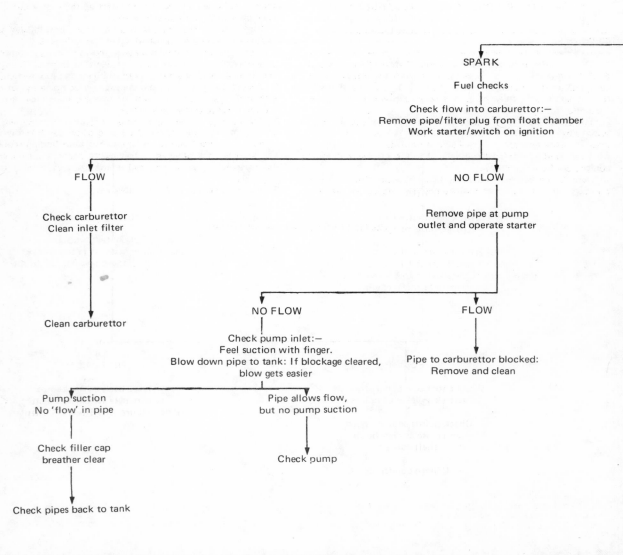

SPARK

Fuel checks

Check flow into carburettor:—
Remove pipe/filter plug from float chamber
Work starter/switch on ignition

FLOW

NO FLOW

Check carburettor
Clean inlet filter

Remove pipe at pump
outlet and operate starter

Clean carburettor

NO FLOW

FLOW

Check pump inlet:—
Feel suction with finger.
Blow down pipe to tank: If blockage cleared,
blow gets easier

Pipe to carburettor blocked:
Remove and clean

Pump suction
No 'flow' in pipe

Pipe allows flow,
but no pump suction

Check filler cap
breather clear

Check pump

Check pipes back to tank

not run

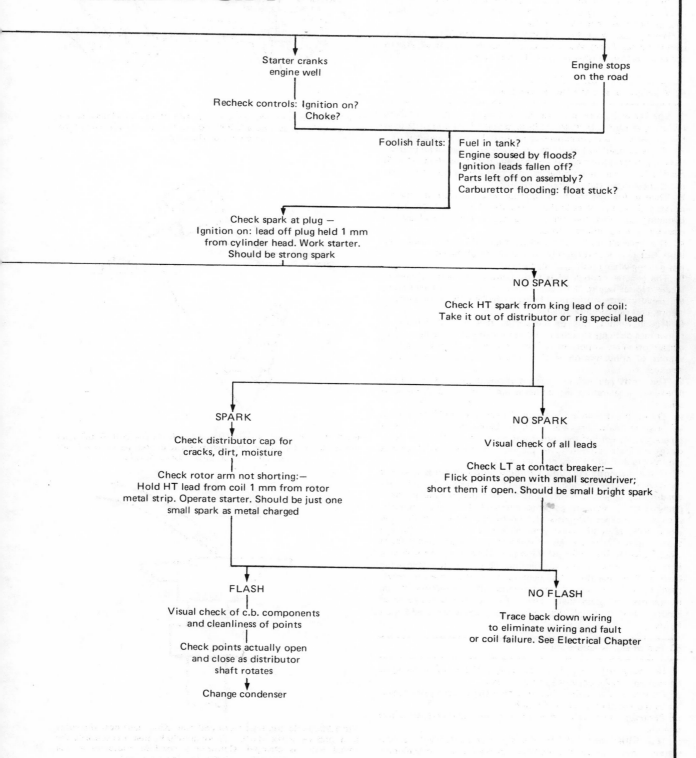

Starter cranks
engine well

Engine stops
on the road

Recheck controls: Ignition on?
Choke?

Foolish faults:
Fuel in tank?
Engine soused by floods?
Ignition leads fallen off?
Parts left off on assembly?
Carburettor flooding: float stuck?

Check spark at plug —
Ignition on: lead off plug held 1 mm
from cylinder head. Work starter.
Should be strong spark

NO SPARK

Check HT spark from king lead of coil:
Take it out of distributor or rig special lead

SPARK

Check distributor cap for
cracks, dirt, moisture

Check rotor arm not shorting:—
Hold HT lead from coil 1 mm from rotor
metal strip. Operate starter. Should be just one
small spark as metal charged

NO SPARK

Visual check of all leads

Check LT at contact breaker:—
Flick points open with small screwdriver;
short them if open. Should be small bright spark

FLASH

Visual check of c.b. components
and cleanliness of points

Check points actually open
and close as distributor
shaft rotates

Change condenser

NO FLASH

Trace back down wiring
to eliminate wiring and fault
or coil failure. See Electrical Chapter

48 Fault-finding: engine runs erratically

1   Erratic running is nearly always a partial fuel blockage. It is therefore best first to eliminate any ignition failures.

2   An ignition fault that gives erratic running will probably be a loose lead. Anything else would give difficult starting. A check should therefore be made of all leads.

3   Having dismissed the ignition system, carefully note the circumstances that provoke the erratic running, and then refer to the fault section of Chapter 3 on the fuel system.

49 Knocks and noises: roughness or smoke

1   The car will often give audible warning of mechanical failure in very good time. If these are heeded when faint and diagnosed then, disaster and more expensive repair bills can be avoided.

2   You will need to know how to interpret noises when you are buying a second hand car. If you are inexperienced then you will need help. A run in a similar car but one known to be in good mechanical order can set your standards.

3   Then as you get to know your car you will learn its normal noises and must be alert to the possibility of new ones appearing. Listening to what the car has to say is helped by ruthless tracking down of minor rattles.

4   The over all noise produced by the FIAT 128 is not very loud. But it is accentuated by the nearness of the engine and its low gearing when cruising at high speed.

5   The general noise level is fairly continuous, and difficult to locate. Noises due to defects are heard through this backround, are usually not continuous, being provoked by some circumstance, and can often be located.

6   Rough running due to the partial failure of a cylinder is sometimes difficult to detect. A smoky exhaust, or excessive oil consumption are important symptoms. Beware of mistaking light vapour of condensation in the exhaust in cold weather as oil smoke.

7   Two tests can help to keep a check on a car's condition. These are acceleration and compression tests, and are described later.

8   The various defects are now tabled. Each is treated individually. In practise faults or wear may, probably will, occur simultaneously. So neither the symptoms nore the faults would be so clear-cut. Tests referred to in the dignosis tables are described with the fault-finding tests on later pages.

9   If the diagnosis tells you somthing serious is amiss it would be wise to get a second opinion. If you decide to get a re-conditioned engine it is sufficient to learn that the old engine is badly worn. If you are going to overhaul the engine yourself, then a more exact diagnosis could help you decide whether the work really is within what you think you can cope with, and that it is not bad enough to warrant a reconditioned one. It would also let you order up the spares in advance. If the engine is in good enough order to continue to run without damaging itself and making the subsequent repair much more expensive, then there is opportunity to prolong the observation of the symptoms, so assess them better. Finally, the ultimate most accurate and thorough diagnosis is to take it apart and look inside.

50 Test of engine acceleration

It is very difficult to judge properly if the engine is giving its correct power. An objective test is needed.

a) Choose a long straight hill up which the car can just accelerate in the speed range 35 to 45 mph.

b) Choose prominent landmarks at beginning and end of the test stretch.

c) If possible time the car over the test stretch with a stop watch. Anyway, note the speedometer reading at the beginning and end.

d) Always enter the test stretch at the same speed. Only do tests

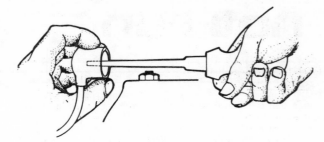

Fig.1.20a On cars with caps on the end of the plug leads, check for a spark by putting a ¼ inch bolt in the cap, and holding it to a bare bit of the engine.

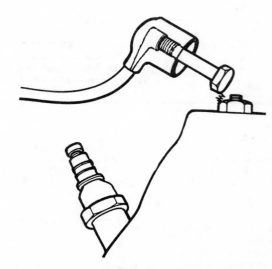

Fig.1.20b To check a spark is coming from the coil, if the lead cannot be pulled out of the distributor cap, arrange a screwdriver to reach into the carbon brush inside.

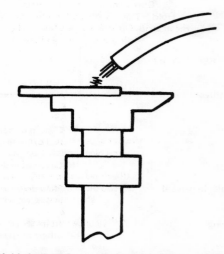

Fig.1.20c Hold the lead from coil (the King lead) near the rotor arm, and work the starter. There should be just one spark as the metal mass is charged. Continuous sparking indicates a leak shorting through the plastic to the shaft.

in conditions of light winds.

e) Do the test a number of times when you know the car is going well. Also try and do it with another similar car known to be in good order. Record these results so that when you are suspicious of the car's performance a test can straight away give useful information.

51 Test of engine compression

Useful information in defect diagnosis is the amount of pressure that can be achieved in the cylinders. This will indicate the state of the pistons in relation to the bores as they must build up the pressure, and also it shows whether the valves are sealing the cylinder properly.

a) An engine compression test gauge is needed. This is the sort of equipment the most enthusiastic owner-mechanic gets, but many owners will have to get a garage to do this test.

b) Warm up the engine. Remove the sparking plugs.

c) Hold the rubber seal of the gauge tightly over the spark plug hole in the cylinder head.

d) Get an assistant to operate the starter whilst holding the throttle open wide. The starter will need to work for about 3 seconds, to allow a reading to settle down on the gauge.

e) Note down the reading.

f) Release the pressure from the gauge, and then do the same test on the other cylinders. After that do all the cylinders for the second time. If the second reading is more than 2% different from the first for a particular cylinder, do a third test to get an average.

g) The readings for all the cylinders should be within 5% of each other. The specific reading does not matter: it is the difference between them that gives the indication of poor compression.

52 Stethoscope for engine noises

A simple stethoscope can be made to listen to odd engine noises.

a) Get a piece of plastic petrol pipe about 3ft long.

b) In one end put a probe of thin metal pipe about 4 inches long.

c) Put the end of the plastic tube in an ear, and search for noises with the metal end.

d) The stethoscope will probably not help in locating major knocks deep in the engine, such as big ends. But it is good for locating noises in such things as the generator.

Symptom	Test/Circumstance	Possible cause
Poor acceleration, otherwise smooth and quiet	Compression test satisfactory	Ignition timing wrong. Brakes binding. Blocked air cleaner. Accelerator linkage maladjusted.
Poor acceleration: Oil consumption and smoke satisfactory. Idle probably rough (continously and rythmically irregular)	Compression test low	Burned exhaust valve. Tappets no clearance.
Oil consumption high, exhaust smoky; some loss of power	Compression test low	Worn pistons, rings and cylinders.
Oil consumption perhaps above normal. Exhaust smoky, particularly after long idle	Compression test satisfactory	Inlet valve stem oil seals incorrectly fitted.
Ditto, with some loss of power	Ditto	Worn valve guides.
Extreme loss of power, engine idle very rough, on three cylinders	Pull off each spark plug lead and replace it in turn (wear thick glove)	Engine misfiring on cylinder whose plug makes no difference. Spark plug faulty.
Ditto	Ditto plus compression test which shows bad cylinder very low	Valve jammed. Piston broken.

Noise	Circumstance	Possible Cause
Engine faults in general	Slow down with engine speed and disappear in neutral with the engine switched off	
Light tapping	At all speeds and loads, though drowned by others at speed	Tappets too wide
Continuous light chatter	If idling very slowly; disappears if clutch disengaged	Gearbox chatter, set idle faster.
Loud hollow knock	Worst cold and on load	Piston slap. Ignore if engine otherwise good Test compression.

Loud solid knock and low oil pressure	At idle when hot. At speed hot. In extreme cases a loud and wild hammering at particular engine speeds. Disconnecting a spark plug alters knock	Big ends excessive clearance. In mild cases new shells will cure. If the engine used when bad, crankshaft will be hammered, in extreme cases the con rod breaks and wrecks engine.
Dull low thudding, and low oil pressure	Worst at speed, hot.	Worn main bearings.
Continuous whining or roaring noises	Dependent on engine speed, but alters in different gears, and when pulling or on over-run	Transmission wear
Continuous roaring	In neutral, engine off.	Wheel bearings.
Continuous swishing occasional clonks	Freewheeling, engine off	Drive shafts.
	Accelerating gently on full lock	Drive shaft constant velocity joints

For other gear grating noises and clonks see Clutch Chapter 5.

Chapter 2 Cooling: Exhaust: Heating

Contents

Specifications

Cooling system capacity	11½ Imp. pints (6½ litres) 14 U.S. pints
Anti-freeze proportion	Follow makers instructions
Fan power	55 watts
Fan cut in temperature	194°F 90°C
Fan switch off temperature	187°F 87°C
Thermostat starts to open	176 - 183°F 80 - 84°C
Travel fully open (205°F, 96°C)	at least .314 in (8 mm)

Water pump

Maximum bearing end play	0.005 in	0.12 mm
Clearance impeller/housing	0.031 - .051 in	0.8 - 1.3 mm
Heater fan power	20 watts	

1 General description

1 The engine is cooled by water, and in most respects the cooling system is conventional. The radiator is at the front, and is normally cooled by the car's forward motion through the air. Because the engine is transverse, the fan cannot be driven in the usual way. Instead, an electric fan is mounted on the radiator. It cuts in automatically when the temperature gets high, such as in traffic, or climbing mountains. Some 128 specifications include a thermometer, but the others only have a high temperature warning light.

2 The rubber 'V' belt, usually called a fan belt, drives the water pump, and is tensioned at the generator in the usual way. This belt is dealt with under Routine Maintenance and in the generator Section of the Electrical Chapter.

3 The fan is controlled by a temperature sensor in the bottom tank of the radiator. This controls a relay, mounted just below the battery, so that the sensor contacts do not have to carry the full fan current load.

4 The heater is mounted behind the engine on the right. It is its bulk that makes that part of the engine compartment inaccessible. The heater uses the engine coolant, and the temperature is controlled by regulating the flow of the water. The heater cannot be properly drained, so when flushing the system, this must be allowed for.

5 The exhaust is a simple system, running down the centre of the floor, and then across at the rear. There is one rigid bracket to the transmission at the front. At the rear flexible brackets allow it to move with the power unit. The Coupe has a dual down pipe at the front.

2 Coolant level check

1 Under normal circumstances the coolant level can be seen at a glance in the expansion tank on the right of the engine compartment. When cold the level will be lower than when hot. The cold level should be maintained about 2.5 ins (6 cm) above the minimum mark on the expansion tank.

2 If the level does not rise and fall in the expansion tank as the engine heats up and cools, then there is an air leak between the tank and the radiator, so the coolant cannot be drawn back in. This leak can either be in the fixing of the expansion pipe, or the seal of the cap on the radiator.

3 If there is suspicion that the expansion system is not keeping the radiator full at all times, the radiator itself should be checked. Anyway, this is a good idea at intervals. If possible this should be done when the engine is cold. If the engine is hot, and there is a crisis, switch off, and allow the engine at least ten minutes to cool slightly. The radiator cap must not be taken off when the temperature of the coolant is above boiling point. The cap is pressurised, so the coolant will not actually boil though above the normal boiling point. But when the cap is opened the pressure is released, and voilent expansion with boiling will give grave risk of scalding. Once it has cooled, open the cap to the

partway position, with some rag covering the hand, and allow the pressure to escape gradually. Whenever the cap is taken off, hot or cold, the radiator header tank should be full, and an air space indicates the expansion system is not working.

4   The system should need topping up very seldom. A need for regular topping up indicates a leak. Topping up should be done with the anti-freeze/water mix.

5   If the system has been drained, recheck the level after the engine has been warmed up. There is likely to have been a pocket of air, so the level will fall. Also check the heater works, and has not got an air-lock.

3   Anti-freeze and inhibitors

1   In cold climates anti-freeze is needed for two reasons. In extreme cases if the coolant in the engine freezes solid it could crack the cylinder block or head. But also in cold weather, with the circulation restricted by the thermostat, and what warm water is getting to the radiator being at the top, the bottom of the radiator could freeze, so block circulation completely, making the coolant trapped in the engine boil.

2   The anti-freeze should be mixed in the proportions advocated by the makers according to the climate. There are two levels of protection. The first cuts risk of damage, as the anti-freeze goes mushy before freezing. But when mushy it does not circulate properly. It gives full protection allowing proper circulation to only a less cold temperature. The normal proportion in temperature climates is 25% anti-freeze by volume, with 33.1/3% for colder. This mix should be used for topping up too, otherwise the mixture will gradually get weaker.

3   Anti-freeze should be left in through the summer. It has an important secondary function, to act as an inhibitor against corrosion. In the cooling system are many different metals, in particular the aluminium of the cylinder head. In contact with the coolant this sets up electrolytic corrosion, accentuated by any dirt in the system. This corrosion can be catastrophically

fast. Reputable anti-freeze of a suitable formula must be used. Whilst FIAT approve other oils as well as their own, their own instructions specify only their own anti-freeze.

4   After about two years the effectiveness of the anti-freeze's inhibitor is used up. It must then be discarded, and the system flushed, and refilled with new. Mix the new with water, half and half. Pour this in, then finally fill to over flowing with water.

5   In warm climates free from frost, an inhibitor should be used. Again a reputable make giving full protection must be chosen and renewal every two years. Inhibitors with dyes are useful for finding leaks, and on some makes the dye shows when the inhibiting ability is finished.

4   Flushing the cooling system

1   Despite the use of inhibitors, the cooling system collects dirt and sludge. Whenever circumstances such as renewing the anti-freeze permit, or when it has been drained for such a job as removing the cylinder head, the system should be flushed. Though the drain taps on radiator and engine be opened, the whole system will not drain, and there is no way of draining the heater.

2   After a journey, so all sludge is well stirred up, open the taps at the bottom of the radiator, and on the rear side of the cylinder block (directly below the carburettor). (photo). Remove the filler cap from the radiator. Put a hose in the filler cap, and turn it on when the hot water is still flowing out so that the change to cold water is gradual.

3   Disconnect the heater pipe at the cylinder head. Turn the heater full on. Transfer the hose to the heater connection. If possible use a short length of metal pipe to connect the hose direct to the heater hose. If none is available, once the hose is on the heater union, and the radiator has had a good flush, turn off the radiator drain so that more flow is available to go through the heater circuit, and ensure water comes out of the disconnected heater hose. (photo).

4   Leave the heater hose disconnected whilst refilling the

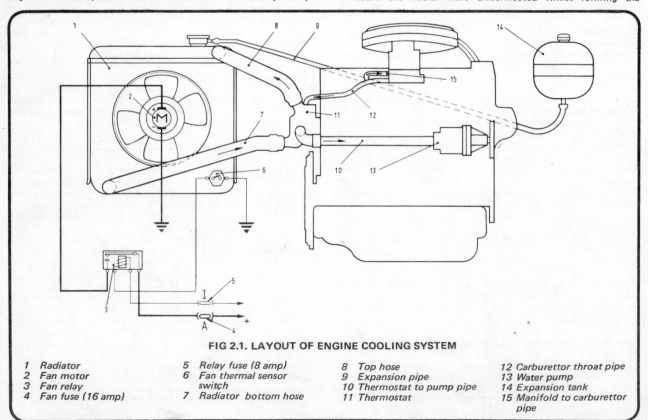

FIG 2.1. LAYOUT OF ENGINE COOLING SYSTEM

1 Radiator	5 Relay fuse (8 amp)	8 Top hose	12 Carburettor throat pipe
2 Fan motor	6 Fan thermal sensor	9 Expansion pipe	13 Water pump
3 Fan relay	switch	10 Thermostat to pump pipe	14 Expansion tank
4 Fan fuse (16 amp)	7 Radiator bottom hose	11 Thermostat	15 Manifold to carburettor pipe

system, till the new coolant begins to come out of the connection, then air is allowed to escape more easily.

5 On old cars, or ones used with very hard water, or without inhibitors, the water passages may become coated with hard deposits that will not come out with normal flushing. In this case use one of the proprietary brands of flushing agents, in accordance with the makers instructions. Afterwards flush out as just described.

6 When the engine has been stripped for a job such as 'decarbonising' there will be dirt that has fallen into the water passage. So when refilling after such work put normal water in first, run the engine, and then flush out, before putting in the anti-freeze or inhibitor.

7 After refilling, start up and allow the engine to warm up. Check the heater works, proving there is no air-lock. Switch off. Check the level: it is likely to have fallen, as some air pocket will have now filled with coolant.

5 Cooling system leaks

1 The fitting of hoses, and their freedom from leaks, will be better if whenever any of the simple clips orginially fitted by FIAT are removed, they are replaced with screw worm ones such as 'Jubliee clips' or 'Cheney connections'

2 New hose connections settle in, and the clips will need re-tightening 500 miles and again at 2,000 miles after fitting.

3 Clean anti-freeze is 'searching', and will leak at weak spots. The system should be very carefully inspected for refilling with anti-freeze.

4 Hoses should be replaced before failure. This particularly applies to the top hose to the radiator, and the two to the heater, as these have the hottest water, and also flex a lot. Unless nearly new such hoses should be renewed when some work demands their removal.

5 Coolant leaks from the cylinder head gasket can give some strange symptons. Water can get in the oil. This can give a rising oil level! Very quickly the oil becomes creamy coloured with the emulsified water. Oil can get into the water, though this is less common due to the pressurised cooling system. If the water is leaking into the combustion chambers, the water will show as excess vapour in the exhaust. Water vapour is always visible in the exhaust when cold, but a leaking head gasket can make it continue when hot. Unlike oil smoke it is white, and very whispy, blown more quickly by the wind.

6 Minor leaks from parts of the engine or the radiator can be successfully cured with proprietory sealants that are put in the coolant. Leaking hoses must be replaced. Bad leaks in metal parts must be properly mended.

6 Thermostat

1 The thermostat is needed in all climates to give quick warm up, and in cold ones to prevent the engine running too cold all the time. It also ensures hot water for the heater.

2 The thermostat has a double acting valve to close off the bye-pass once the main passage is open. If there was no bye-pass system the coolant would be stagnant, so the top of the engine would heat too much compared with the bottom.

3 The thermostat is of the wax capsule type. If it fails it is most likely to do so in the closed position, and give immediate and bad overheating. Should it stick in the open position the engine will run cold, and take a long time to warm up. On normal cars without thermometers this will only show by poor output from the heater. Though the car will run well, it is harmful to it, as parts are the wrong fit, and condensation of combustion by-products occurs. Also more fuel is used.

4 If there is sudden severe overheating on a journey then the thermostat is suspect.

5 To remove the thermostat, first allow the engine to cool well below boiling point. Then open the radiator drain tap, and let out just over half the coolant, to get the level below the bottom of the thermostat.

6 Disconnect the bottom radiator hose at the thermostat. If you have small hands and a suitable spanner now remove the cover on the bottom of the thermostat housing. Then wriggle the thermostat itself out between the bottom of its housing and the top of the transmission. (photo).

7 If in trouble working on the housing still on the engine remove all the water hoses from the housing. Then unbolt the housing from the engine. Then the cover is easily removed.

8 The action of the thermostat can be checked by heating it up in a saucepan of water. The opening action should be seen as a definite movement well before the water boils.

9 If the thermostat jams shut on the road, it must be removed then and there. Trying to continue with the engine overheating will damage it. If no replacement is available, then the engine must be run without the thermostat. There will not then be any valve to shut the bye-pass. There will be a tendency for the circulation to take the shortest route, and not go through the radiator, resulting in overheating. If driving on after removing the thermostat, the temperature warning light may come back on. The cure for this will be to seal off the bye-pass passage in the thermostat housing. A wooden plug should be cut, and driven into the hole dividing the upper and lower parts of it. Alternatively a more secure block could be made by clamping two washers together from either side.

4.2 The drain for the cylinder block is on the rear face in line with the exhaust

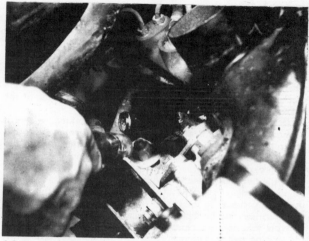

4.3 The heater pipe union makes a good point for attaching a hose for flushing out, and venting trapped air when filling.

CLOSED	PARTLY OPEN	FULLY OPEN
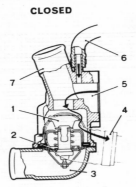	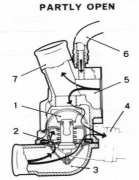	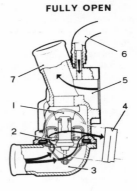

FIG 2.2. THERMOSTAT OPERATION

1 Top valve
2 Bottom valve
3 Union from radiator

4 Outlet to pump
5 Entry from cylinder

   bottom
   head
6 Pipe from carburettor
   throat heater

7 Union to radiator
   top

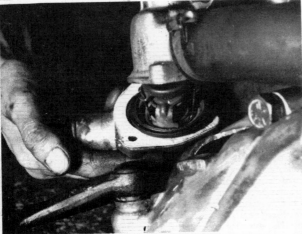

6.6 The thermostat can be got out by removing the radiator bottom hose, then taking off the housing bottom.

6.7 But accessability is improved if the whole housing is taken off

7 Electric fan

1   When the car is halted, it is possible to hear the fan cut in. An enthusiastic owner may like to rig up a warning light to show when it is working: such a person too will probably fit a thermometer, which will enable the correct functioning of the whole system to be monitored properly.

2   It is worthwhile checking that the fan is working, so that it does not remain with a defect undented for some time, and result in a crisis. To check the fan operation the temperature should be raised by running the engine at a fast idle with the car stationary, preferably after climbing a steep hill.

3   If the fan does not cut in, then refer to Chapter 9 for electrical fault finding in general. The test bulb should be put across the relay contacts to see if that is functioning. The contacts at the sensor can also be shorted out to eliminate that.

4   Note that only the sensor circuit to the relay is controlled by the ignition switch. The main feed through the relay is direct. If the relay system fails the leads can be temporarily joined together, but then will need disconnecting when the engine is switched off.

7.4 The electric fan is switched on by a sensor in the radiator bottom link

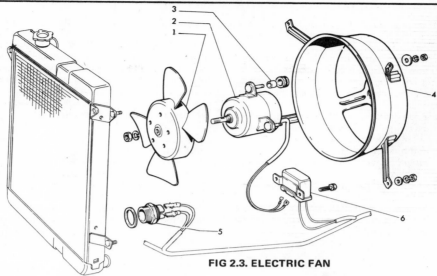

FIG 2.3. ELECTRIC FAN

1 Fan	3 Motor mounts	5 Thermal sensor
2 Fan motor	4 Fan cowl	switch
		6 Relay

8 Radiator removal and repair

1 The radiator will sometimes be removed to give access to the bonnet hinges. This is dealt with in Chapter 12.

2 To remove the radiator first drain the coolant. Disconnect the leads to the fan sensor at the bottom. Disconnect the fan wires at the relay below the battery mounting. Take off the two hoses from the top and the bottom of the radiator. Undo the small pipe from the filler to the expansion tank.

3 Undo the two mounting bolts at the top of the radiator. (photo).

4 Lift the radiator up out of the rubber padded rest at the bottom.

5 If the radiator core is leaking, then it is best to get this repaired by professional radiator repairers. There are specialist firms who do this. The core is made of thin metal, and easily damaged by an unskilled repairer.

6 If the radiator is ever removed, the opportunity should be taken to clean it inside and out. The bottom tank should be swilled out, the debris being tipped out of the bottom hose union, and the radiator not turned upside down, lest the thin passages get blocked. If the radiator is old and dirty, and has to remain off the car for a day or so, it must not be allowed to dry out. The unions must be blocked and the filler cap kept on. Otherwise the deposits will harden, and prove impossible to remove. Hose dead insects etc out of the air passages. Carefully straighten any of the cooling fins that might have been bent.

9 Overhaul of the water pump

1 The water pump is likely to need overhaul for worn or noisy bearings, or if the gland is leaking. There is a drain hole between the gland and the bearings so any leak can get out without contaminating the bearing grease, so ruining them. Gland leaks are usually worse when the engine is not running. Once started a leak is likely to get worse quickly, so should be dealt with soon. Worn bearings are likely to be noted first due to noise. To check them the pulley should be rocked firmly, when any free movement can be felt despite the belt. But if the bearings are noisy yet there is not apparently any free play, then the belt should be removed so that the pump can be rotated by hand to check the smoothness of the bearings.

2 Removal of the pump forms part of the engine dismantling procedures, and is in Chapter 1/11. (photo).

3 Whenever the pump is dismantled, even though the bearings

8.3 The radiator is easily removed after taking off the hoses, unplugging the fan wires, and taking out the two mounting bolts at the top.

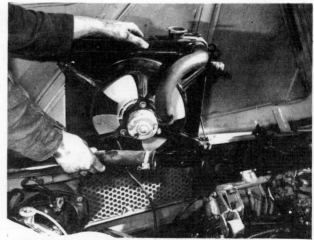

8.4 The radiator bottom sits in a rubber lined bracket

are the cause, the gland (or seal) should be replaced.

4   Having removed the pump from the engine, take off the nuts and split the two halves of the pump.

5   The pump shaft is an interference fit in the impeller, bearings, and pulley boss. How the pump is dismantled depends on whether only the gland needs replacement, or the bearings as well, and what puller or press is available to get everything apart. (See Fig.2.4).

6   Assuming complete dismantling is required, proceed as follows. Supporting it close in at the boss, press the shaft out of the pulley. Pull the impeller off the other end of the shaft.

7   Take out the bearing stop screw.

8   From the impeller end, press the shaft with the bearings out of the cover half of the housing.

9   Press the shaft out of the bearings, taking off the spacer, the circlip, and the shouldered ring.

10 Do not immerse the bearings in cleaning fluid. They are 'sealed'. Liquid will get in, but a thorough clean will be impracticable , and it will be impossible to get new grease in.

11 Check all the parts. Get a new gland, two new grommets, and a new gasket. Scrape all water deposits out of the housing and off the impeller.

12 To reassemble start by inserting the new grommets in their grooves by each bearing. Fit the circlip to the shaft, then the shouldered ring, bearings and spacer. Fit the shaft and bearing

assembly into the cover. Fit the stop screw. Press on the pulley.

13 Fit the new gland (seal), seating it in its location in the cover. Press the impeller onto the shaft. FIAT have special press tools to get everything in the right place. Without these the impeller must be put on part way, and then the housing held in place to see how far the impeller must go down the shaft to give the correct clearance. See again Fig.2.4.

14 The impeller clearance can be checked through the water passage in the side of the pump.

10 Exhaust system

1   In detail the Coupe exhaust is very different from that of the Saloon and Estate cars. But to work on they are very similar.

2   At the front there is the connection to the exhaust manifold.

3   Just down the pipe from this a bracket to the transmission holds the pipe steady, so the manifold joint is not stressed as the engine moves on its mountings. The pipe then runs back towards the rear axle, where are the two silencers. Here the pipe is supported by flexible mountings with hooks. (photo).

4   In the case of the Coupe the pipe starts as a double one, joining under the front floor. It has a flanged joint to the manifold, instead of the conical one on the saloon/estate. (photos).

9.2 The water pump is held on by the four large bolts. Removal needs the manifolds off first. See Chapter 1/11.

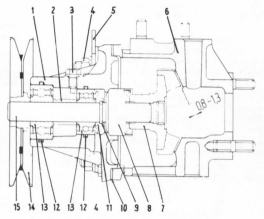

FIG 2.4. SECTION OF WATER PUMP

1	Pump cover	8	Gland (Seal)
2	Bearing spacer	9	Circlip
3	Bearing stop screw	10	Gasket
4	Cover nuts	11	Shouldered ring
5	Lifting bracket	12	Grommets
6	Housing	13	Bearing
7	Impeller	14	Pulley
		15	Shaft

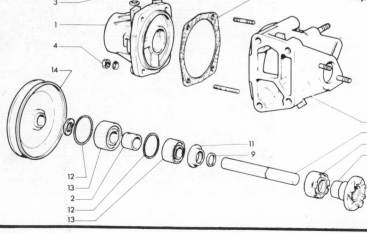

FIG 2.5. EXPLODED VIEW OF WATER PUMP

1	Pump cover	9	Circlip
2	Bearing spacer	10	Gasket
3	Bearing stop screw	11	Shouldered ring
4	Cover nuts	12	Grommets
5	Lifting bracket	13	Bearings
6	Housing	14	Pulley
7	Impeller	15	Shaft
8	Gland (Seal)		

5   More often than it is removed for its own sake, the exhaust will have to be disconnected at the manifold. If the engine is being removed, so the support bracket to the transmission undone, then the front end of the pipe must be supported by string to save over-stressing the pipe and mountings at the rear.

6   To remove the whole system, it should be disconnected at the front first, and temporarily supported till the rear mountings are undone.

7   When a leak comes in the exhaust, short term repairs can sometimes be made. But a hole usually occurs only as the first part of general failure. Unless plenty of firm metal is left repairs cannot last long. New exhausts are relatively inexpensive, compared with the money that can be wasted on short term palliatives. Stainless steel replacements, at twice the cost of mild steel ones, are well worth the extra cost, as life is many times more.

8   When fitting a new exhaust, use new clips and flexible mountings. These will have aged too, and the disturbance of dismantling the exhaust will not leave them long to live.

11 Heater

1   The heater draws water from the water pump, and returns it to the thermostat.

2   The heater hoses will often need to be disconnected for work on the engine. But there is no need to remove the heater itself. If working in the area below it, access can usually be gained by leaning across the car from the left. However, the air intake can be removed without the heater itself quite readily.

3   The item most likely to need attention is the water valve. This may fail internally, not stopping all flow, so in hot weather cold ventilation is impossible, or it may develop a water leak to the outside.

4   When working on other parts of the cooling system the water valve of the heater should be open, that is the left lever fully down, to allow flow for draining, flushing or filling.

5   To remove the valve it is best to remove the heater body, as it is so inaccessible. Drain the coolant. Disconnect the two heater hoses at the heater (or if thought easier, at the far end).

6   Disconnect the link to the air admission shutter in the intake at the bolt and nut halfway along. (photo). Undo the clips holding the air intake to the heater radiator. Take out the screw in the centre of the air intake, and lift it out.

7   Undo the cable from the valve. Take out the heater radiator.

8   Take the valve off the radiator.

9   The foregoing dismantling is also necessary to reach the heater fan.

10.3 Apart from the joint to the manifold, and the bracket to the transmission, the exhaust is held up by simple flexibly mounted hooks

10.4a The Coupe and Rally have a twin, long separation, down pipe, with a flanged joint to the manifold.

10.4b The twin pipes join near the gear lever. The rear mountings are the same as the saloon.

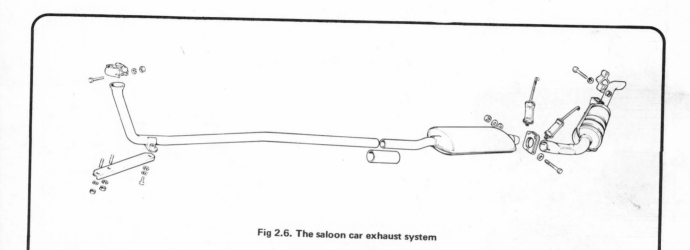
Fig 2.6. The saloon car exhaust system

12 Fault-finding

Symptom	Reason/s	Remedy
Loss of coolant	Leak in system. Cracked block or head	Examine all hoses, connections, drain taps, radiator and heater for leakage when the engine is cold, then when hot and under pressure. Tighten clips, renew hoses and repair radiator as necessary.
Loss of coolant from radiator into expansion bottle	Defective radiator pressure cap Leaking expansion pipe Overheating Blown cylinder head gasket causing excess pressure in cooling system forcing coolant past radiator cap into expansion tank	Examine, renew if necessary. Refix pipe. Check reasons for overheating. Remove cylinder head for examination.
Overheating	Insufficient coolant in system Water pump not turning properly due to slack belt Kinked or collapsed water hoses causing restriction to circulation of coolant Faulty thermostat (not opening properly) Engine out of tune Blocked radiator either internally or externally Cylinder head gasket blown forcing coolant out of system New engine not run-in	Top up radiator and expansion tank. Tighten belt. Renew hose as required. Fit new thermostat. Check ignition and carburettor settings. Flush out and clean cooling fins. Remove head and renew gasket. Drive gently until run-in.
Engine running too cool	Faulty thermostat	Fit new thermostat.

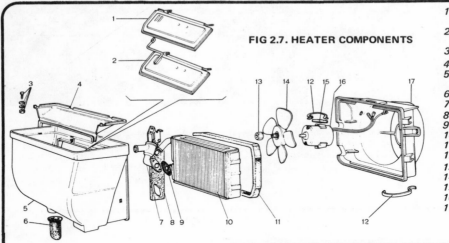

FIG 2.7. HEATER COMPONENTS

1 Upper shutter for air to car interior
2 Lower shutter for air to heater radiator
3 Air intake fixing screw
4 Water shield
5 Air intake and body
6 Water drain
7 Water valve
8 Gasket
9 Valve gasket
10 Heater radiator
11 Gasket
12 Spring clips
13 Fan nut
14 Fan
15 Rubber pad
16 Motor
17 Fan housing

FIG 2.8. HEATING AND VENTILATION CONTROLS

1 Upper shutter cable
2 Water valve and lower shutter cable
3 Lock plate
4 Screw
5 Clip
6 Fastener
7 Clip
8 Screw
9 Lever support
10 Plate
11 Warm air

admission knob
12 Fresh air knob
13 Washers
14 Grommets
15 Plate
16 Washers
17 Levers
18 Cotters
19 Lock plate

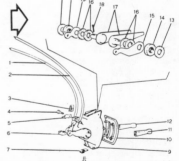

11.6 The air intake trunking is removed first, by disconnecting the link to the shutter, removing the clips, and a bolt in its cowling.

Chapter 3
Fuel system, carburettors and emissions control

Contents

Specifications

Carburettor types:

Saloon and estate cars 1116 cc	Weber 32 ICEV
	Weber or Holley Europa 32 ICEV 10
	Solex C32 DISA
	Solex C32 DISA 20
	Manufacturer depends on supply
Rally/coupes 1290 cc/1116 cc	Weber 32 DMTR or 32 DMTR 20
Fuel pump	Mechanical or electrical dependent on market

Air cleaner	Paper element)
	Oil bath) dependent on market

Idle speed - normal cars	750 rpm
emission controlled	800 - 900 rpm
emission controlled cars' fast idle	1550 - 1650 rpm

Setting data for Weber and Holley Europa 321 CEV (Variations for 321 CEV 10 in brackets):

	mm
Bore	32
Starting device	Manual choke
Primary venturi	24
Auxiliary venturi	4
Main jet	1.25
Idle jet	0.40
Main air correction jet	1.50
Idle air correction jet	1.60
Accelerator pump jet	0.40
Power jet	1.10
Power air correction jet	1.00 (1.40)
Power mixture orifice	2.00
Needle valve seat	1.50
Emulsion tube	F48
Weight of float	10.5 g
Throttle valve opening (starting)	Nil (0.80)
Starting device choke throttle opening	Nil (4.5)

Float level								mm	
— distance between cover (vertical),) metal float								11	
with gasket, and ... ...) plastic float								36	
— float travel) metal float								Nil	(7)
) plastic float								10	

Setting data for Solex C32 DISA (C32 DISA 20 variations in brackets)

								mm	
Bore								32	
Main venturi								24	
Auxiliary venturi								5	
Main jet								1.40	
Idle jet								0.52	
Main air correction jet								1.90	
Idle air correction jet								1.00	
Accelerator pump jet								0.45	
Accelerator pump relief orifice								0.40	(Nil)
Power jet								0.50	
Well								3.50	(3.70)
Level								21 to 22	(22 to 24)
Needle valve seat								1.60	
Weight of float								9 g	

Setting data for Weber 32 DMTR (32 DMTR 20 variations in brackets)

	1st barrel	2nd barrel
Barrel diameter	32 mm	32 mm
Venturi diameter	22 mm	22 mm
Main jet diameter	1.05 mm (1.10 mm)	1.15 mm
Idle jet diameter	0.50 mm	0.70 mm
Main air metering jet diameter	1.95 mm (2.10 mm)	2.00 mm (1.90 mm)
Idle air metering jet diameter	1.00 mm (1.10 mm)	0.70 mm
Pump jet diameter	0.40 mm	
Diffuser	F30	F30
Starter system	Throttle	Throttle
Needle valve seat		1.5 mm
Primary throttle opening (starter on)	0.75 to 0.80 mm (0.80 to 0.85 mm)	

Float level: distance from cover face, in vertical position, with
gasket ... ...   6 mm

1 General description

1 The FIAT 128 has a downdraught carburettor. Normally this
is a single barrel model. But on the Rally and Coupe a double
barrel one is used. The choke is a manual throttle type. The
carburettors are manufactured by Weber, Holley, and Solex,
dependant on the supply situation.
2 The fuel pump is on the majority of cars a mechanical one
mounted on the front of the engine and driven by an eccentric
on the auxiliary shaft. Some cars have an electric pump mounted
at the rear, dependant on the country to which they are going.
3 Some cars have a circulatory circuit for the final supply pipe.
A return pipe from the carburettor takes back to the tank petrol
that is not used by the carburettor. This prevents stagnant petrol
evaporating in hot weather, particularly at high altitudes, which
would cause fuel vapour locks.
4 To meet the emissions control regulations of the USA, cars
going to North America have an emissions control regulator
system for the carburettor, which includes a fast idle control.
They also have a fuel vapour absorption system.

2 General carburettor function

1 The general method of operation as described below is similar
on the various types, though in this case the Weber 321 CEV is
chosen. (See Fig.3.1).
2 For normal running, the fuel (See Fig.3.1) passes through the
needle valve (8) to the bowl (13). Here the float (12), hinged on

its pin (10), regulates the rise and fall of the needle (9) so that
the fuel level in the bowl remains constant; the needle (9) is
attached to the float tongue (12) by means of the recall hook
(11).

The fuel then passes from the bowl (13) into the well (15) via
the main jet (14). It is then mixed with air drawn in through the
air bleed jet (3) and the air jet (6) and passed through the holes
in the emulsion tube (19). The air/fuel emulsion is then ejected
through the spray outlet (22) to reach the carburation area,
consisting of the auxiliary (21) and primary (20) venturi.

The carburettor is provided with an **enrichment circuit**.

Fuel passes from the bowl (13) through the passage (17) and
the jet (5) and mixes with air drawn in via the calibrated orifice
(4).

This mixture passes through the passage (2) and the calibrated orifice (1) into the carburettor throat during fast running.
3 Fig.3.1 also shows the crankcase ventilation device in the idle
running (A) and normal running (B) positions. This device
consists of a rotating valve (25) entrained by the throttle shaft
(16) and the lever (18). This valve channels the blow-by gas from
the duct (23) via the slot (24) to below the throttle valve (17).
During idle running, gas is drawn in through the calibrated
orifice (26).
4 When idling, or progressing from idle to normal running, fuel
passes from the well (15) to the idle jet (33) via the passage (32).

It is then emulsified with air drawn in through the calibrated
bush (34), the passage (31) and the idling feed orifice (27),
which can be adjusted by means of the screw (28) The air/fuel
mixture enters the carburettor throat downstream from the
throttle (17).

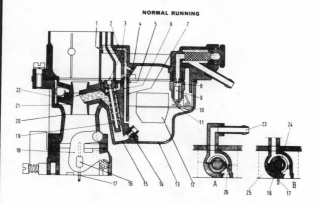

NORMAL RUNNING

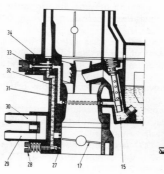

IDLE AND PROGRESSION

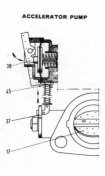

ACCELERATOR PUMP

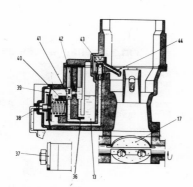

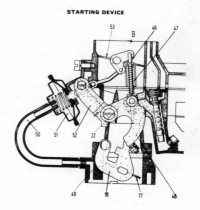

STARTING DEVICE

FIG.3.1 WEBER 32 ICEV CARBURETTOR OF SALOON AND ESTATE CARS

1   Power mixture orifice.
2   Power mixture passage
3   Air bleed jet
4   Air intake calibrated orifice
5   Power fuel jet
6   Air intake jet
7   Power fuel passage
8   Needle valve
9   Needle
10 Float hinge pin
11 Needle recall hook on float tongue
12 Float
13 Fuel bowl
14 Main jet
15 Emulsion tube well
16 Throttle shaft
17 Throttle valve

18 Crankcase ventilation device control lever
19 Emulsion tube
20 Primary venturi
21 Auxiliary venturi
22 Spray outlet
23 Blow-by gas duct
24 Normal running blow-by gas slot
25 Rotating valve
26 Idle blow-by gas calibrated orifice
27 Idle feed orifice
28 Idle mixture adjustment screw
29 30 Hot water pipes for heating throat
31 Idle feed passage
32 Fuel passage

33 Idle jet
34 Idle air jet
35 Progression orifices
36 Delivery passage
37 Throttle valve control lever
38 Accelerator pump control lever
39 Diaphragm
40 Suction spring
41 Ball valve
42 Accelerator pump excess fuel jet
43 Delivery valve
44 Accelerator pump nozzle
45 Throttle rapid opening cushion spring
46 Rod
47 Calibrated spring

48 Lobe
49 Depression passage
50 Depression tube
51 Diaphragm device
52 Choke throttle control lever
53 Choke throttle

Blow-by gas and oil fumes re-circulation device:

A   Idling operation
B   Normal running operation

Starting device:

A   Device in operation
B   Device cut out

As the throttle (17) is gradually opened from the idling position, the mixture is also drawn in via the progression orifices (35), so that a steady increase in power is given.

The area around the idling feed passage is heated by water running through pipes (29, 30) set in parallel to the engine cooling system. This is done to prevent the formation of ice in the idling area and near the progression orifices during cold weather.

5   Quick response is needed for acceleration. When the throttle (17) is opened by means of the linkage (37, 38) and the spring (45), the diaphragm (39) injects fuel into the carburettor throat via the passage (36), the delivery valve (43) and the nozzle (44).

Abrupt throttle movements are stored by the spring (45) and the delivery of fuel is prolonged.

Excess fuel delivered by the accelerator pump is fed back into the bowl (13) through the calibrated bushing (42), together with fumes from the pump chamber.

When the throttle (17) is closed, the lever (38) releases the diaphragm (39), allowing the suction spring (40) to draw fuel from the bowl (13) via the ball valve (41).

6   To start from cold, a rich mixture is needed, as the fuel is not evaporating properly.

When the choke control is operated, the lever (52) is in position A, the choke throttle (53) blocks the carburettor air inlet, while the throttle (17) is opened a little way by means of the lobe (48) of lever (52) and by lever (18).

The spray outlet (22) therefore provides a suitable mixture for rapid starting.

As soon as the engine fires, depression partly opens the choke throttle (53) against the action of the calibrated spring (47). Depression downstream from the throttle (17) is felt by the diaphragm device (51) via the passage (49) and the tube (50), resulting in further weakening of the mixture. This ensures that the engine will pass smoothly over to normal running.

When the correct running temperature is reached, the choke control is pushed back, the device is cut out completely (position B). The choke throttle (53) is now held fully open by the rod (46) and the throttle (17) takes up its normal idling position.

7   On the double barrelled carburettor of the Rally and Coupe only the primary barrel is used when the accelerator pedal is pressed partway down. As the pedal is pushed further the throttle begins to open. The secondary idle passages give the necessary progression feed to make this a smooth transition. Then when the pedal is pushed to the floor, and the secondary throttle is wide, it has its own air bleed arrangements, and is a separate, second carburettor.

3   Carburettor inlet filter

1   In the engine fault finding Section reference is made to testing that petrol is flowing to the carburettor by removing the filter plug. In Routine Maintenance the cleaning of the filter is called for under the 6,000 mile task 3.8.

2   The plugs are large hexagon nuts on the float chambers, near the fuel inlet. They are shown in the diagrams of the various carburettors. After the plug has been taken out the filter can be withdrawn, and washed in petrol.

3   The cleaning of the filter at 6,000 miles is a frequency set for places where there is a high risk of dirt or water in the fuel. Once it has been cleaned, the amount of dirt found, and the general experience for that particular locality must be the guide when deciding if this task can be left for double this mileage, which will prove satisfactory using clean fuel supplies.

4   Pump and line filters

1   Filters are fitted in the fuel pumps. Also on cars for various markets, including North America, filters are fitted in the fuel line.

2   On mechanical pumps the filter is reached by taking off the

FIG.3.2 WEBER 32 ICEV GENERAL VIEW

1 Idle mixture adjustment screw	4 Filter inspection plug
2 Idle speed adjustment screw	5 Diaphragm device for partial release of the choke by depression
3 Idle jet holder	

FIG.3.3 WEBER 32 ICEV COVER AND MAIN BODY

1 Choke	9 Main jet
2 Mixture enrichment device	10 Accelerator pump
3 Floats	11 Air bleed jet
4 Needle stop mounted on float tongue	12 Accelerator pump jet
5 Fuel inlet union	13 Blow-by gas duct
6 Filter inspection plug	14 Spray outlet
7 Cover	15 Hot water pipes
8 Carburettor body	16 Idle mixture adjustment screw
	17 Depression pipe

dome, after removing the central screw. The filter disc should be washed in clean petrol. Check the dome's gasket before re-assembly.

3 On electric pumps the filter disc is between the main body and bottom part. Before stripping the pump it is essential that the pump is quite clean. If this cannot be guaranteed, it is better to leave the filter, as provided refuelling is done from clean supplies, its area is large enough to run a long time.

4 The line filter is to the right of the engine, above the right mudguard, just before the pipe reaches the carburettor. It is changed, and the old one thrown away.

5 Pump and line filter cleaning and replacement is item 5.5 of the 18,000 mile task.

5 Carburettor partial dismantling and cleaning

1 As item 3.8 of the 6,000 mile task is the job of cleaning the carburettor. This is set by FIAT. But it is a frequency realistic only if refuelling from dirty sources. A car given clean fuel should run twice this mileage with no problem. This 12,000 mile task is Routine Maintenance item 4.2.

2 To clean the carburettor, first remove the air cleaner, (photo).

3 Refer to the appropriate picture for the type of carburettor fitted. Remove the filter plug. Undo the fuel pipe into the carburettor, and return pipe and those with fuel recirculation. Unclip the choke to throttle interconnection.

4 Undo the screws holding the top down onto the carburettor body, and brackets that span the two parts.

5 Lift the top up carefully, so as to bring the float out of the float chamber without bending it. Put it down where it cannot get damaged, or the float pivot come out.

6 Mop out the fuel, and any dirt, from the bottom of the float chamber. Be careful the dirt is not swilled into any duct to the jets.

7 If the carburettor is found to be very dirty, then the jets must be removed. These should be blown through to clean. In extreme cases, it will be necessary to remove the carburettor, so that it can be cleaned under good conditions, completely dismantled on a bench. See Section 7.

8 See also Section 15 for the maintenance of the crankcase fumes system, which involves stripping the control valve on the carburettor, by the throttle.

6 Air cleaner

1 For most markets a paper element filter is used. For dusty countries this would need uneconomically frequent replacement, and supplies of new elements might be difficult, so oil bath types are used.

2 The paper element is changed by undoing the top of the cleaner, and lifting out the element. When handling the new one ensure no dirt is put on the inside surface. This must be watched very carefully when removing an old element that is to be refitted after work on the engine.

3 The oil bath type is serviced by removing the large element, tipping out the oil in the bottom, cleaning out the sludge, and refilling with engine oil to the level mark. The oil flow in the filter element will normally keep this clean, but if it is dirty, wash it in clean petrol.

4 The normal frequency of service of the air cleaner is 6,000 miles. This applies to a country with sealed roads, but a dry climate with a bit of dust about. If the car is used on dirt roads then the frequency must be doubled. If used on sealed roads in a damp climate, the frequency can be halved.

5 The air cleaner has two air inlets. One is the normal one for cold air, by a pipe drawing from the front of the car. In cold weather to reduce the liability carburettor icing, and give good driveability, the air can be drawn from the hot area around the exhaust manifold. On the 1116 cc engine a lever on the outside of the cleaner allows this change over to be done simply. On the

1290 cc one the top must be removed to make the change. The oil bath type of cleaner only has a cold inlet.

6 It is often necessary to remove the complete air cleaner to improve accessibility to the engine. Pull off the oil breather pipe. Undo the steady bracket from the cylinder head. Take off the air cleaner top, and lift out the element. Remove the two nuts holding the body to the top of the carburettor. Lift off the air cleaner. Cover the carburettor's air intake to prevent anything falling into the engine.

7 Carburettor removal and dismantling

1 Do not undertake this job until you have bought a manifold gasket, and set of gaskets, washers, and diaphragms for the carburettor.

2 Very often the carburettor will be removed as part of a more general overhaul. Sometimes it will come out still in position on the inlet manifold. It has to be removed from the engine to take off the cylinder head with ordinary spanners, as the camshaft housing must come off first.

3 It should only be necessary to remove the carburettor for its own sake on cars that have run great mileages. Then it can be worked on in clean and comfort, so a thorough job done.

4 Drain off enough coolant to lower the level below the inlet manifold.

5 Remove the spare wheel and the air cleaner.

6 Unclip the throttle linkage at the throttle, and unclip the cross rod from its pivot on the engine. Unclamp the inner and outer choke cables. (photo).

7 Take off the two water hoses to the carburettor throat.

8 Take off the fuel inlet pipe at the float chamber, and the crankcase ventilation pipe near the throttle.

9 On cars so fitted, disconnect the wires to the fast idle actuator.

10 Take off the two nuts holding the carburettor down to the manifold. Hold the drip tray so its gasket is not torn, and lift the carburettor off. Or if so required, undo the drip tray drain from the left end of the manifold, and take that off too.

11 Cover the inlet manifold inlet to prevent anything falling into the engine.

12 Befores dismantling the carburettor, refer to its diagram. Clean the outside very thoroughly, but keep the carburettor upright, so any dirt inside will be prevented from washing into passages to the jets.

13 Take off the external fittings. Take out the screws holding the two halves together.

14 Clean out the float chamber, and the filter.

15 Take out all the jets, laying them out in systematic order so they will not get muddled up.

16 Clean all jets, by blowing through them. On no account must they be poked at with wire or a pin, as they are machined to very close tolerance, and even a slight rounding of a corner will vary the amount of petrol that will flow.

17 Clean out all the passages in the body.

18 Examine the float and needle valve. If the latter is badly worn it will need replacement. Shake the float to check it has no leak. Diaphragms, in such things as the accelerator pump, should be replaced unless in very good condition.

19 Reassemble carefully, using new gaskets etc.

20 The idle will need resetting. In order to get the car to start, screw the throttle stop out till the throttle is shut, then in one turn. The mixture screw should be screwed in gently as far as it will go, and then out 1½ turns.

21 Start up with the air cleaner off, so the movement of the choke can be seen when the throttle is blipped. The function of the accelerator pump can be sensed by judging the engine's response. On some models it is adjustable, and should be set to the minimum pump action consistant with a good pick up when the engine is thoroughly warmed up. Some hesitation when cold should be accepted.

5.2a The air cleaner has a bracket on the engine,

5.2b as well as the nuts inside, on the carburettor. Also pull off the breather pipes underneath when lifting it up.

5.5 Lift the top off gently so the float is not damaged, then the inside of the carburettor can be cleaned with it still on the engine.

7.6 When taking the carburettor off, the choke control must be unclamped, but the throttle is a snap connection.

7.7 As well as fuel, the pipes for the coolant heating the carburettor throat, on the left, have to be disconnected.

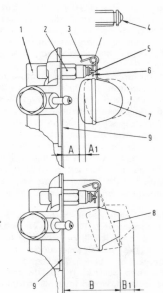

FIG.3.4 WEBER 32 ICEV FLOAT LEVEL SETTING

1 Carburettor cover	4 Movable ball of needle vavle	7 Metal float
2 Needle valve	5 Stop	8 Plastic float
3 Lug	6 Tongue	9 Gasket

A = .433 in (11 mm): distance between cover (with gasket) and metal float
A' = .275 in (7 mm): metal float travel.
B = 1.417 in (36 mm): distance between cover (with gasket) and plastic float.
B' = .334 in (8.5 mm): plastic float travel.

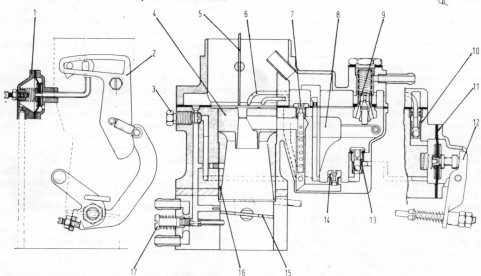

FIG.3.5 DIAGRAMATIC SECTION OF SOLEX C32 DISA ALTERNATIVE CARBURETTOR FOR SALOONS AND ESTATE CARS

1 Lean mixture device	5 Choke	9 Needle valve	13 Accelerator pump valve
2 Cold starting control lever	6 Accelerator pump nozzle	10 Accelerator pump jet	14 Main jet
3 Idle jet	7 Emulsion tube	11 Accelerator pump diaphragm	15 Throttle
4 Auxiliary venturi	8 Float	12 Diaphragm control lever	16 Main venturi

17 Idle mixture adjustment screw

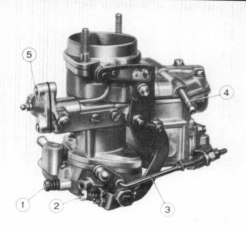

FIG.3.6a SOLEX C32 DISA RIGHT SIDE

1 Idle mixture adjustment   rod
  screw   4 Fuel delivery pipe union
2 Throttle stop screw   5 Lean mixture vacuum device
3 Accelerator pump control

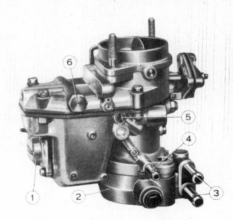

FIG.3.6b SOLEX C32 DISA LEFT SIDE

1 Accelerator pump   4 Blow-by gas duct
2 Lower housing   5 Idle jet
3 Hot water pipes for heating 6 Filter plug
  area around idle feed passage

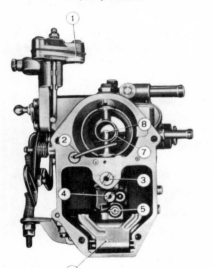

FIG.3.6c SOLEX COVER AND HOUSING

1 Lean mixture vacuum device
2 Accelerator pump nozzle
3 Emulsion tube
4 Main jet
5 Pump pick-up valve
6 Float
7 Auxiliary venturi
8 Spray outlet
9 Needle valve
10 Fuel delivery pipe union
11 Rich mixture nozzle
12 Starting device choke throttle
13 Bowl fumes recirculation
   outlet

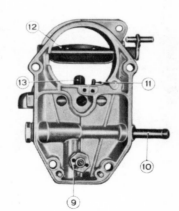

**FIG.3.7 THE WEBER 32 DMTR TWO BARRELLED CAR-
BURETTOR**

1 Idle mixture adjusting screw 4 Throttle opening adjusting
2 Idle adjusting screw (by-pass)   screw (locked in factory)
3 Choke

**FIG.3.8 FLOAT LEVEL ADJUSTMENT OF THE WEBER
32 DMTR**

1 Carburettor cover   6 Movable ball
2 Needle valve   7 Tang
3 Lug   8 Float arm
4 Needle   9 Float
5 Return hook   10 Gasket

a = .236 in (6 mm) = distance between float and cover with gasket, in vertical position.
b = .590 in (15 mm) = maximum distance of float from cover
with gasket
$b-a$ = .354 in (9 mm) = float travel.

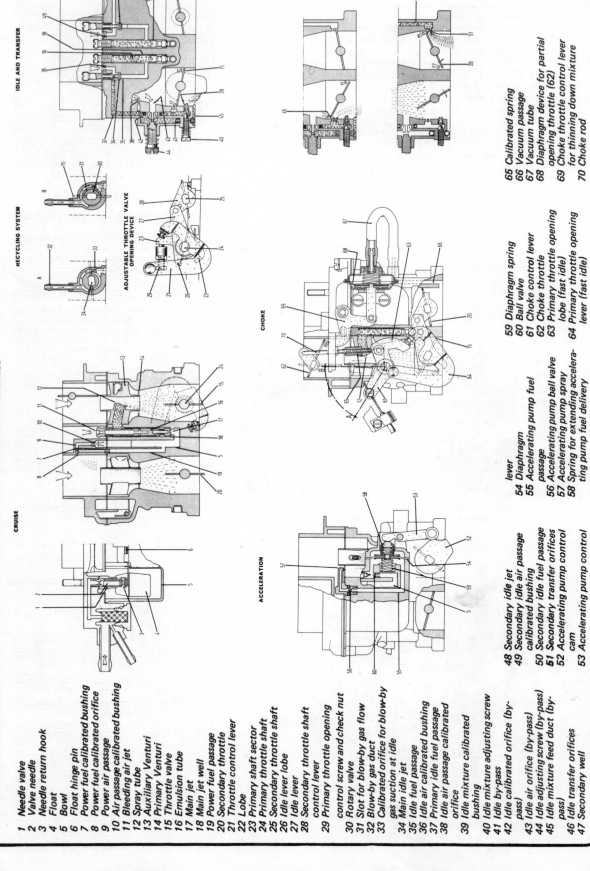

FIG.3.9 THE WEBER 32 DMTR CARBURETTOR FITTED TO RALLY AND 1300 COUPE ENGINES

IDLE AND TRANSFER

RECYCLING SYSTEM

ADJUSTABLE THROTTLE VALVE OPENING DEVICE

CRUISE

CHOKE

ACCELERATION

1 Needle valve
2 Valve needle
3 Needle return hook
4 Float
5 Bowl
6 Float hinge pin
7 Power fuel calibrated bushing
8 Power fuel calibrated orifice
9 Power air passage
10 Air passage calibrated bushing
11 Bleeding air jet
12 Spray tube
13 Auxiliary Venturi
14 Primary Venturi
15 Throttle valve
16 Emulsion tube
17 Main jet
18 Main jet well
19 Power fuel passage
20 Secondary throttle
21 Throttle control lever
22 Lobe
23 Primary shaft sector
24 Primary throttle shaft
25 Secondary throttle shaft
26 Idle lever lobe
27 Idle lever
28 Secondary throttle shaft control lever
29 Primary throttle opening control screw and check nut
30 Rotary valve
31 Slot for blow-by gas flow
32 Blow-by gas duct
33 Calibrated orifice for blow-by gas suction at idle
34 Main idle jet
35 Idle fuel passage
36 Idle air calibrated bushing
37 Primary idle fuel passage
38 Idle air passage calibrated orifice
39 Idle mixture calibrated bushing
40 Idle mixture adjusting screw
41 Idle by-pass
42 Idle calibrated orifice (by-pass)
43 Idle air orifice (by-pass)
44 Idle adjusting screw (by-pass)
45 Idle mixture feed duct (by-pass)
46 Idle transfer orifices
47 Secondary well

48 Secondary idle jet
49 Secondary idle air passage calibrated bushing
50 Secondary idle fuel passage
51 Secondary transfer orifices
52 Accelerating pump control cam
53 Accelerating pump control lever
54 Diaphragm
55 Accelerating pump fuel passage
56 Accelerating pump ball valve
57 Accelerating pump spray
58 Spring for extending accelerating pump fuel delivery

59 Diaphragm spring
60 Ball valve
61 Choke control lever
62 Choke throttle
63 Primary throttle opening lobe (fast idle)
64 Primary throttle opening lever (fast idle)
65 Calibrated spring
66 Vacuum passage
67 Vacuum tube
68 Diaphragm device for partial opening throttle (62)
69 Choke throttle control lever
for thinning down mixture
70 Choke rod

8 Idling adjustment

1 From time to time the idling of the engine will become erratic, and need resetting. When the carburettor has been dismantled it will have been upset. Major variations in the idle will make themselves apparent. But sometimes the settings will work gradually wrong and go unnoticed, so checking the idle is item 3. 19 of the 6,000 miles task.

2 Warm up the engine. Ideally the idle should be reset during a journey, so the temperature is thoroughly stabilised.

3 Adjust the throttle stop screw so the idle speed is correct. As a guide the "No charge" warning light should just come on.

4 Screw the mixture adjustment screw gradually in and out to find the point at which the engine runs the fastest consistent with a steady exhaust note. This may make the engine speed increase: In this case unscrew the throttle stop to restore the speed, and then recheck the mixture screw.

5 The positions of the two screws differ on the various models of carburettors fitted. Which is which can be seen from the pictures, but also deduced by looking at the carburettor. The throttle stop is one against which the throttle comes to rest when the accelerator pedal is released. The mixture adjustment screw is in the throat of the carburettor, near the inlet manifold joint. On emissions controlled cars there is a third screw. This is on the actuator for the electrically controlled fast idle system.

6 The fast idle for the emissions control can be checked by pressing the button on the switch near the bonnet. This is discussed more fully in Section 13.

7 There is an interconnection between the choke linkage and the throttle so that the latter is automatcially opened to give a suitable setting for starting up, and then for warming up The engine will not idle on the normal throttle stop when cold, and anyway it is kinder to the engine to run it at a slightly brisker speed of about 1,200 rpm when cold. When starting up after dismantling this warm up position allows the engine to run despite the fact that the idle setting will have been lost, and only set roughly, as described in the previous Section.

9 Mechanical fuel pump: removal and refitting

1 Before removing the pump get a selection of gaskets for the joint to the engine, and either a pump overhaul set or reconditioned pump if it is faulty.

2 Clean the outside of the pump, and the cylinder block around the joint.

3 Remove the inlet and outlet pipes from the pump.

4 Undo the two nuts holding the pump to the engine, and take off the washers.

5 Pull off the pump, and the plastic spacer. (photos).

6 Take the actuating rod out of the cylinder block.

7 When refitting the pump, first have a trial fit of the spacer with a gasket side to check that the actuating rod protrudes between 0.59 and 0.61 in (15 - 15.5 mm). If too much protrudes the pump may be damaged. If too little protrudes pump output may be low. Adjust the gaskets used to get the setting correct. Gaskets are available in three thicknesses. Smear the gaskets with grease before finally assembling.

8 Start up and check for leaks.

10 Dismantling the mechanical fuel pump

1 The pump will need partial dismantling to clean the filter and remove sediment. This was described in Section 3. Here full dismantling is considered, either as a result of failure, or as preventative maintenance after some 60,000 miles.

2 Remove the pump from the engine.

3 Take off the domed filter cover.

4 Undo the ring of screws holding the two halves of the body together. Prise the body apart. It is unwise to undertake this unless new diaphragms are available, as they are likely to get torn.

8.5 The throttle stop is on the throttle. Here is shown the idle mixture screw, near the manifold flange.

9.5 The mechanical pump

9.7a is worked by a rod from the auxiliary shaft.

9.7b The amount it sticks out is controlled by the thickness of the gasket.

5   Carefully take out the valves, but only if suspect.

6   Push out the pin for the actuating lever, and take it and its spring out, and unhook the diaphragm.

7   The diaphragms are in two layers, one to do the pumping, and one to prevent fuel leaking into the engine.

8   Use a new gasket under the domed cover, new diaphragms, and if necessary new valves.

9   Assemble the diaphragms so they are spread without unfair stretch. Tighten the screws holding the body together evenly.

11   Electrical fuel pump

1   Some cars are fitted with electrical fuel pump mounted at the rear of the car. These make fault finding much easier, as the pump will work whenever the ignition is switched on, so flow can be checked without having to work the starter.

2   If the pump fails to work, a temporary paliative is to thump it. Once there is a definite failure, the pump should be removed, the outside cleaned, and then work done on a clean bench.

3   To remove the pump, clean the dirt around the pipe unions, and the electric leads. Use either water and detergent, or an aerosol of easing oil. Undo the electrical connections and the two pipes. Release the pump body from its bracket, after undoing the bolts through the shield.

4   The two parts of the pump can be split to give access to the filter.

5   If the electric action or the diaphragm and valves fail, it is recommended a new unit is fitted. The two separate halves of the pump are itemised as spares, but it is usual only to stock the whole, as if one has failed, the other is likely to be near the end of its life.

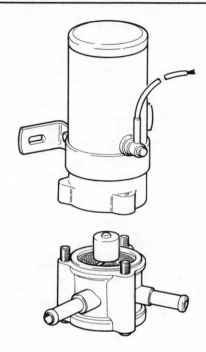

Fig.3.10 The electric fuel pump

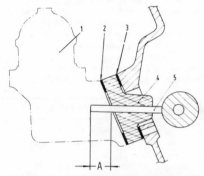

FIG.3.11 MECHANICAL FUEL PUMP INSTALLATION

1   *Pump*
2   *Gasket between pump and insulating support*
3   *Gasket between insulating support and crankcase (spares are supplied in the following*

thicknesses: .012, .027 and .047 in - 0.3, 0.7 and 1.2mm)
4   *Insulating support*
5   *Rod*
A   *= .59 to .61 in (15 to 15.5 mm)*

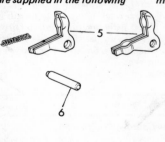

FIG.3.12 THE MECHANICAL FUEL PUMP

1 *Domed cover*	4 *Alternative types of diaphragm assemblies*	5 *Alternative actuating levers*	7 *Spacer*
2 *Filter*		6 *Lever pivot*	8 *Main body*
3 *Upper body*			

12 Fuel tank removal

1 If there is a lot of fuel in the tank, drain it out to lighten it.
2 Disconnect the battery positive lead.
3 Undo the filler and venting pipes in the boot.
4 Under the car scrape the dirt and paint of the screws for the tank shield, and those holding the tank itself. Remove the shield if fitted.
5 Pull the flexible pipe off the metal one just in front of the cross member by the tank.
6 Undo the screws holding the tank. Lower the tank slightly, until the gauge wire fixed to the top can be reached, and disconnected. On cars with vapour control absorption systems, there are the three vapour pipes to do too.
7 Lower the tank fully.
8 The tank should be shaken violently to loosen all dirt, tipped out, and then swilled out with petrol/engine oil mixture a number of times.
9 Any leaks should be repaired with solder. Special attention should be paid to the seams.
10 The outside should be repainted with car underneath protective paint.
11 When refitting, grease the securing screws before assembly so the threads will not rust. After fitting, wipe them dry and paint with underneath paint.

13 Fuel vapour evaporation absorption system

1 The evaporation of fuel from the tank is one of the bigger sources of pollution. To prevent this, the fuel cap is sealed. Air is allowed in by the venting system when the engine is running, to let the fuel flow out. But when the engine is not running, and fuel evaporates, particularly when parked in the sun, the vapour is absorbed into charcoal in a canister. In the pipe from the tank to the canister is a catch tank to separate out liquid fuel and pass this back to the tank, (photo).
2 Once the engine is started up, air is drawn through the absorption canister to purge it of the absorbed fuel, and the vapour is drawn into the engine with the crankcase fumes, and burned.
3 The absorption canister is an upright cylinder in the engine compartment, to the right of the camshaft belt cover. (photo).
4 In course of time the absorption canister looses its efficiency and should be replaced. This is an 18,000 mile task as item 5.4 in the Routine Maintenance.
5 It will also be useful to remove the canister to improve accessibility in the right part of the engine compartment.
6 To remove the canister, note the run of the various pipes. Then disconnect them. Then slacken the mounting bolts, and remove the canister.

7 Refit the canister the same way up. Do not get the pipes muddled. The vapour and fumes go in at the bottom, and the purge pipe out at the top.

14 Emission control carburettor system

1 This engine is so efficient that it meets the emissions regulations of the USA at the time of writing with very few modifications. One of the moments when engines give much pollution is on the over-run, when the very small amount of mixture coming into the engine, under very low pressure, gives bad combustion.
2 Fitted to the carburettor is an electrically operated fast idle valve. Its wiring comes from fuse A and the ignition circuit. It is controlled by a switch at the front of the engine compartment close to the bonnet, by the clutch pedal, and the 3rd/4th selector in the gearbox. The bonnet switch has a button sticking out. When this is pressed the system can be made to function. (photo).
3 On the actuator on the carburettor is an adjuster screw. Adjust this when the engine is warm, to give a fast idle with the system switched on of 1,550 - 1,650 rpm.
4 For such emissions controlled cars the normal idle is 800-900 rmp, and at this speed the Carbon Monoxide should be 1.5 - 2.5%.
5 Before making any alterations to any such engine settings, reference should be made to local regulations regarding tests to be made, and any seals required. Setting may need an exhaust gas analyser to measure accurately enough to meet the regulations.

15 Crankcase ventilation

1 Engine gasses that blow by the pistons must be ventilated, and condensation products drawn out of the crankcase. The ventilation system draws the fumes up the large pipe in front of the engine. The fumes are then drawn through the carburettor to be burned in the engine.
2 When the engine is on full throttle it is sufficient to send the fumes in direct in the main stream of air. But the flow needs better control when the engine is idling.
3 To give this control there is a valve on the carburettor by the throttle.
4 It is Routine Maintenance 12,000 mile task item 4.3 to clean this valve.
5 Release the valve by undoing the nut on the end of the throttle spindle.
6 The valve must be cleaned in a carbon solvent, and washed off rather than scraped. FIAT recommend 70% paraffin (kerosene) and 30% butylcellosolva.

13.1 A liquid separator allows only fumes to go from fuel tank to absorption canister near the engine. Venting system has a small three way valve.

13.3 White arrow shows absorption canister, nearby is electric valve for emissions control. Hidden behind that is fuel line filter. Also arrowed is front switch for fast idle emissions control.

14.2 Black arrow shows canister from the other side, and white arrow, the fast idle actuator on carburettor

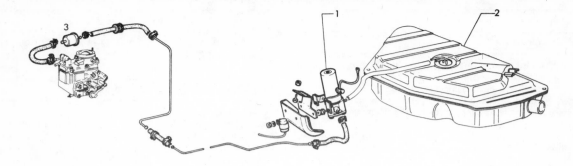

FIG.3.13 ELECTRIC FUEL PUMP AND INSTALLATION

1 Pump. 2 Fuel tank with connections for fuel vapour absorption and second pipe to carburettor for Venturi. 3 Fuel line filter

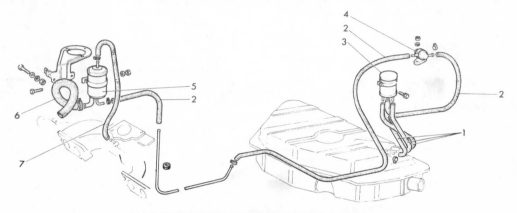

FIG.3.14 THE FUEL VAPOUR CONTROL SYSTEM

1	Vapour pipes from tank		canister	4	Three way check valve	6	Fume pipe
2	Vapour pipes to absorption	3	Liquid separator	5	Absorption canister	7	Purge pipe

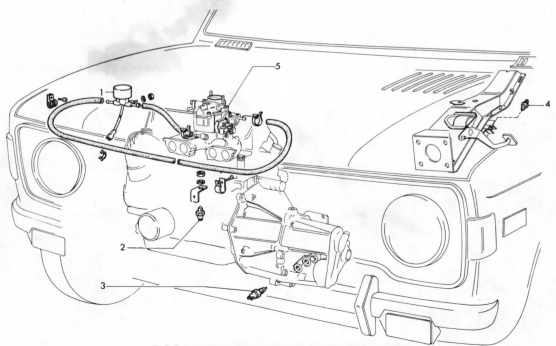

FIG.3.15 EXHAUST EMISSION CONTROL DEVICE

1	Electric valve	3	3rd/4th gear switch	5	Carburettor with fast idle valve
2	Front switch	4	Clutch switch		

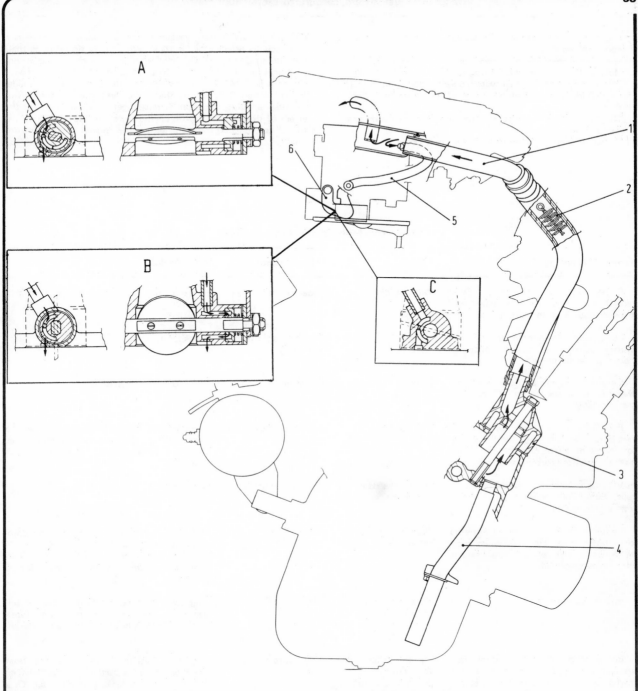

FIG.3.16 DIAGRAM OF BLOW-BY GAS AND OIL FUMES RECIRCULATION DEVICE

1 Engine to air cleaner pipe
2 Backfire suppressor
3 Crankcase breather
4 Crankcase breather to sump oil return pipe
5 Air cleaner to carburettor pipe
6 Crankcase blow-by gas and oil fumes device control lever

A — Throttle closed: blow-by gases are drawn into the inlet manifold through the calibrated orifice.
B — Throttle open: part of the blow-by gases is passed into the inlet manifold; the remainder enters the air cleaner downstream from the filter element.
C — Section through idling blow-by gas calibrated pick-up orifice.

16 Fault-finding

1   Most of the fault-finding relating to the fuel system was given in Chapter one, with the fuel system checks taking up much of the fault-finding chart. The chart was concerned with failure to start.

2   The fuel system can also produce exasperating faults giving erratic running.

3   Tabled here are various problems that may occur .

4   On cars fitted with emissions control equipment there is a tendency to at once blame these. Whilst they do produce their own defects, more often than not the problem will be a conventional one. So that the effect of the emissions control device can be judged, when all is in working order tests should be made, so later when fault-finding the proper response is known. With the engine idling, and bonnet raised, get an assistant to try the effect of pressing the button on the switch by the bonnet, whilst the clutch is used, and the gear lever moved in the 3rd/4th position.

Fuel system faults giving erratic running

Starting and running	Idling	Effect of choke	Probable defect
1 Starts well cold on choke. Only starts hot on wide throttle. Runs well at speed. Poor pick-up on part throttle.	Will not idle	Does not help	Blocked idle jet and/or passages in carburettor.
2 Starts well hot or cold. Coughs and splutters when large throttle opening tried: Can hardly move.	Idles well	Will help a bit to get car going	Blocked main jet.
3 Very difficult to start cold: Has to be "warmed up on the starter". Once warm goes perfectly.	Normal	No effect	Blocked starter jet/passages.
4 Engine tends to stall. Difficult to start hot. Goes well. High fuel consumption. Smell of petrol, and possibly petrol in drip tray under carburettor.	Will not idle	Makes matters worse	Carburettor flooding: Float jammed. Needle valve stuck or damaged or dirt on seating. Float set wrong; level too high in float chamber.
5 Varying symptoms. Sometimes cures itself. Sometimes goes in jerks, other times engine cuts out.	Sometimes does, others not	Sometimes helps	Water in fuel.
6 Difficult to restart hot. In extreme hot weather may cut out when moving. Worse in mountains. Engine restarts when allowed to cool.	Once restarted behaves well	Makes little difference	Fuel vapour lock due to hot weather combining with engine overheating. Check fan working. Check water pump 'V' belt. Perhaps ignition timing wrong. Obstruction to air flow.
7 Engine won't restart.	Once restarted, behaves well	Makes matters worse	Plugs wet with petrol. Slowly press accelerator to floor; hold it there and work starter. (Not really a fault, just a temporary crisis).
8 Engine starts well hot or cold, then runs well initially, but peters out. Driving slowly may allow it to recover if symptoms mild.	Initially idles well. Will not idle after petering out unless symptoms mild.	Will not rescue engine	Engine is initially running on the float chamber. There is a partial blockage between needle valve and tank. Perhaps filter. Or a weak pump.
9 Ditto.	Idles well	Helps a bit	Dirt getting sucked into main jet, but falling back out of it when flow stops. e.g. flake of dirt; wisp of rag. If latter, take out jet and burn it out.
10 Ditto but damp cold weather. Cures itself if given a couple of minutes rest.	Probably won't idle	Probably will not help	Carburettor icing. Check air cleaner in winter position. Buy top quality fuel. Partially blank off radiator. Check thermostat.
11 Coupe and Rally only: Car behaves well on up to half throttle. Full throttle gives - a Minor hesitation b Major flat spot	Not applicable	Cures hesitation only	Blockage in second barrel system. a In "idle" progression jets b In main jet of secondary system

Chapter 4 Ignition system

Contents

Specifications

Distributor

Type	Marelli or Ducellier
Timing marks	On camshaft belt cover, at 10° , 5° and 0° BTDC
Timing — Europe:	Static $\qquad$ 10° BTDC
	At 700 rpm $\qquad$ 10° BTDC
USA:	At 850 rpm $\qquad$ TDC
Centrifugal advance	Starts at 900 rpm $\pm$ 200 rpm
	Complete at 4,700 rpm = 27° - 29°
Firing order	1 3 4 2
Contact breaker gap	.014 - .017 in $\qquad$ (0.37 - 0.43 mm)
Contact dwell	$55^o \pm 3^o$
Distributor rotation	Clockwise

Spark plugs

Type	Champion N9Y Marelli CW 240 LP Bosch W200T30
Gap	.020 - .024 in $\qquad$ (0.5 - 0.6 mm)

Coil types and resistances at 68^oF (20^oC)

Make	Primary	Secondary
Marelli BE 200B	3.1 — 3.4 ohm	6,750 — 8,250 ohm
Martinetti G 52S	3.0 — 3.3 ohm	6,500 — 8,000 ohm
Bosch K 12V	3.0 — 3.4 ohm	7,000 — 9,300 ohm

Condenser	0.22 - 0.23 microfared at 50 - 100 Hz
Resistance terminals to earth	About 50 megohms at 50 V. d.c.

1 General description

1 For the engine to run correctly It is necessary for an electrical spark to ignite the fuel/air mixture in the combustion chamber at exactly the right moment in relation to engine speed and load. The ignition system is based on feeding low tension voltage from the battery to the coil where it is converted to high tension voltage. The high tension voltage is powerful enough to jump the spark plug gap in the cylinders under high compression pressures, providing that the system is in good condition and that all adjustments are correct.

2 The ignition system is divided into two circuits, the low tension circuit and the high tension circuit.

The low tension (sometimes known as the primary) circuit consists of the battery, lead to the control box, lead to the ignition switch, lead from the ignition switch to the low tension or primary coil windings, and the lead from the low tension coil windings to the contact breaker points and condenser in the distributor.

The high tension circuit consists of the high tension or secondary coil windings, the heavy ignition lead from the centre of the coil to the centre of the distributor cap, the rotor arm, and the spark plug leads and spark plugs.

The system functions in the following manner: High tension voltage is generated in the coil by the interruption of the low tension circuit. The interruption is effected by the opening of the contact breaker points in this low tension circuit. High

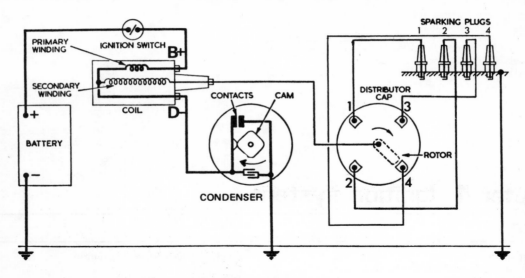

Fig.4.1 Ignition system layout

tension voltage is fed from the centre of the coil via the carbon brush in the centre of the distributor cap to the rotor arm of the distributor.

The rotor arm revolves at half engine speed inside the distributor cap, and each time it comes in line with one of the four metal segments in the cap, which are connected to the spark plug leads, the opening of the contact breaker points causes the high tension voltage to build up, jump the gap from the rotor arm to the appropriate metal segment, and so via the spark plug lead to the spark plug, where it finally jumps the spark plug gap before going to earth.

3 The ignition is advanced and retarded automatically, to ensure the spark occurs at just the right instant for the particular load at the prevailing engine speed.

The ignition advance is controlled mechanically. The mechanical governor mechanism comprises two weights, which move out from the distributor shaft as the engine speed rises, due to centrifugal force. As they move outwards they rotate the cam relative to the distributor shaft, and so advance the spark. The weights are held in position by two springs and it is the tension of the springs which is largely responsible for correct spark advancement.

4 Maintenance of the ignition system is part of the 6,000 mile (10,000 km) task. Lack of maintenance of the ignition system is the prime cause of difficult starting. In particular, cleanliness of the leads and distributor cap is vital.

2 Contact breaker cleaning and adjustment

1 Mechanical wear of the contact breaker reduces the gap. Electrical wear builds up a lump of burned metal on one of the contacts. This prevents the gap being measured for re-adjustment, and also spoils the electric circuit.

2 At 6,000 mile intervals the points must be removed for cleaning, or replacement. They can be cleaned once, then the next time replacement points should be fitted.

3 Unclip and remove the distributor cap. Pull off the rotor arm.

4 Slacken the insulated terminal on the side of the distributor body enough for the contact breaker lead to slide out. Undo the two screws holding the contact breaker to the distributor plate, and lift out both the moving and the fixed contacts, (photo).

5 Clean the points by rubbing the surfaces on a fine abrasive such as an oil stone. The point surface should be shaped to a

2.4 Two screws hold the contact breaker to the distributor plate.

2.7 Having replaced the cleaned points, leave the screws slack so the points can be moved stiffly to the correct gap.

gentle convex curve, so that they will be able to touch each other fairly. All the lump burned onto one contact must be removed. It is not necessary to go on until all traces of the hole have been removed from the other. There is enough metal on the contacts to allow this to be done once. At alternate services, fit new points. Wash debris off cleaned points, and preservative of new ones.

6 Whilst reassembling, lubricate the distributor as detailed in the next section.

7 Now adjust the contact breaker gap. With electronic test equipment this can be done by measuring the well, in accordance with the instructions of the tester. For normal adjustment, turn the engine over by putting the car in top gear, and moving it forward till the contact breaker points are open as wide as they go, with the heel of the moving contact on the top of the cam. Insert a feeler for 0.015 in (0.4 mm) between the contacts. (photo). Slacken the clamping screws so the fixed contact can just be moved. Prise it into position so that the feeler is lightly brushed by the contacts. Carefully tighten the screws so as not to disturb the contact. Recheck the gap, trying feelers slightly larger and smaller to see it is right. Turn the engine over to come up on another cam, to recheck. With an old distributor some variation must be expected from cam to cam. The gap is going to close slightly as the heel of the contact wears. So the gap must start big enough. But if the gap is too large, the dwell will not be long enough: This means there will be insufficient time for the magnetic field to build up in the coil to give a good spark.

8 Now reset the timing as described in Section 4.

9 Wipe the rotor arm and distributor cap inside clean. Check the metal segments are not badly burned, nor have been in metal to metal contact due to incorrect fitting of the rotor arm. If badly worn, they will need replacement. Clean the outside of the distributor cap, and all the leads.

3 Distributor lubrication

1 At the 6,000 mile service, whilst the contact breaker points are being cleaned, the distributor should be lubricated. This lubrication is important for the correct mechanical function of the distributor, but excess lubrication will ruin the electric circuits, and give difficult starting.

2 Whilst the contact breaker is off, squirt some engine oil into the bottom part of the distributor, onto the centrifugal advance mechanism below the plate.

3 Wet with oil the felt pad on the top of the distributor spindle, normally covered by the rotor arm. (photo)

4 Put just a drip of oil on the pivot for the moving contact.

5 Smear a little general purpose grease (Castrol LM Grease) onto the cam, and the heel of the moving contact breaker.

4 Ignition timing resetting

1 As the contact breaker heel wears, and with the variations of different sets, the timing must be reset whenever the contact breaker points are cleaned or replaced. If this is not done engine power and efficiency will be lowered, and the idling may be uneven or unreliable. If the timing is retarded the idle will be smooth, but slow. If advanced, it will tend to be fast, but uneven. Variations of at least 3° are needed to make the idle appear wrong. But such variations will be showing more important loss of efficiency in fuel consumption, power, and exhaust emissions if measured with suitable equipment. If the timing has been completely lost, as opposed to needing resetting, refer first to the next Section.

2 For static timing turn the engine over by putting the car in gear and moving it forwards, till the first, the 10° mark on the camshaft belt cover is opposite the notch in the crankshaft belt pulley. Do not turn the engine backwards, as then backlash in the distributor drive will upset the timing. (See Fig.4.2).

3 With the engine at this position the points should be at the moment of opening. The ideal way to see when the points open is to wire a 12 volt bulb across the contact breaker points, using

3.3 A little oil (and grease on the cam) is important. Too much will give difficult starting.

FIG.4.2 IGNITION TIMING MARKS USING THE CRANKSHAFT 'V' BELT PULLEY AND THE CAMSHAFT BELT COVER

1 10° Before top dead centre
2 5° BTDC
3 TDC

the wire to the coil from the switch, having taken the wire off the coil. (See Section 10:2).

4   Slacken the nut on the distributor clamping plate.

5   Turn the distributor slightly in the direction of rotation of the cam (clockwise) to make sure the points are shut. Then carefully turn it anti-clockwise to advance the ignition, against the direction of rotation, until the points open, as shown by the light going out. If not using a light, then with the ignition on, a spark can sometimes be seen at the points, or if an ammeter is fitted, an assistant can watch this for a flicker, the ignition being on.

6   Reclamp the distributor.

7   Now recheck, by turning the engine over, forwards again, till the timing notch on the pulley is coming up to the mark again. Watch the timing light and the pulley. Turn the engine smoothly and slowly, and see where the notch was when the timing light went out. It should of course be by the 10° BTDC mark.

8   The timing can be set with the engine running, using a stroboscope. This method is more accurate, and such accuracy is needed to meet the American emissions regulations.

9   Connect up the timing light to No 1 cylinder plug lead in accordance with the makers instructions. Start up the engine. Check the idle speed is correct with a tachometer. Shine the light on the timing marks. Slacken the distributor, and move it as required to get the correct relationship of the notch on the pulley with the mark on the cover, as 'frozen' by the light. Reclamp the distributor. Speed up the engine, and check the automatic advance is working.

10 Unless an accurate tachometer is in use, setting the timing by stroboscope will be inaccurate, as the automatic advance is varying the timing as the engine speeds up.

5   Distributor removal and replacement

1   If the distributor is removed, the timing will be lost. It is quite straight forward to set it up again, but do not take it out unless you realise what is involved.

2   If there will be no need to turn the engine over whilst the distributor is out, then the problem can be eased. To do this, turn the engine over until the timing notch in the crankshaft pulley is opposite the timing mark on the camshaft felt cover, and the dot on the camshaft pulley is just past 6 o'clock, and opposite a pointer on the engine mounting. Take off the distributor cap. Note to which segment the rotor arm is pointing. It should be cylinder number 4. (photo) (See also Chapter 1, photo 37.4.a).

3   Undo the nut on the clamp holding the distributor down into the engine. Take off the clamp.

4   Pull the distributor out of the engine. Take care as the spindle comes out of the cylinder block in case the drive gear has come as well, so it is not knocked off the end of the shaft.

5   If the gear did not come out, and needs to do so, fish it out with a finger, if long ones, or with a piece of wood a little fatter than a pencil, sharpened to a gradual taper.

6   When refitting the distributor, first oil the gear, and put it back in place with the piece of wood/finger.

7   Reset the contact breaker points, as this is much easier done with the distributor on the bench. (See Section 2).

8   If the engine has not been turned over since the distributor was removed, put the rotor arm at the appropriate position for cylinder No 4.

9   If the engine has been turned over, turn it again until the crankshaft pulley timing mark is lined up with the 10° mark on the camshaft belt cover, and at the same time the camshaft pulley is just coming up to its mark, so No.4 cylinder is at the top of its compression stroke. This is shown by both its cams being well away from the valves, whilst the valves of No.1 cylinder are at overlap, exhaust just closing, and inlet opening. (See Fig.4.2 and the photo 5.2). Set the distributor so that the rotor arm will point to the segment in the cap for No.4 cylinder.

10 Slide the distributor down into the engine, turning the spindle slightly to engage the splines in the gear.

11 Fit the clamping plate, and put on the nut finger tight.

12 Wire up the timing light and set the static timing as described in Section 4. If it is intended to use a stroboscope, still set the timing now, so it is accurate enough to start the engine.

13 Refit the distributor cap, checking all the leads do go to the correct plugs, in the firing order 1 3 4 2.

6   Distributor dismantling and inspection

1   Apart from the contact points the other parts of a distributor which deteriorate with age and use, are the cap, the rotor, the shaft bushes, and the bob weight springs.

2   The cap must have no flaws or cracks and the 4 HT terminal contacts should not be severely corroded. The centre spring loaded carbon contact is replaceable. If in any doubt about the cap buy a new one.

3   The rotor deteriorates minimally but with age the metal conductor tip may corrode. It should not be cracked or chipped and the metal conductor must not be loose. If in doubt renew it. Always fit a new rotor if fitting a new cap.

4   To gain access to the centrifugal advance mechanism refer to Figures 4.3 and 4.4 for the details of the Marelli and Ducellier distributors.

5.1 Removing the distributor involves retiming the engine. But this is not difficult

5.2 This camshaft pulley timing mark can be seen through the small hole in the belt cover. It gives ignition for No 4 cylinder.

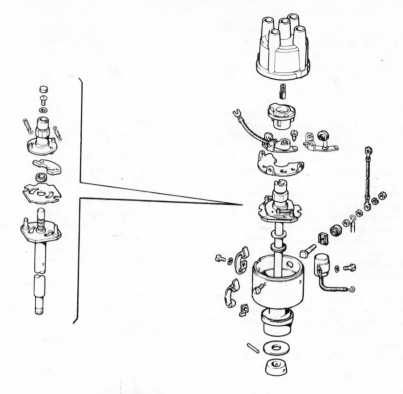

Fig.4.3 The parts of the Marelli distributor

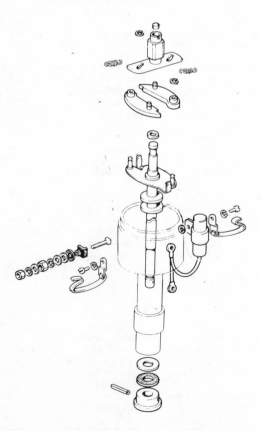

Fig.4.4 The Ducellier distributor fitted to some cars according to parts supply availability

5 Remove the contact breaker. Take out completely the insulated terminal from the side of the distributor, noting how the insulators are fitted. Remove the screws that hold the plate on which is mounted the contact breaker, and lift out the plate.

6 There is no way to test the bob weight springs other than by checking the performance of the distributor on special test equipment, so if in doubt fit new springs anyway. If the springs are loose where they loop over the posts it is more than possible that the post grooves are worn in which case the various parts which include the shaft will need renewal. Wear to this extent would mean that a new distributor is probably the best solution in the long run. Be sure to make an exact note of both the engine number and any serial number on the distributor when ordering.

7 The cam, with its lugs for the centrifugal advance mechanism, fits as a sleeve over the spindle. To remove it, first prise out the felt oil wick at the top. Hold the bottom of the shaft in a padded vice, and undo the screw at the top (it is a washer on the Ducellier). Take off the centrifugal advance springs, being careful not to stretch them. Note how the bob-weights are fitted, then pull the cam up, off the spindle. Before reassembly, put plenty of engine oil on the bearing between the cam and spindle, as not much comes from the wick.

8 If the main shaft is slack in its bushes or the cam on the spindle, allowing sideways play it means that the contact points gap setting can only be a compromise because the cam position relative to the cam follower on the moving point arm is not constant. It is not practical to re-bush the distributor body unless you have a friend who can bore and bush it for you. The shaft can be removed by driving out the roll pin from the retaining collar at the bottom. (The collar also acts as an oil slinger to prevent excess engine oil creeping up the shaft).

7 Condenser removal, testing and replacement

1 The purpose of the condenser (sometimes known as capacitor) is to ensure that when the contact breaker points open there is no sparking across them which would weaken the spark and cause rapid deterioration of the points.

2 The condenser is fitted in parallel with the contact breaker points. If it develops a short circuit, it will cause ignition failure as the points will be prevented from interrupting the low tension circuit.

3 If the engine becomes very difficult to start or begins to misfire whilst running and the breaker points show signs of excessive burning, then suspect the condenser has failed with open circuit. A further test can be made by separating the points by hand with the ignition switched on. If this is accompanied by a bright spark at the contact points it is indicative that the condenser has failed.

4 Without special test equipment the only sure way to diagnose condenser trouble is to replace a suspected unit with a new one and note if there is any improvement.

5 To remove the condenser from the distributor, take out the screw which secures it to the distributor body and slacken the insulated terminal nut enough to remove the wire connection tag.

6 When fitting the condenser it is vital to ensure that the fixing screw is secure and the condenser tightly held. The lead must be secure on the terminal with no chance of short circuiting.

8 Spark plugs and high tension leads

1 The correct functioning of the spark plugs is vital for the correct running and efficiency of the engine. The plugs fitted as standard are listed in the 'Specifications' at the beginning of this Chapter.

2 At intervals of 6,000 miles/6 months the plugs should be removed, examined, cleaned or if worn excessively, renewed. The condition of the spark plug will also tell much about the overall condition of the engine.

3 If the insulator nose of the spark plug is clean and white, with no deposits, this is indicative of a weak mixture, or too hot

a plug. (A hot plug transfers heat away from the electrode slowly - a cold plug transfers it away quickly).

4 If the tip of the insulator nose is covered with sooty black deposits, then this is indicative that the mixture is too rich. Should the plug be black and oily, then it is likely that the engine is fairly worn, as well as the mixture being rich.

5 If the insulator nose is covered with light tan to greyish brown deposits, then the mixture is correct and it is likely that the engine is in good condition and correctly tuned.

6 If there are any traces of long brown tapering stains on the outside of the white portion of the plug, then the plug will have to be renewed, as this shows that there is a faulty joint between the plug body and the insulator, and compression is being allowed to leak away, any chips or cracks also mean that the plug should be renewed.

7 Clean around the plug seats in the cylinder head before removing the plugs to prevent dirt getting into the cylinder. Plugs should be cleaned by a sand blasting machine, which will free them from carbon more thoroughly than cleaning by hand. The machine will also test the behaviour of the plugs under compression. Any plug that fails to spark at the recommended pressure should be renewed. It is recommended a new set of plugs is fitted, then the others can be taken later for cleaning, when more convenient. The two sets are then used concurrently, plugs can only last about 12,000 miles before their points are burned too far. So they will not require cleaning often, as replacement will be at alternate services.

8 The spark plug gap is of considerable importance, as, if it is too large or too small the size of the spark and its efficiency will be seriously impaired. The spark plug gap should be set to the gap shown in the Specifications for the best results.

9 To set it, measure the gap with a feeler gauge, and then bend open, or close, the outer plug electrode until the correct gap is achieved. The centre electrode should never be bent as this may crack the insulation and cause plug failure, if nothing worse.

10 When replacing the plug see that the washer is intact and carbon free, also the shoulder of the plug under the washer. Make sure also that the plug seat in the cylinder head is quite clean.

11 Replace the leads from the distributor in the correct firing order, which is 1-3-4-2; No.1 cylinder being the one nearest the camshaft belt.

12 The plug leads require no routine attention other than being kept clean and wiped over regularly. At intervals, say twice yearly, pull each lead off the plug in turn and also from the distributor cap. Water can seep down into these joints giving rise to a white corrosive deposit which must be carefully removed from the brass connectors at the end of each cable, using an aersol such as WD40, to prevent corrosion and dispense damp.

9 Distributor cap, rotor arm, and HT leads

1 The distributor cap, leads, and the rotor arm distribute the high tension to the plugs. They should all last long mileages without replacement. But in a very short mileage their state can be responsible for frustration and annoyance.

2 If the components of the HT circuit are dirty, they will attract damp. This damp will allow the HT current to leak away. This will give difficulty in starting the engine when cold. All this is agravated as when cold and damp the battery only gives a slightly low voltage. The oil will be thick, so making the starter take more voltage and current, even so only cranking the engine slowly. The voltage drop due to the starter's demands means reduced voltage in the primary circuit, so a corresponding fall in that in the secondary, the HT. This at the very time when a strong spark is needed to fire the cold cylinder.

3 It is but a temporary palliative to spray the ignition leads with an aerosol damp repellant. The leads, the spark plug insulators, the outside and the inside of the distributor cap, and the rotor arm must be clean and dry. In winter this will need doing at least at 3,000 mile intervals.

4 Some plug leads are 'resistive'. They are made of cotton

White deposits and damaged porcelain insulation
indicating overheating

Broken porcelain insulation due to bent central
electrode

Electrodes burnt away due to wrong heat value or
chronic pre-ignition (pinking

Excessive black deposits caused by over-rich
mixture or wrong heat value

Mild white deposits and electrode burnt indicating
too weak a fuel mixture

Plug in sound condition with light greyish brown
deposits

Fig. 4.5 Sample spark plug conditions

impregnated with carbon, to give the necessary radio interference suppression with separate suppressors. After a time flexing makes the leads break down inside. If difficult starting persists, then new leads, with normal metal core, and suppressor end fittings, could effect a cure. End fittings should not be taken off the resistive wire, as it is difficult to fit them so that a good contact is achieved.

10 The coil

1   Coils normally run the life of the car. The most usual reason for a coil to fail is after being left with the ignition switched on but the engine not running. There is then constant current flowing, instead of the intermittent flow when the contact breaker is opening. The coil then overheats, and the insulation is damaged.

2   The contact breaker points should preferably not be flicked without a lead from the coil centre to some earth, otherwise the opening of the points will give a HT spark which, finding no proper circuit, could break down the insulation in the coil. When connecting a timing light for setting the ignition, this should come from the switch side of the coil, the coil itself being disconnected.

3   If the coil seems suspect after fault-finding, the measurement of the resistance of the primary and secondary windings can establish the matter definitely. But if an ohmmeter is not available, then it will be necessary to try a new one.

11 Fault-finding

1   Faults in the ignition system are dealt with on the fault–finding chart at the end of Chapter 1. Usually ignition faults results in failured to start or a breakdown on the road.

2   Random erratic running due to the ignition having a loose connection can result in jerks. The only way to cure this is to check all leads for security.

3   If the car starts well, but misfires at high engine speed, then the contact breaker, or the coil are suspect. If the contact breaker lacks lubrication, or its spring is weak, it cannot follow the cam at speed. If the breaker gap is too large, at high engine speed the coil will not have time to build up its magnetic field sufficiently. Similarly if the coil has suffered a partial failure, it will be weak.

4   Difficult starting from cold has already been discussed in Section 9. The solution when this occurs is to try a push start. If this gets the engine going easily, then either the ignition is weak, perhaps through dirt and damp, or the battery is weak, either needing a charge, or replacement.

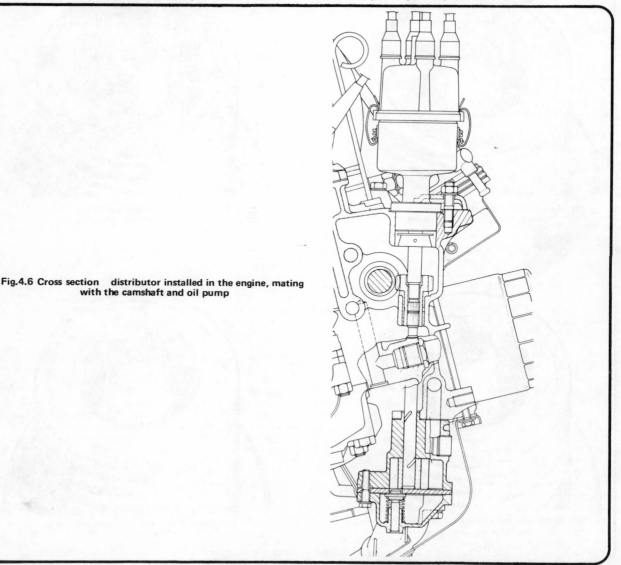

Fig.4.6 Cross section   distributor installed in the engine, mating with the camshaft and oil pump

Chapter 5 Clutch

Contents

Specifications

Type	Single dry plate, diaphragm spring
Withdrawal mechanism	Cable
Lining outer diameter	7 5/32 in (181.5 mm)
Lining inner diameter	5 in (127 mm)
Max. runout of driven plate friction linings	01 in (0.25 mm)
Clutch pedal free travel, corresponding to a clearance of .079 in (2 mm) between friction ring and throwout sleeve ...	1 in (25 mm)
Travel of release flange, corresponding to a pressure plate displacement not less than .055 in (1.4 mm)	.315 in (8 mm)

Tightening torques:-

Clutch to flywheel	11 lbf. ft	1.5 kg m
Clutch withdrawal fork to pivot	18 lbf. ft	2.5 kg m

1 General description

1 All models covered by this manual are fitted with a single dry plate diaphragm clutch. The unit comprises a steel cover which is dowelled and bolted to the face of the flywheel and contains the pressure plate; pressure plate diaphragm spring; and fulcrum rings.

2 The clutch disc is free to slide along the splined gearbox input shaft and is held in position between the flywheel and the pressure plate by the pressure of the pressure plate spring. Friction lining material is riveted to the clutch disc and it has a spring cushioned hub to absorb transmission shocks.

3 The circular diaphragm spring is mounted on shouldered pins and held in place in the cover by two fulcrum rings and rivets.

4 The clutch is actuated by cable .

5 Unlike in-line engines and gearboxes, the shaft through the clutch into the gearbox does not have a spigot bearing in the end of the crankshaft.

2 Clutch - removal and inspection

1 Remove the transmission (see Chapter 6).

2 Mark the position of the clutch cover relative to the flywheel.

3 Slacken off the bolts holding the cover to the flywheel in a diagonal sequence, undoing each bolt a little at a time. This keeps the pressure even all round the diaphragm spring and prevents distortion. When all the pressure is released on the bolts, remove them, lift the cover off the dowel pegs and take it off together with the friction plate which is between it and the flywheel.

4 Examine the diaphragm spring for signs of distortion or fracture.

5 Examine the pressure plate for signs of scoring or abnormal wear.

6 If either the spring of the plate is defective it will be necessary to replace the complete assembly with an exchange unit. The assembly can only be taken to pieces with special equipment and, in any case, individual parts of the assembly are not obtainable as regular spares.

7 Examine the friction plate for indications of uneven wear and scoring of the friction surfaces. Contamination by oil will also show as hard and blackened areas which can cause defective operation. If there has been a leak from engine or transmission this must be cured before reassembling the clutch. If the clearance between the heads of the securing rivets and the face of the friction lining material is less than 0.5 mm/.020 inches it would be worthwhile to fit a new plate. Around the hub of the friction disc are six springs acting as shock absorbers between the hub and the friction area. These should be intact and tightly in position.

8 The face of the flywheel should be examined for signs of scoring or uneven wear and, if necessary, it will have to be renewed or reconditioned. See Chapter 1 for details of flywheel removal.

9 Also check the clutch withdrawal bearing (Section 4) before reassembly.

10 Clutch parts are relatively cheap compared with the great labour of removal, so it is best to replace parts if there is any doubt.

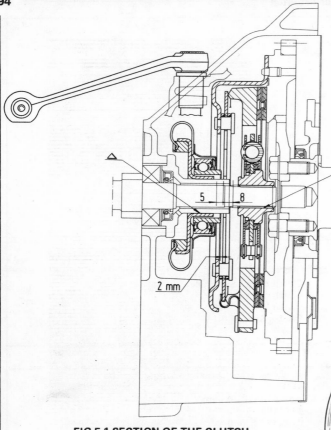

FIG.5.1 SECTION OF THE CLUTCH

The dimension given are:- 2 mm = clutch free travel: 5 mm = maximum acceptable movement with worn linings: 8 mm = declutching travel. The triangular marks are the sliding parts of the withdrawal mechanism. Use the special FIAT KG 15 lubricant, or leave dry.

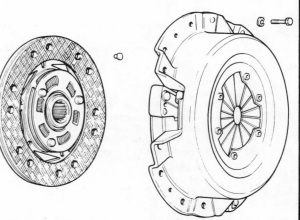

FIG.5.2 THE TWO PARTS OF THE CLUTCH

On the left the friction, or driven plate: On the right the cover assembly with spring and pressure plate.

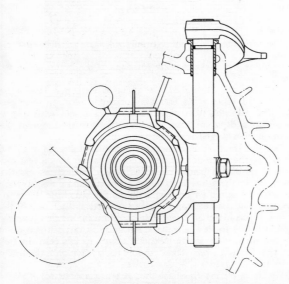

FIG.5.3 CLUTCH WITHDRAWAL FORK AND SHAFT

The bush for the shaft should be lubricated with a molybdenum disulphide grease if dismantled. (Castrol MS 3 Grease)

3 Refitting the clutch

1 Hold the clutch friction, or driven plate up against the flywheel. The disc holding the cushion springs must be away from the flywheel (photos).

2 Put the clutch cover assembly over the plate, lining up the dowel holes, and fit the bolts. Tighten the bolts finger tight, just enough to take the weight of the friction plate between the pressure plate and the flywheel.

3 Now centralise the clutch plate. The splines in the plate must be accurately lined up with the end of the crankshaft, otherwise when the clutch is clamped up tight, and the friction plate cannot be moved, the shaft will not fit through, and reassembly of transmission to engine will be impossible. FIAT use a special mandrel that fits into the end of the crankshaft. The alignment can be done satisfactorily using a metal or wooden bar, and checking carefully by eye.

4 Tighten the bolts round the edge of the clutch cover carefully and diagonally, gradually compressing the clutch spring.

5 Refit the transmission as described in Chapter 6.

4 Clutch withdrawal or release mechanism

1 To release the clutch, so that the drive is disengaged, the pressure plate is 'withdrawn' from the flywheel. The driver's pedal action, through the cable, pulls on the withdrawal lever on the outside of the transmission case, and the fork inside pushes the withdrawal bearing against the clutch.

2 The pivot for the lever fork should outlast the car.

3 The withdrawal or release bearing should not give trouble either. But should it fail the transmission must be removed from the car to reach it. So when the transmission is out, even though for some other work, the bearing should be looked at very critically, and if there is any doubt it should be renewed.

4 The bearing is clipped to the withdrawal fork (photo). It should not be immersed in cleaning fluid, as it is sealed. Liquid will get in, but can not be dried out, nor can new lubricant be got in. The bearing should be rotated. It should be completely smooth in action, but the smooth resistance of the grease should be felt. It should not make any noise.

5 When fitting a new bearing the clips and the bearing surfaces of the fork should be lubricated with grease.

6 If the bearing is suspected, but the transmission is still in the car, the bearings failure can only be assessed by noise. If the actual bearings are breaking up, this will be shown by a squawking or groaning noise when the clutch pedal is pressed down. If the bearing is loose, it may rattle at speed, and this rattle be quietened of the pedal is lightly pressed to hold the bearing. The car should not be driven in this condition, for if the bearing breaks up, repair is likely to be expensive, as other parts will be damaged.

5 Clutch cable replacement

1 Should the cable show signs of incipient failure such as frayed ends of broken cable strands, it should be replaced. The broken ends of cable may jam up in the outer cable, and prevent proper action. Also it is rather difficult to continue a journey when the cable has broken.

2 Unhook the spring from the withdrawal lever.

3 Take off the locknut and adjusting nut from the end of the cable. (See Fig.5.4).

4 Inside the car take the circlip off the end of the cable pin on the pedal. (See Fig.5.6).

5 Take out the two bolts holding the outer cable abutment to the scuttle (fire wall) in front of the driver, from the engine side.

6 Remove the cable.

7 Use a new grommet at the clutch end of the cable. Fit the new cable, and adjust the free play as given in the next section.

3.1 The clutch driven plate must go with the mounting for the cushion springs away from the flywheel.

3.2 It must be centralised with the flywheel.

3.3 Here a socket spanner extension is being used as a centralising tool.

4.4 The clutch withdrawal bearing is clipped to the fork.

6 Clutch adjustment

1   As the friction linings on the clutch plate wear, the pressure plate moves closer to the flywheel, and the withdrawal mechanism must move back to allow for this movement. There must always be clearance between the withdrawal mechanism and the clutch, otherwise the full clutch spring pressure will not be available, and the clutch will slip, and quickly ruin itself. Also the life of the withdrawal bearing will be shortened.

2   The small clearance of 2 mm at the clutch itself appears as 1 inch (25 mm) at the pedal. (See Fig.5.5).

3   This free movement at the pedal can be felt as movement against only the pull-off spring on the clutch withdrawal lever, before the firmer pressure needed to free the clutch itself.

4   Adjust by undoing the lock nut, and moving the adjuster nut on the end of the cable. To increase the free play, move the nut nearer the end of the cable. (photo).

5   If the free play always needs adjustment at the stated mileage intervals, 6,000 miles (10,000 km) it is suggested you review your driving technique. See the next section. For many drivers wear in the clutch linings just about balances stretch and wear in the clutch withdrawal mechanism, and no adjustment is ever needed.

7 Clutch life

1   Some drivers allow their clutches to outlast the engine and transmission. Others need new ones almost as often and regularly as their 12,000 mile service. The clutch is one of the prime examples of a component cheap to buy, but expensive (or lengthy for the home mechanic) to fit.

2   The short life is due to abuse.

3   Common abuses can be avoided as follows.

4   Do not sit for long periods, such as at traffic lights, with the clutch disengaged. Put the gearbox in neatral until the lights go yellow. This extends the withdrawal bearing life.

5   Always remove the foot completely from the clutch pedal once under way. Riding the clutch lightly ruins the withdrawal bearing. Riding it heavily allows it to slip, so quickly wears out the lining.

6   Whenever the clutch is disengaged, hold it completley so, the pedal down as far as it will go. You see drivers holding the car on a hill by slipping the clutch. This wears it quickly.

7   Always move off in first gear.

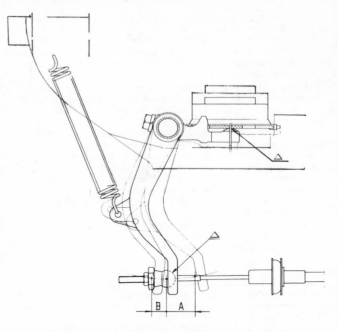

FIG.5.4 CLUTCH WITHDRAWAL LEVER AND FORK

A = Clutch release travel   *B = Adjustment due to wear*

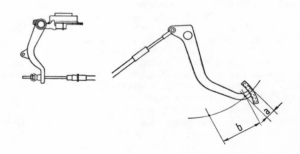

FIG.5.5 CLUTCH PEDAL MOVEMENT

a   = Free travel of 1 in (25mm)

b   = Release travel of 4.02in (102mm)

6.4 The clutch free play is adjusted by the nut and locknut on the end of the cable.

8 Fault diagnosis and remedies

Symptom	Reason/s	Remedy
Judder when taking up drive	Loose engine/gearbox mountings or over flexible mountings Badly worn friction surfaces or friction plate contaminated with oil carbon deposit Worn splines in the friction plate hub or on the gearbox input shaft Badly worn transmission or drive shafts	Check and tighten all mounting bolts and replace any 'soft' or broken mountings. Remove transmission and replace clutch parts as required. Rectify the oil leak which caused contamination. Renew friction plate and/or input shaft. Renew bearings and shafts.
Clutch drag (or failure to disengage) so that gears cannot be meshed	Clutch actuating cable clearance too great Clutch friction disc sticking because of rust on splines (usually apparent after standing idle for some length of time) Damaged or misaligned pressure plate assembly	Adjust clearance. As temporary remedy engage top gear, apply handbrake, depress clutch and start engine. (If very badly stuck engine will not turn). When running rev up engine and slip clutch until disengagement is normally possible. Renew friction plate at earliest opportunity. Replace pressure plate assembly.
Clutch slip - (increase in engine speed does not result in increase in car speed - especially on hills)	Clutch actuating clearance from fork too small resulting in partially disengaged clutch at all times Clutch friction surfaces worn out (beyond further adjustment of operating cable) or clutch surfaces oil soaked Damaged clutch spring	Adjust clearance. Replace friction plate and remedy source of oil leakage. Fit reconditioned assembly.

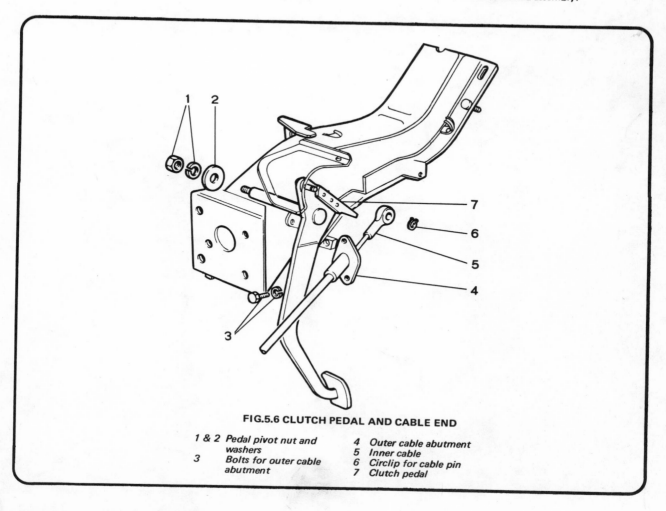

FIG.5.6 CLUTCH PEDAL AND CABLE END

1 & 2	Pedal pivot nut and washers	4	Outer cable abutment
3	Bolts for outer cable abutment	5	Inner cable
		6	Circlip for cable pin
		7	Clutch pedal

Chapter 6 Transmission

Contents

Specifications

Speeds ...		Four forward and one reverse
Synchromesh, spring ring type ...		1st, 2nd, 3rd and 4th gears
Gear type:	forward ...	Constant mesh, helical toothed
	reverse ...	Straight toothed, with sliding idler gear
Gear ratios:	first ...	3.583 to 1
	second ...	2.235 to 1
	third ...	1.454 to 1
	fourth ...	1.037 to 1
	reverse ...	3.714 to 1
Final drive gears ...		Helical-toothed
Final drive ratio:	Saloon ...	4.077 to 1 (13/53)
	Estate ...	4.416 to 1 (12/53)

		1st	2nd	3rd	4th	rev.
Overall ratios: Gears ...						
(Saloon) Reduction ratio: 1 ...		14.61	9.11	5.93	4.23	15.14

Differential case bearings ...	Two
Bearing type ...	Taper roller
Bearing pre-load setting ...	By shims
Side to planet gear backlash adjustment ...	By thrust washers
Road speed in top gear (saloon and coupe) ...	15 mph (24¼ km/hr)
(estate car) ...	14 mph (22½ km/hr)

Lubricant

Temperate climate ...		Engine oil (Castrol GTX)
Hot climates ...		SAE 90 (not EP) (Castrol ST90)
Capacity ...		5½ Imp. pints 3.15 litre 6 2/3 U.S. pints
Gear backlash ...	.004 - .008 in	(0.1 - 0.2 mm)
Clearance reverse idler to shaft ...	.003 - .006 in	(0.08 - 0.15 mm)
Clearance other gears to second shaft ...	.001 - .003 in	(0.04 - 0.08 mm)

Ball bearings:

Side play; maximum ...	.002 in	(0.05 mm)
End play; maximum ...	.02 in	(0.50 mm)
Differential preload: Interference of ...	.003 in	(0.08 mm)
Preload shims: Seven thicknesses ...	0.50 - 1.10 mm	

Synchronizer ring, seated outer diameter:

1st/2nd gear ...	3.004 ± .008 in	(76.30 ± 0.2 mm)
3rd/4th gear ...	2.607 ± .008 in	(66.22 ± 0.2 mm)

Tightening Torques:

Differential halves/crownwheel: 10 mm	...	...	...	...	51 lb f. ft	7 kg m
Differential halves/crownwheel: 8 mm	...	...	...	...	36 lb f. ft	5 kg m
Bolts securing selector forks and levers to rods (Size M6)						
(10 mm AF)	...	...	...	...	14½ lb f. ft	2 kg m
Other nuts/bolts (Size M6) (10 mm AF)	...	...	...	...	7 lb f. ft	1 kg m
Nuts; Gearbox casing to clutch housing	...	...	...	...	18 lb f. ft	2.5 kg m
Nuts, differential flange to transmission	...	...	...	...	18 lb f. ft	2.5 kg m
Bolt and nuts, Transmission to engine	...	...	...	...	58 lb f. ft	8 kg m

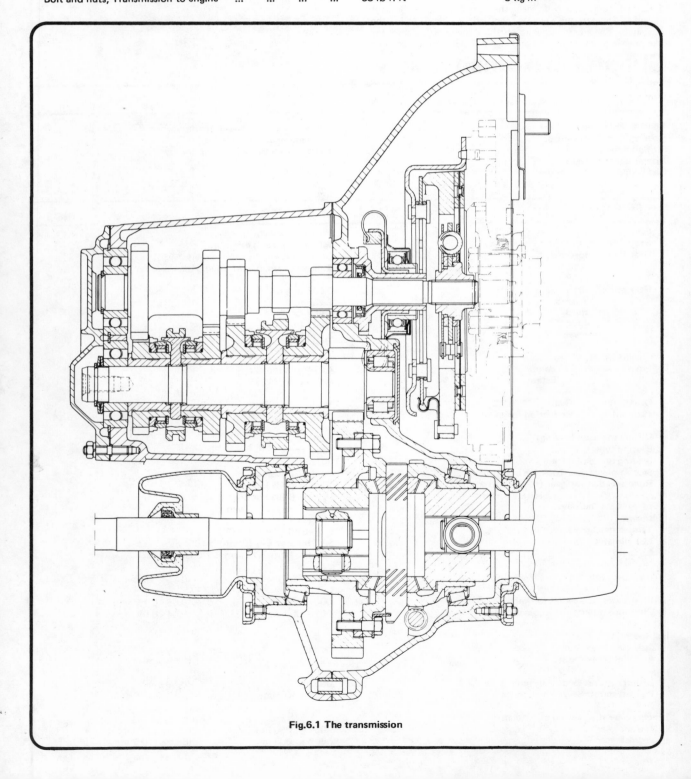

Fig.6.1 The transmission

1 General description

1 Two items of the transmission, the clutch and the drive shafts, are dealt with in separate Chapters. In this one the combined gear box, final drive and differential are described.

2 Figure 6.1 shows the three shaft layout of the transmission on the left end of the engine. Because the components are arranged so differently from gearboxes in-line with the engine, the normal names, such as main shaft, and lay shaft, are not applicable. The top shaft, in line with the engine, is called the input shaft. The next one, with all the sliding dog clutches for engaging the gears, is the 'second shaft'. Below this is the final drive with differential.

3 The synchromesh is of the Porsche ring type, having a self assisting and clash-proof action.

4 The transmission can be removed from the car leaving the engine in place. (photos). Contrariwise the engine cannot be removed without the transmission, and as this involves disconnecting the drive shafts, it is responsible for much of the labour of engine removal. The transmission must be removed to give access to the clutch. Removal of the transmission, unlike that of the engine, does not involve use of lifting tackle, but two good jacks, and plenty of stout timber blocks will be needed. The most likely reason to remove the transmission is to cure an oil leak, or to overhaul the clutch. If the transmission itself is badly worn, then its overhaul is quite possible without special tools. But to be sure of a successful outcome, with absence of noise, then the overhaul must be exceedingly thorough. The cost and the difficulty in obtaining all the parts makes the case for fitting a FIAT reconditioned unit worth while. This could be ordered before dismantling the car.

2 Removing the transmission: engine in place

1 Drain the transmission oil.

2 Remove the spare wheel.

3 Disconnect the battery, undo its clamp, and remove it.

4 Under the car remove the bracket from the transmission to the exhaust. (photo). Undo the earthing strip from transmission to body.

5 Remove the shields under the car. The front one is straightforward. The left hand one has two inaccessible bolts above the drive shaft. The right hand one need not be removed.

6 Disconnect the gear change linkage at the single bolt just before the rod goes inside the transmission casing. Tie the link to the gear lever up to the car with some string.

7 Remove the solenoid wire, and the heavy cable from the starter motor. Unbolt the starter, and take it off the engine.

8 Undo the nut and lock nut on the end of the clutch cable, and disconnect it from the clutch withdrawal lever. Tuck the cable up out of the way.

9 Remove the shield on top of the transmission. (This one is not fitted to cars going to some markets).

10 Disconnect the speedometer from the transmission casing.

11 Disconnect the wires to the various switches on the transmission casing. These vary on versions for various markets. For America there are two on the front not fitted for Europe. These control such things as the seat belt warning system, and the emissions control 3rd/4th gear switch. There is another underneath for the reverse light. Note the colours of the wires going to each.

12 Now prepare for the removal of the drive shafts. First remove the hub cap from the wheel, and whilst the car is still on the ground, undo the nuts on the other end of the drive shafts.

13 Jack the car up until the wheels, hanging free on the suspension, are 1 foot (30 cm) clear of the ground. Put firm supports under the strong points of the body just behind the wheel arches. Put extra blocks for safety incase the car should shift. There will now be room to work underneath, and lift the transmission clear after it has been lowered to the ground.

14 Clean the area around the inner end of the drive shafts, so

1.4a The transmission can be removed leaving the engine in the car.

1.4b It slides off the left, after the engine has been lowered a little so it will clear the wheel arch.

1.4c The drive shaft and anti-roll bar have to be removed.

2.4 The exhaust bracket and gear linkage must be disconnected, and the bearer removed from the beam.

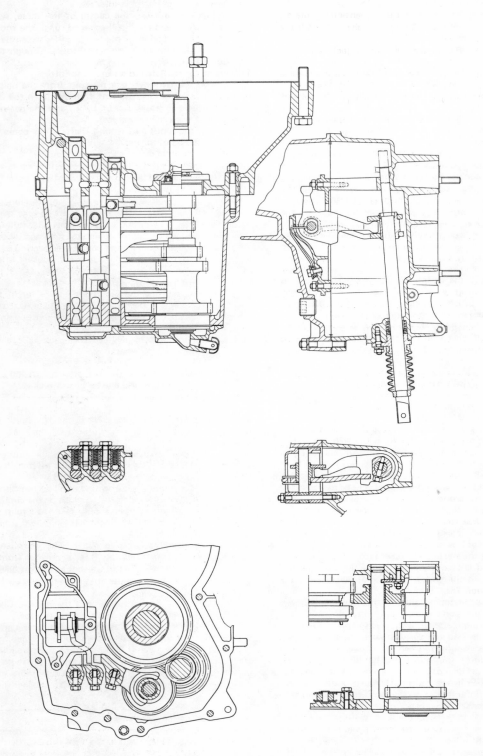

Fig.6.2 Sections of the gear selection mechanism

when the rubber boots are removed, no dirt will get in.

15 Remove the drive shafts, as described in Chapter 7. The method involving the dismantling of the suspension should be used, as the anti-roll bar must be removed to give room for the transmission to slide off the engine.

16 Take the weight of the power unit with a jack under the transmission.

17 Undo the small bolt securing the shield over the flywheel to the transmission flywheel housing.

18 Undo the three nuts holding the triangular bearer bracket to the transmission.

19 Undo the two bolts holding the bearer to the support bracket beam under the engine.

20 Take off the triangular bearer bracket and rubber mounting, and the flywheel shield. Leave the beam behind. If in difficulty due to the inaccessibility of some of the bolts, take the beam off with the bracket, but then put it back on its own afterwards.

21 Lower the jack so the engine is resting on the beam. This is done this way so that the transmission will be low enough to slide clear to the left under the wheel arch, yet the engine is still held up. Leave the jack under the transmission for now.

22 Undo the nuts and bolts holding the transmission to the engine. Support the weight of the transmission, so it does not hang on the clutch. The jack can do this.

23 Withdraw the transmission to the left, and once the stud is out of the dowel to the rear, and the input shaft clear of the clutch, lower it to the ground.

3 Removal of the components from the casing

1 Clean the outside of the casing, and the inside of the clutch housing, checking in the dirt for runs indicating oil leaks, particularly from the core plug.

2 Take the clutch pull-off spring off the clutch withdrawal lever. Pivot the lever round so the withdrawal bearing is nearer, and unclip it from the fork.

3 Remove the nuts with spring washers on the studs inside the clutch housing that hold it onto the gearbox casing. (photo).

4 Stand the transmission up on end, clutch housing downwards.

5 Remove the nuts on the studs holding the end cover, now at the top, of the gearbox. Take off the cover, and the old gasket, (photos).

6 Take off the two bolts holding the plate over the detents.

7 Take out the three springs. Note one is green and two are blue. The green one is the shortest, and is for reverse.

8 Remove the three detent balls.

9 Take off the inner circlips, on the end of the input and second shafts. Note that the one on the second shaft has behind it two belleville washers. These put a heavy load on the circlip. If it will not readily come out of its groove, then the load must be taken off it using a clamp. This clamp will definitely be needed for assembly. See Section 7:5.

10 The belleville washers can be compressed by screwing into the threaded end of the shaft one of the bolts that holds the transmission to the engine, using a large socket spanner to press down on the belleville washers. Between the socket and the washer must go a semicircle of steel so the socket clears the circlip, and through the gap in it the ends of the circlip can be reached.

11 Having removed the circlips from both shafts, see if the two bearings will come off the shafts and out of the casing readily, prising with screwdrivers. If they do not, leave them on the shafts for now, but take off the large circlips round the outer races.

12 Remove the nuts on the other studs on the outside holding the gearbox casing to the clutch housing.

13 Pull the gearbox casing up off the shafts and selector rods.

14 Remove the nut holding the locking plate for the reverse idler shaft, on the face at present uppermost of the gearbox side of the clutch housing.

15 Take out the reverse shaft.

16 Remove the bolts securing the three selector forks and the selector levers to the three selector rods.

17 Pull the reverse selector rod up, out of the housing, and lift off the reverse fork with the idler gear.

18 Pull up the 3rd/4th, the centre of the three, selector rod, leaving the fork and lever still engaged, until the rod is clear of its seat, then the rod with the fork and lever can be lifted out. Keep the rods with their levers and forks. Though they cannot be muddled up, it saves sorting out later.

19 Repeat for the 1st/2nd selectors. (photo).

20 Remove the two interlock plungers from the passages either side of the central, 3rd/4th rod. Remove from the 3rd/4th rod the thin interlock plunger. Put these, and the detent balls in a small box so they cannot get lost.

21 Lift out the input and second shafts. They come most easily as a pair, because of the gears being in mesh.

22 Lift out the final drive/differential. (photo).

23 It is recommended the gear selector linkage is removed so that new seals can be fitted. Undo the three bolts holding the selector pivot to the housing.

24 Take out the bolt holding the finger on the inner end of the selector rod. On the outside of the housing take off the flange guiding the rod, on which the rubber boot fits. Pull out the rod, retrieving from inside the spring and oil seals and washers.

25 Take out of the housing the engine end bearing (roller) of the second shaft. It might just tip out if the housing is turned over.

26 Turn the housing over, and from inside the clutch housing take off the oil seal for the input shaft, in its carrier.

27 The outer races for the final drive can be left in the housing and casing unless it is decided to replace them. Unless they need replacing, the preload plate on the casing, with behind it a shim, need not be removed.

28 There is no need to take the bearings off the input shaft unless they are being renewed.

4 Dismantling the gear clusters on the second shaft

1 If the bearing has not yet been removed when taking the shaft out of the gearbox, take it off now, by holding the outer race in the hand, and hitting the end of the shaft with a soft hammer. (photos).

2 One by one take the gears with their bushes, and the gear-engaging dog-clutches on their hubs off the shaft, keeping them in order, and the same way round.

3 If the synchromesh was in good order, do not dismantle it, as reassembly is difficult due to the strength of the circlip.

4 To strip the synchromesh, simply take the circlip off the gear wheel side. See how all the rings, half rings, and stops, fit inside and then lift them out.

5 Keep all parts laid out in order. Though many parts are interchangeable. Otherwise how they go obvious from examining them and from the pictures in this book; it saves having to work everything out. It is also better to put everything back just where it came from.

6 Reassembly of the components is the reverse. Check that all is correct by referring to the drawings and photos.

7 To refit the circlip on a synchromesh unit is a great struggle. Mount the gear wheel in a soft jawed, clean vice, gripping the flanks of the gear wheel. Part the circlip with circlip pliers, or else prise it apart with a screw driver, to get it part way into position. Then work all the way round with more screwdrivers, to force it into position. An assistant with another screwdriver is almost essential.

5 Dismantling the differential

1 The differential cage acts as the final drive carrier.

2 Undo the ring of bolts holding the final drive wheel to the differential, and the two halves of the differential cage together.

3 This will also release the locking plate for the planet pinion shaft. (photos).

4 Lift off the final drive wheel.

5 Mark the two halves of the differential cage, with punch dots, for reassembly.

6 Prise the two halves apart. Remove the shaft and the two planet pinions.

7 Take out the two bevel side gears, with their thrust washers, from the two halves of the cage. Leave the taper roller bearings in place unless they are being renewed.

8 Reassembly is the reverse. The backlash of the side and planet gears should be .004 - .008 in (0.1 - 0.2 mm). It can be adjusted by fitting thicker thrust washers behind the side gears. Tighten the bolts evenly, gradually, and diagonally, to the specified torque. If new bearings are being fitted, drive them into place carefully and evenly, only doing so by the inner race, not by the rollers. Setting the preload of these bearings is described in Section 7.

9 If new parts are fitted it should be noted that the size of the bolts holding the two halves of the differential and the final drive gear together were increased in size from 8 to 10 mm from Saloon No 411638 and Estate car No 472315. Thus all parts, including the planet pinion lock plate are compatible. The estate car also has a different final drive wheel from the saloon due to its lower gearing.

6 Inspection and renewal of components

1 Check all the components for signs of damage. All the gear teeth should be smooth and shiny, without any chips. The ball and rollers of the bearings should be unblemished.

2 The races of the final drive taper roller bearings, still in the casing, should be a smooth, even colour without any mark. As the lubricant does not have the Extreme Pressure Additives necessary with hypoid gears of conventional rear axles, these bearings are likely to last well. But should either the rollers or the races be marked at all, then the complete bearing must be replaced. In this case the outer races must be extracted from the casing, and the rollers with the inner races pulled off the differential cage halves. The latter is strong, so it will be simple to prise them off. But the casing being soft, great care must be taken to pull the outer races out straight. FIAT have a special puller. It would be advisable to get this job done by your agent.

3 Check the clearance of the gear wheels on their hubs against specification.

4 Check the synchromesh rings. The rings have a triple function. As the gear engaging clutch is moved towards the gear wheel to engage it, the speeds will not be the same. The ring will rub on the clutch, and try to get the gear wheel going at the correct speed. It will also expand, as it will be carried round against its abutment by the movement of the gear wheel in relation to the clutch. This expansion is assisted by the inner half-rings. (photos). Having expanded, it rubs even harder, so giving a form of self-servo action to increase the synchronising effort, this servo effect increasing with the driver's pull on the gear lever. As the ring has expanded, the clutch cannot slide along until it touches the teeth on the gear wheel, so the ring also prevents the gears clashing. Once the clutch and gear wheel are going at the same speed, the ring contracts, and allows the clutch to slide over the gear wheel. Some idea as to the state of the synchromesh rings will have been gained from the feel of the gears when driving. Once the gears are removed from the box they can be seen without actually being dismantled. Look at the way the outer surface is convex, in the Section in Fig.6.1. If this shape has gone, the rings must definitely be replaced. If the gear wheels are being renewed, then the synchromesh should be too. One point easy to miss in examining the gears is fracture of the small ends of the teeth that are on the outside of the synchro ring, and are an extension of the teeth for the clutch to engage. If any of these are chipped the gear must be renewed, as the ring may break the others, and tear a way out.

5 Check the casings for any cracks. If there are leaks at a core plug, a new one must be fitted. This must be tapped judiciously into place, hard enough to expand it, but not hard enough to distort it too much. It should be bedded in with sealing compound. If a plug is not available, or if its security is doubted after fitting, 'weld' the plug into place with a layer of an epoxy

3.3 Remove the nuts inside the clutch housing.

3.5 Then turn it up on end and start dismantling by removing the end cover.

3.6 Retrieve the three springs and three detent balls.

3.11 It will probably be easier to remove the big circlips from both bearings,

3.13 and leave them behind on their shafts when lifting off the casing.

3.14 Take out the locking plate for the reverse idler shaft, and take out the shaft.

3.17 Then the reverse idler can be taken off with its selector rod.

3.18 Next comes the 3rd/4th selector rod, once the bolts holding its fork and its lever have been taken out.

3.19 Last the 1st/2nd rod, and the fork and lever.

3.20 Then retrieve the two interlock plunger from between the passages. There is also a thin plunger in the end of the 3rd/4th selector rod.

3.21 Lift out the input and second shafts complete.

3.22 The differential/final drive just lifts out now.

4.1a Now that the second shaft is out of the casing, it is easier to get off the circlip against the considerable pressure of the belleville washers next to it.

4.1b Then drive the shaft out of the bearing.

4.2a Slide the gear wheels and synchromesh dog-clutch units off,

4.2b noting how everything goes.

5.2 The differential cage is clamped together by this ring of bolts.

5.3 Two of the bolts hold the lock plate for the planet pinions' shaft.

5.4 Undoing them allows the whole assembly to come apart.

5.6 The planet pinions come off their shaft.

5.7 Both bevel side gears have a washer behind to take side thrust, and set the back lash with the teeth of the planet pinions.

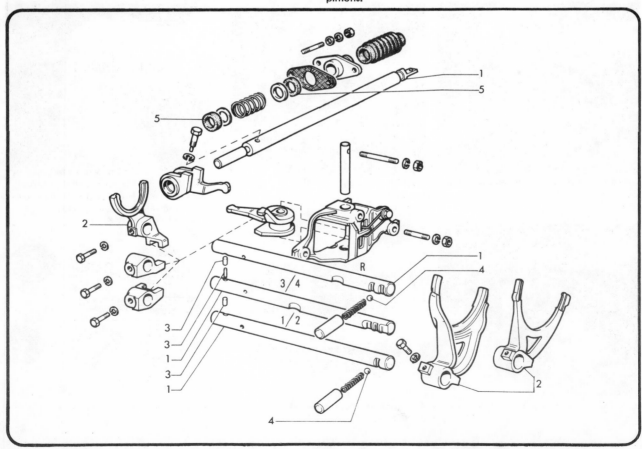

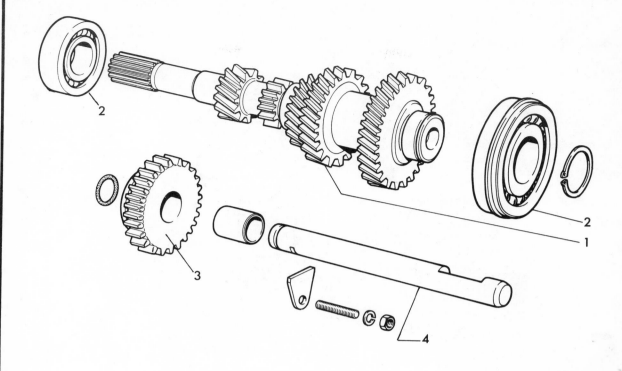

FIG.6.4 INPUT AND REVERSE SHAFTS

1 Input shaft with integral
  gears

2 Input shaft ball bearings

3 Reverse idler gear

4 Idler shaft

FIG.6.3 THE GEAR SELECTOR PARTS

1 Selector rods
2 Selector forks
3 Interlock plungers

4 Detent balls, only two of
  three shown
5 Rod oil seals

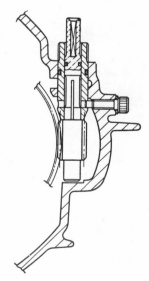

Fig.6.5 Speedometer driven gear in housing

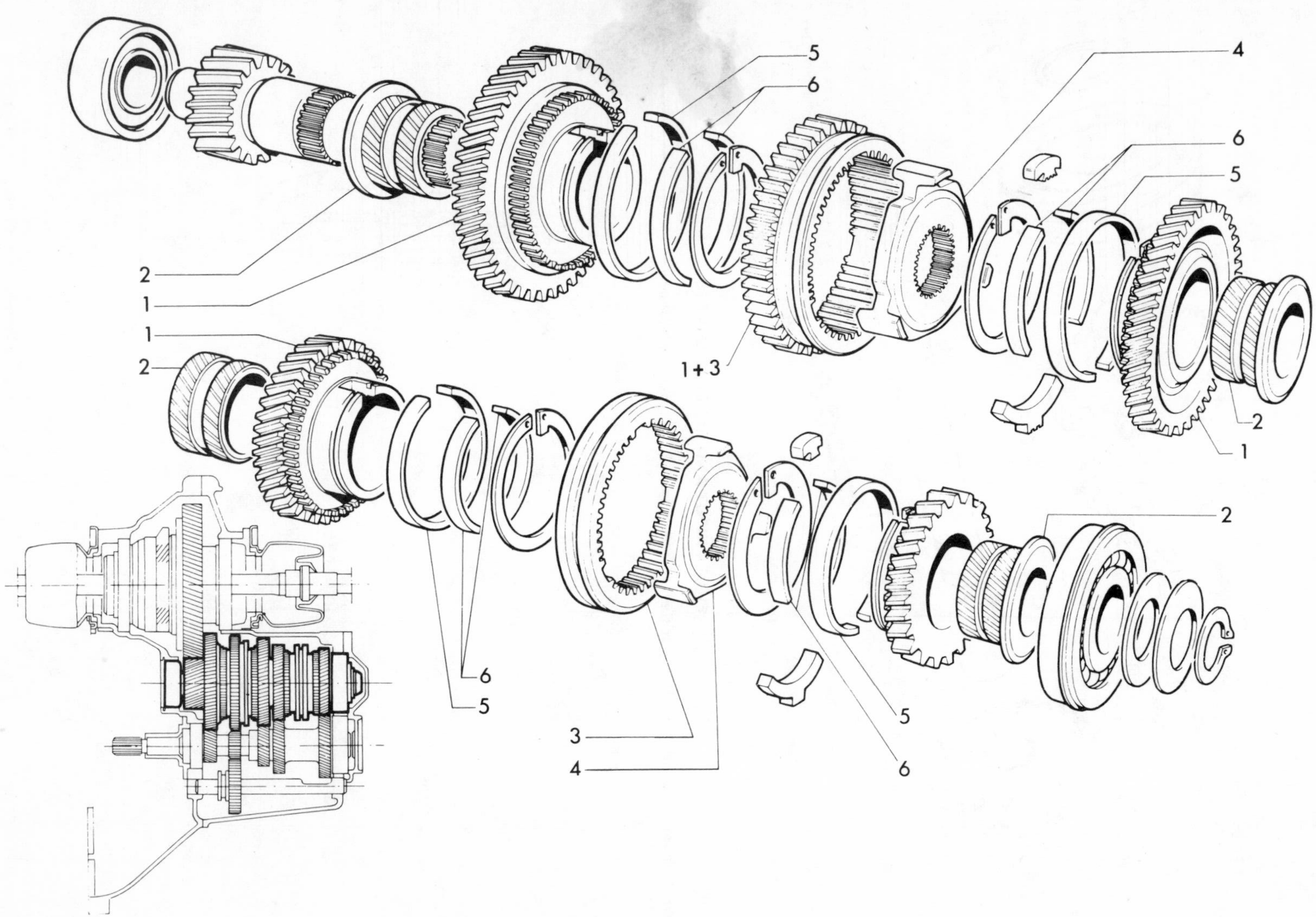

FIG.6.6 PARTS OF THE GEAR 'CLUSTER' MOUNTED ON THE 'SECOND' SHAFT

1 Gear wheels   2 Gear hubs   3 Dog clutch sliding sleeves   4 Hubs for clutch sleeves   5 Synchromesh spring rings   6 Expander half rings

two part glue such as Araldite, round its rim. This glue will need two days to cure properly before the transmission is filled with oil.

6 Unless the transmission is fairly new, the oil seals and the boot should be renewed where the selector rod enters the housing. Early cars only had one sealing ring. Later ones have one at either end of the spring. Note that the metal washers go next to the spring, and the seals next to the housing.

7 Whilst working on the transmission, check the rubbers in the noise insulating joint in the gear lever linkage. This can make the lever movement soggy if soft.

7 Reassembly of the transmission

1 Refit all the differential components and the final drive gear wheel to the differential cage, so it is ready as a sub-assembly. Use appropriate thrust washers behind the bevel side gears to get the correct backlash with the planet gears.

2 Fit all the gear wheels, with their synchromesh units already assembled, on their bushes and hubs respectively onto the second shaft. Refer to the drawings to get everything in the correct order and the right way round. (photos).

3 Fit the bearing on the end of the second shaft, with the groove for the circlip in the outer race outermost. Use some piping over the shaft on the inner race to drive it down.

4 Fit the two belleville washers, their outer rims next to each other, on the end of the shaft.

5 Fit the circlip. For this to get into its groove against the considerable pressure of the pair of washers, the latter must be compressed by a clamp. The end of the shaft is internally threaded, and the bolts fixing the transmission to the engine are the same thread. Select a socket just large enough to span the shaft but press on the circlip. The bolts are a bit long, so another socket makes a handy distance piece to use up the extra length of bolt. Screw in the bolt to push the two washers and the circlip down the shaft, watching carefully at the gap in the circlip to see when it is lined up with the groove in the shaft. Tap the circlip, which is trapped by the socket, with a small screwdriver, to push it into the groove. Release the press.

6 Insert the roller bearing for the second shaft in the clutch housing. Fit both bearings to the input shaft, and the circlip to the end, if these have been removed for renewal.

7 Refit the gear selector rod to the housing with the new seals inside and rubber boot outside.

8 Put the differential into the housing.

9 Fit the gear selector linkage bracket onto its studs, engaging the lever with the rod linkage.

10 Fit the input and second shafts with their bearings, as a pair so the gears can be meshed, into the housing, the two shafts standing on their bearings in the housing. The large circlips should be removed from the upper bearings (those at the left end of the shafts) outside races so that the casing can be fitted over the bearings.

11 Put the reverse idler gear in its selector fork, and the fork on the selector rod, and put them in position in the housing, and then fit the revrse shaft to the idler. Lock the reverse shaft with its plate, and the fork with its bolt.

12 Put in an interlock plunger into the passage between the reverse and 3rd/4th selector rods. To get in, glue it with a lump of grease to a screwdriver, and lower it into place.

13 Fit the 3rd/4th selector rod, with fork and lever. This rod can be recognised by the small hole through the end for the thin interlock plunger. Do not forget to fit this little plunger before fitting the rod. Lodge the lever and fork in place in the selectors and synchro clutch respectively. Then slide the rod down into the housing. Fit the bolts to secure the lever and the fork to the rod.

14 Fit the next interlock plunger into the passage between 3rd/4th and 1st/2nd selector rods.

15 Fit the 1st/2nd selector fork into its clutch groove, and swivel it into place. Pass its selector rod through it and the lever into its seat. Bolt the fork and lever to their rod.

16 The selector rods should now all be in place with the grooves for the detents all in line at the top. (photo).

17 Fit the new gasket to the housing.

18 Fit the gearbox casing, lowering it down over the input and second shafts, the differential, and the selector rods. If the differential bearings have been replaced, the outer races should of course be in place, but the bearings preload plate should not be fitted yet to the casing, (photo).

19 Fit the nuts to the studs holding the casing to the housing that are at present uppermost, on the outside.

20 If the differential bearings have been removed, now set the bearing preload. Put two shims above the bearing race then fit the bearing plate, and tighten it gently down to push the bearing into place. This will be helped if a gear is engaged, and the gears rotated by the input shaft, to allow everything to roll into place. As there are two shims fitted the flange of the plate should not go right down. Release the nuts, so the plate is still in contact through the shims with the bearing, by its own weight only, and not strained. Measure the gap between the flange and its seat on the casing. This can be done by inserting feelers between the two, (photo). Remove the plate, and measure the total thickness of the shims in use. Select a shim that will leave a gap of 0.003 in (0.08 mm) between plate and casing with no load on the fixing nuts. When the nuts are tightened, this interference will give the correct preload on the bearings, as the plate is pulled down onto the casing. FIAT do the measuring with gauges, and this is shown in Fig.6.7.

21 Fit the large circlips to the outer races of the bearings on the ends of the input and second shafts. The bearings may need levering up a little, bringing their shafts with them, to get the grooves clear.

22 Fit the three detent balls and their springs. The one odd spring, the green one, goes in the left hole, for reverse. (photo). Put on the new gasket, and fit the cover.

23 Fit the new gasket to the end of the casing, and put on the end plate.

24 Turn the transmission over, clutch end up.

25 Fit the nuts with their spring washers to the large studs inside the clutch housing.

26 Fit the new oil seal into its carrier, so that its lips will be towards the gear box. Fit it carefully over the input shaft, and bolt it in place, using a new gasket between it and the housing.

27 Clip the clutch withdrawal race into place on its fork, putting a trace of grease on its seats.

8 Refitting the transmission to the car

1 The transmission having been assembled, check nothing is left to be done. The drive shafts, with their inner and outer joints, and rubber boots should be ready, but not fitted to the transmission. The oil should be put in later too.

2 The clutch must have been centralised as described in Chapter 5/3.

3 Offer up the transmission to the engine, holding it square. Slide the stud on the rear into the tubular dowel, and the shaft through the clutch. An assistant can help by turning the engine over slightly by a spanner on the crankshaft pulley nut, to allow the splines to line up and engage.

4 As the transmission goes into place, keep the weight supported, so it does not hang on the clutch.

5 Fit the bolts and the nut holding the engine and transmission together. Tighten the top one first so that it takes the weight of the transmission.

6 Put a jack under the transmission, and lift the left end of the power unit to get it level.

7 Fit the shield to the bottom of the flywheel housing, and then the bearer bracket to both power unit and the beam.

8 Lower the jack. Check the power unit is sitting properly in its bearers, and all are properly secured.

9 Refit the drive shafts and front suspension as described in Chapter 7.

10 Refit the exhaust bracket. Reconnect the earthing strip. Couple up the gear lever to the selector rod.

6.4a To slide along, the clutch must compress the synchro ring. This is going at a different speed, with the gear wheel, so is carried round.

6.4b till its end is against the stop, when it expands more,

6.4c helped by the half rings inside. So the gear cannot be engaged,

6.4d till the speeds are the same, when the ring will relax, and allow the clutch to slide over.

7.2 With all the gears etc on the shafts, they should look like this.

7.3 Fit the bearing, then the two belleville washers back to back, followed by the circlip.

7.4 A transmission-to-engine bolt has a suitable thread to make a press to squeeze the belleville washers,

7.5 till the circlip is level with its groove, and can be tapped into it.

7.6 Fit the second shaft's roller bearing,

7.8 Then the final drive.

7.9 After fitting the gear selector rod with its new seals, put on the lever bracket

7.10 The input and second shafts go in as a pair.

7.11a Then the reverse idler in its selector fork, on the selector rod.

7.11b Followed by the shaft.

7.13 In the 3rd/4th selector rod must be this thin interlock plunger.

7.14 A fat interlock plunger must go into the passages between the reverse and 3rd/4th rods, and as shown here, between 3rd/4th and 1st/2nd selector rods. Use grease as glue.

7.15 Thread the 1st/2nd fork into position

7.16 Finally all the gears and rods should be in place,

7.17 and look like this.

7.18 Then the casing can go on.

7.20a If the differential bearings have been renewed, the casing should be fitted with the bearing plate off.

7.20b Measure the thickness of shim needed to give specified preload. Then fit it under the plate.

7.21 On the bearings on the ends of the shafts, fit the large circlips. The bearings may need prising up a little, in the special slots provided so the end face is not burred.

7.22 Fit the three detent balls, then the springs, the one green one, shorter than the other two, is for reverse.

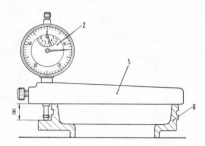

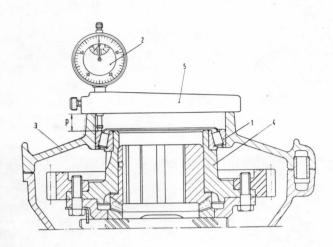

FIG.6.7 FIAT METHOD OF SETTING DIFFERENTIAL PRELOAD

1	Taper roller bearing outer race	2	Dial gauge	4 Differential cage	gauge
		3	Transmission casing	5 FIAT tool for holding dial	6 Bearing cover plate

P = distance bearing face to plate mounting face.
H = height of plate.
S = shim thickness.
S = P − H + 0.003 in (0.08 mm)

The bearing must be settled before taking the measurement P, by applying a load until the gauge shows a yeild of 0.0016 in (0.08 mm)

Fig.6.8 The gear lever, its pivot and guards, and linkage.

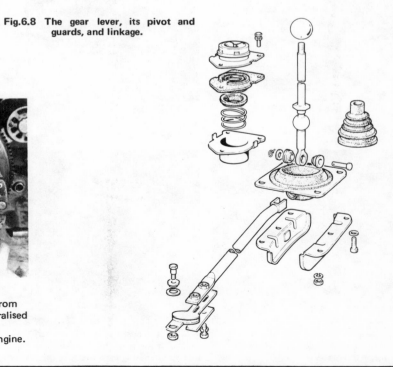

8.2 If the clutch has been removed from the flywheel, the plate must be centralised as described in chapter 5, before the transmission can be refitted to the engine.

11 Lower the car to the ground.

12 Fill the transmission with oil.

13 Refit the starter motor. Connect its heavy cable, and solenoid wire.

14 Connect up the various wires to the switches for the emissions control and reverse light etc.

15 Refit the speedometer cable.

16 Connect up the clutch cable. Refit the pull of string to the lever. Adjust the free play as given in Chapter 5, to 1 in (25 mm) free movement at the pedal.

17 Refit the battery and connect it up.

18 Road test the car. Afterwards check all bolts for tightness, particularly the mountings, and those holding the transmission to the engine. Check for leaks. Check the oil level. When all is correct, refit the shield underneath and on top.

19 If the gear lever action is wrong, its position should be adjusted at the clamp on the link with two bolts, just behind the rubber bonded joint. The holes are elongated. It should be set so that the lever is central.

9 Lubricant

1 Routine Maintenance gives the changing of transmission oil as a 12,000 mile, (20,000 km) task. Some manufacturers claim there is no need to change the oil, as it will last the life of the transmission. This may be so, but the life can be longer if the oil is changed. Changing the oil removes particles of metal worn off the gears and synchromesh mechanism. It also removes oil contaminated by damp. The oil should be changed 500 miles after the transmission has been dismantled. This will remove any metal worn off new components as they settle in, and any bits of dirt inadvertently left in the transmission.

2 The oil should be drained after a journey, so it flows easily, and any dirt will be stirred up. Remove the plug on the left of the final drive part of the casing. Allow the oil to drain fully. Clean the plug before removal, and again before refitting.

3 Fill to the level of the plug on the front.

4 The official FIAT oil for world wide use is an SAE 90 oil. One of EP, extreme pressure, should not be used. As there is not a bevel final drive, the EP quality is not necessary, and so the side effects of the EP additives on bearings can be avoided. FIAT England recommend the use of engine oil in the transmission. This is common practice. It will run a trace cooler, and use slightly less fuel, whilst being a little noiser, compared with the SAE 90 oil.

10 Fault - finding

1 There will often be noises from the transmission. The important thing is to be able to decide whether a noise is normal or not: whether the transmission needs dismantling, or is safe for continued use.

2 If it is decided there is a definite fault in the transmission, what it actually is can be discovered when it is removed and stripped for examination.

3 If subdued whining comes on gradually, there is a good chance the transmission will last a long time to come. Whining or moaning appearing suddenly, or becoming loud, should be examined straight away.

4 If thumping or grating noises appear, stop at once. If bits of metal are loose inside, then the whole transmission, including the casing, could quickly be wrecked.

5 The FIAT 128 can make one noise which is alarming but harmless. When idling, there can be quite a loud chattering from the gears. This will stop if the clutch is disengaged. The engine vibrations start the gears chattering at a critical speed of slow idling. The cure is to set the idle a little faster.

6 Whining is usually gear teeth at an incorrect distance apart. Roaring, rushing or moaning is bearing failure. Thumping or grating noises suggest a hunk out of a tooth.

7 Final drive noises are only heard on the move. Noise on tight corners, if not the drive shafts, the most likely cause, could be excessive tightness or play in the bevel side gears or the planet gears of the differential.

8 Faults within the gear box can be tracked down by noting the change according to the gear selected.

9 In neutral, with the clutch engaged, gearbox noises can be heard. Noises that come when the clutch is disengaged are probably either the clutch withdrawal mechanism, or could be associated with the fact that when the clutch is disengaged, the crankshaft is pushed hard. This can either cause noise, or if the crankshaft end float is excessive, stop it. The fault will often be in the semi-circular thrust bearings in No 5 main bearing.

10 If there is a complete failure, the circumstances in which it occurs will give a clue as to its reason. It could be a mechanical failure, but also the selector mechanism could be the cause.

Castrol GRADES

Castrol Engine Oils

Castrol GTX

An ultra high performance SAE 20W/50 motor oil which exceeds the latest API MS requirements and manufacturers' specifications. Castrol GTX with liquid tungsten† generously protects engines at the extreme limits of performance, and combines both good cold starting with oil consumption control. Approved by leading car makers.

Castrol XL 20/50

Contains liquid tungsten†; well suited to the majority of conditions giving good oil consumption control in both new and old cars.

Castrolite (Multi-grade)

This is the lightest multi-grade oil of the Castrol motor oil family containing liquid tungsten†. It is best suited to ensure easy winter starting and for those car models whose manufacturers specify lighter weight oils.

Castrol Grand Prix

An SAE 50 engine oil for use where a heavy, full-bodied lubricant is required.

Castrol Two-Stroke-Four

A premium SAE 30 motor oil possessing good detergency characteristics and corrosion inhibitors, coupled with low ash forming tendency and excellent anti-scuff properties. It is suitable for all two-stroke motor-cycles, and for two-stroke and small four-stroke horticultural machines.

Castrol CR (Multi-grade)

A high quality engine oil of the SAE-20W/30 multi-grade type, suited to mixed fleet operations.

Castrol CRI 10, 20, 30

Primarily for diesel engines, a range of heavily fortified, fully detergent oils, covering the requirements of DEF 2101-D and Supplement 1 specifications.

Castrol CRB 20, 30

Primarily for diesel engines, heavily fortified, fully detergent oils, covering the requirements of MIL-L-2104B.

Castrol R 40

Primarily designed and developed for highly stressed racing engines. Castrol 'R' should not be mixed with any other oil nor with any grade of Castrol.
†*Liquid Tungsten is an oil soluble long chain tertiary alkyl primary amine tungstate covered by British Patent No. 882,295.*

Castrol Gear Oils

Castrol Hypoy (90 EP)

A light-bodied powerful extreme pressure gear oil for use in hypoid rear axles and in some gearboxes.

Castrol Gear Oils (continued)

Castrol Hypoy Light (80 EP)

A very light-bodied powerful extreme pressure gear oil for use in hypoid rear axles in cold climates and in some gearboxes.

Castrol Hypoy B (90 EP)

A light-bodied powerful extreme pressure gear oil that complies with the requirements of the MIL-L-2105B specification, for use in certain gearboxes and rear axles.

Castrol Hi-Press (140 EP)

A heavy-bodied extreme pressure gear oil for use in spiral bevel rear axles and some gearboxes.

Castrol ST (90)

A light-bodied gear oil with fortifying additives

Castrol D (140)

A heavy full-bodied gear oil with fortifying additives.

Castrol Thio-Hypoy FD (90 EP)

A light-bodied powerful extreme pressure gear oil. This is a special oil for running-in certain hypoid gears.

Automatic Transmission Fluids

Castrol TQF

(Automatic Transmission Fluid)

Approved for use in all Borg-Warner Automatic Transmission Units. Castrol TQF also meets Ford specification M2C 33F.

Castrol TQ Dexron®

(Automatic Transmission Fluid)

Complies with the requirements of Dexron® Automatic Transmission Fluids as laid down by General Motors Corporation.

Castrol Greases

Castrol LM

A multi-purpose high melting point lithium based grease approved for most automotive applications including chassis and wheel bearing lubrication.

Castrol MS3

A high melting point lithium based grease containing molybdenum disulphide.

Castrol BNS

A high melting point grease for use where recommended by certain manufacturers in front wheel bearings when disc brakes are fitted.

Castrol Greases (continued)

Castrol CL

A semi-fluid calcium based grease, which is both waterproof and adhesive, intended for chassis lubrication.

Castrol Medium

A medium consistency calcium based grease.

Castrol Heavy

A heavy consistency calcium based grease.

Castrol PH

A white grease for plunger housings and other moving parts on brake mechanisms. *It must NOT be allowed to come into contact with brake fluid when applied to the moving parts of hydraulic brakes.*

Castrol Graphited Grease

A graphited grease for the lubrication of transmission chains.

Castrol Under-Water Grease

A grease for the under-water gears of outboard motors.

Anti-Freeze

Castrol Anti-Freeze

Contains anti-corrosion additives with ethylene glycol. Recommended for the cooling systems of all petrol and diesel engines.

Speciality Products

Castrol Girling Damper Oil Thin

The oil for Girling piston type hydraulic dampers.

Castrol Shockol

A light viscosity oil for use in some piston type shock absorbers and in some hydraulic systems employing synthetic rubber seals. It must not be used in braking systems.

Castrol Penetrating Oil

A leaf spring lubricant possessing a high degree of penetration and providing protection against rust.

Castrol Solvent Flushing Oil

A light-bodied solvent oil, designed for flushing engines, rear axles, gearboxes and gearcasings.

Castrollo

An upper cylinder lubricant for use in the proportion of 1 fluid ounce to two gallons of fuel.

Everyman Oil

A light-bodied machine oil containing anti-corrosion additives for both general use and cycle lubrication.

Chapter 7 Drive shafts

Contents

Specifications

Shaft joints

Outer end:	Constant velocity, RZEPPA type
Inner end	Sliding, TRIPODE type

Lubricant

Constant velocity joints	Molybdenum disulphide grease 3.3 oz (95 g)	(Castrol MS 3)
Tripode joints	Transmission oil	

Tightening Torques:

Hub nut, outer end of shaft	101 lb f. ft	(14 kg m)
Early type shaft coupling sleeve	33 lb f. ft	(4.5 kg m)
Inner end oil retainer boot to casing	7 lb f. ft	(1 kg m)

1 General description

1 From the final drive and differential under the engine the drive is taken out to the two front wheels by a pair of drive shafts. Because the transmission is to the left of the engine, a long shaft is needed on the right side, (and a short on the left).
2 At the inner ends of the shafts are universal joints of the 'Tripode' type. These allow for axial movement as well as misalignment as the wheels move on the suspension.
3 At the outer ends are constant velocity joints of the Rzeppa type. These allow for the movement up and down of the wheel on the suspension, and the swivelling of the steering.
4 The main part of the shaft fits into the joints at the two ends by splines, held by circlips. Rubber boots keep in the lubricant, and the road dirt out.

5 The 'Tripode' joints work in the bevel side gears of the differential, and are lubricated by the transmission oil. The constant velocity joints are packed for life with molybdenum disulphide grease.
6 Provided the rubber boots keep out the dirt the constant velocity joints last well, though on cars used in towns or hills, with a high proportion of driving hard in low gears, they are unlikely to last as long as the rest of the transmission. The 'Tripode' joints should last the life of the transmission.
7 The drive shafts have to be removed to take out the engine and transmission. Early cars were fitted with shafts with a joint part way along, specially to ease this. However, this joint was a weak point, so now one-piece shafts are used. There are two ways of removing these later shafts. Either they can be removed complete with the constant velocity joint, or taken out of the joint. The former method is lengthy, but usually easier, particularly for the first time.

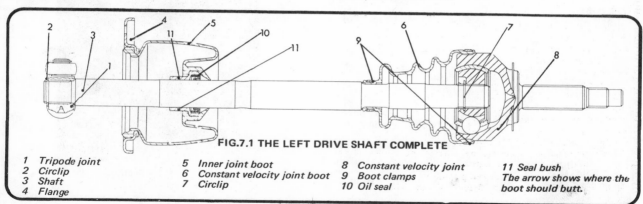

FIG.7.1 THE LEFT DRIVE SHAFT COMPLETE

1 Tripode joint	5 Inner joint boot	8 Constant velocity joint	11 Seal bush
2 Circlip	6 Constant velocity joint boot	9 Boot clamps	The arrow shows where the
3 Shaft	7 Circlip	10 Oil seal	boot should butt.
4 Flange			

2   Removing the drive shafts complete, as an assembly

1   This method involves taking the drive shafts off with the constant velocity joint still on the outer end. This avoids having to open its dirt excluding boot, and is particularly appropriate if there is nothing wrong with the shafts, but they have to be removed, as perhaps the transmission is being taken out. The penalty is that quite a lot of dismantling of the suspension is involved. For the person who has not worked on the car before it is the most straight forward method, as that involving the removal of the shaft from the constant velocity joint is difficult if it is not known exactly what to look for inside.

2   The suspension has to be partially dismantled. In this section is described only the minimum necessary to get off the shafts. However if other jobs then have to be done on the suspension, the work is well on the way having removed the drive shafts.

3   With the front wheels still on the ground and hand brake applied, remove the hub caps, and slacken the nuts on the outer ends of the drive shafts. Squirt onto the shaft splines in the hub an aerosol of rust solvent, which can be soaking in whilst works proceeds. (photo).

4   Jack up both front wheels, and support the car firmly on stands under the reinforced points of the body just behind the front wheels. It must be very firm and at a good height so it is safe and comfortable to work underneath.

5   Remove the front wheel.

6   Remove the brake caliper from the hub by pulling out the two spring clips and wedges. See Chapter 8 for details. Tie the caliper up so the flexible hose will not get strained.

7   Remove the steering ball joint from the steering arm. See Chapter 10 for the method of persuading this to come off.

8   Take the nut completely off the end of the drive shaft, and its flat washer. Give another squirt of the rust solvent to the splines.

9   Under the car clean the area around the seat for the rubber boot at the inner end of the drive shaft, on the transmission casing. But note that if the drive shafts are only being disconnected to remove the front suspension, then this need not be done, and the shafts can be simply undone at the outer end, and left in the transmission.

10 Get an oil drain tray handy.

11 Undo the three bolts holding the rubber boot at the inner end of the shaft. Quite a large proportion of the transmission oil will pour out.

12 Undo the two bolts securing the front suspension strut to the top of the steering knuckle.

13 Put a hand behind the hub and push the drive shaft towards the transmission as hard as possible. Then pull the steering knuckle outwards away from the strut, so that the drive shaft starts to come out of the hub. Initially it may be necessary to drive the shaft back, if the splines are badly rusted. In this case put an old nut on the end of the shaft to protect the threads. If the shaft is stiff in the hub, put in more penetrating oil, and work it too and fro to ease it. Finally to get the shaft out of the hub, pull the steering knuckle down and turn it to full steering lock, (photo).

14 If you get absolutely stuck, the drive shaft can be taken off with the hub. Only two more things need to be undone. Then the shaft can be got out of the hub on the bench. Undo the nut on the end of the anti-roll bar, and take out the pivot bolt at the inner end of the suspension arm. See Chapter 11 for details. However this should not normally be necessary.

15 Having disconnected the outer end of the shaft, it can be drawn out of the transmission. Do this gently, as sometimes, particularly on early cars, the circlips on the 'Tripode' joints come off, and the needle roller bearings fall out and into the transmission. Also keep the 'Tripode' joint out of the dirt.

16 Reassembly is the reverse process. Grease the outer end of the drive shaft, the suspension bolts, and the steering ball joint pin, so another time they will be easier to remove.

17 Refill the transmission with oil, when the car is back on level ground.

2.3 The large nut in the centre of the front hub holds the drive shaft. Both sides are normal right-hand threads.

2.13 After undoing the suspension strut and steering ball-joint, the knuckle can be turned enough to pull the shaft out.

2.15a At the inner end clean the dirt off before undoing the boot, and put a can to catch the oil. Refill the transmission oil afterwards.

2.15b Sometimes the inner, 'Tripode', joint comes apart and spill out its needle rollers, if taken out without care.

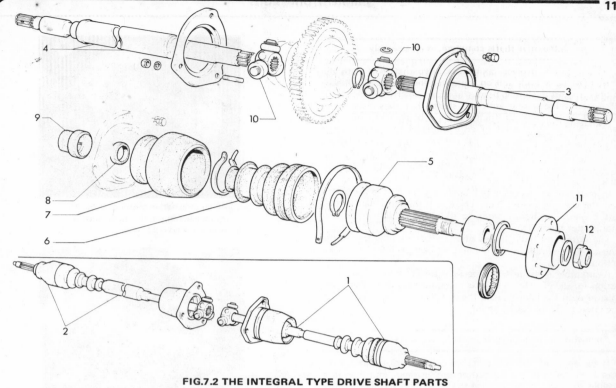

FIG.7.2 THE INTEGRAL TYPE DRIVE SHAFT PARTS

1 & 2	The left and right shaft assemblies	**5**	Constant velocity joint	**8**	Oil seal
3 & 4	The left and right shafts	**6**	CVJ boot	**9**	Seal bush
		7	Boot	**10**	Tripode joints

11 Hub
12 Nut with staking collar

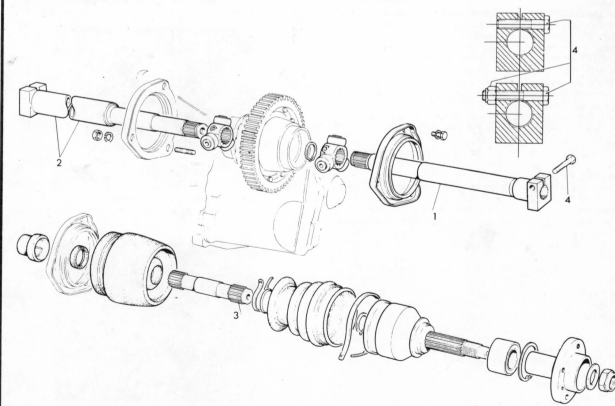

FIG.7.3 EARLY SLEEVED SHAFTS

1 & 2 Shaft main part with sleeve, for left and right   **3** Stub shaft   **4** Original and subsequent pinch bolts

18 If an assistant is available, the nuts can be tightened on the ends of the shafts by applying the foot brake. Otherwise they too must be done when the car is back on the ground. New nuts should be used, and tightened to a torque of 101 lbf ft (14 kg m). Then stake the nut by hammering its collar into the groove in the shaft with a punch (or blunt screw driver).

3 Removing the early jointed shafts in two parts

1 Early shafts had a sleeve joint to ease removal (See Fig.7.3)
2 All the preliminary arrangements are the same as described in the previous section. But do not dismantle the brakes, steering ball joint or suspension strut.
3 Instead remove the pinch bolt clamping the joint in the shaft. Turn the steering to full lock. Then push the inner half of the shaft towards the transmission, to slide off the splines on the outer part of the shaft.
4 The outer and inner halves of the shaft are now free to be removed, if required. In this context see paragraph 8 of the next Section.
5 Reassembly is the reverse process. Again refer to the previous Section for details. However, it is recommended these shafts are replaced with the later type, as the joint works loose. Tighten its pinch bolt to 33 lbf ft (4.5 kg m).

4 Removing the later integral shafts in two parts

1 If the constant velocity joints are going to be replaced, then there is no harm in risking getting dirt in them, and then it is possible to take off the integral shafts without dismantling the suspension. However a circlip has to be removed which is difficult to see, as it is smothered in black grease, and it is very difficult to get at. This method is useful if the splines are seized in the hub.
2 All the preliminary arrangements are as in Section 2. But do not dismantle the brakes, steering ball joint, or suspension.
3 Turn the steering fully inwards. Clean all round the boot at the outer end of the shaft. Take off the clip holding the boot to the joint. Peel the boot back down the shaft. Scrape all the grease off the constant velocity joint.
4 Locate the cut out of the inner part of the constant velocity joint, and the ends of the circlip. The hub may need rotating to bring it round. (photo).
5 Part the circlip. This is almost impossible without circlip pliers, particularly working under the car, and is why this method is not recommended.
6 Holding the circlip parted, pull the shaft towards the transmission to get the groove away from the circlip. Once it has moved, ease the circlip.
7 Check the steering is still on full lock, then pull the shaft on towards the transmission, and out of the inner race of the constant velocity joint. There has been the case where the shaft would not come out, as there was not room, and the two bolts at the bottom of the suspension strut still had to be removed, to allow the hub to move out a bit. But apparently this is not normal.
8 Once the main part of the shaft has been withdrawn from the constant velocity joint at the outer end, then the two parts can be taken off as may be necessary. The way these are released was described in Section 2. If removing the engine or transmission there is no need to disturb the constant velocity joint in the hub, just the inner part should be taken out. If it is the constant velocity joint that needs replacement, then there is no need to take off the rubber boot at the inner end, with consequent draining of transmission oil. Indeed, even if taking out the engine or transmission, once the shafts have been split, they can be tied inwards towards the transmission, with string and no further stripping done, if preferred.
9 Reassembly is the reverse porcess. Take special care with the new joints that no dirt gets in. Refill the joints and seal the rubber boot as described in Section 6.
10 Refer to Section 2 for other aspects of reassembly.

4.3 As an alternative method, after very thorough cleaning, the rubber boot is undone and peeled back,

4.4 and the gap in the circlip found, which is not as easy to see as here when it is still on the car.

4.6 The circlip can be parted and the shaft pulled out of the constant velocity joint.

4.8 Then the joint can be pulled out without having to disconnect the front suspension.

5 Examining and renewing parts

1 The need to replace the constant velocity joints can usually be assessed without removing them. If the rubber boot has failed, the joint is almost certain to do so too soon after, unless the hole was spotted, and a new boot fitted, in very good time. By failure, it is not meant that the joint breaks. But they will become noisy, particularly at full lock. The clicking noise, later becoming a tearing noise, is a sign of excessive wear inside the joint.

2 The shaft splines and the inner 'Tripode' joint should outlast perhaps two constant velocity joints. Their condition should be examined when taken out for other reasons.

3 The shafts are not serviced as complete assemblies, so indivdual parts must be ordered as required. The constant velocity joints do come complete, though without the rubber boot. It is not practible, nor are the parts available, to renovate the constant velocity joints.

4 The shafts and joints will last well provided the remarks in the next Section on the care of them is heeded.

6 Lubrication and rubber boots

1 No specific maintenance tasks have to be done on the drive shafts or their joints. But the visual examination of the condition of the rubber boots is an important item of the check underneath the car in the 3,000 miles (5,000 km) task.

2 The rubber boot on the constant velocity joint at the outer end of the shaft must be examined to ensure there are no tears or slits in it, and that it is properly secured to the joint and the shaft, by clips at its fat and thin ends.

3 The constant velocity joint is lubricated with a molybdenum disulphide grease, such as Castrol MS 3 Grease. Normally this will not need renewing. If the rubber boot is removed, either for replacement, or when splitting the drive shaft at the constant velocity joint, then the old grease should be wiped out with clean rag to take out any dirt. Ensure complete cleanliness when doing this, or more dirt will get in, and the joint will not last long. Then pack in new grease, pushing it well in around the joint balls, and leaving a coating on the outside on the splines. Then put on the rubber boot, with a trace of grease inside it and on the shaft. Do not fill the boot with grease. Too much grease will prevent the boot from working as a concertina as the steering turns.

4 Secure the boot to the rim of the joint, making sure the moulded groove of the boot is in the groove of the joint. See Fig. 6.1. The small end of the boot should butt against the shoulder on the shaft. For preference use the metal tape straps. If these are not available, put round two turns of soft copper wire, and twist the ends together with pliers to draw the wire firmly round the boot, but not so tight it cuts into the rubber, or is under such tension it will break after a short time. Bend the twisted ends backwards, the way they will tend to go due to shaft rotation, so they lie out of the way.

5 The 'Tripode' joint at the inner end of the shaft is lubricated by the transmission oil, so no attention need be paid to that. The rubber boot at the inner end must seal in the transmission oil. Two aspects of the boot are therefore important. The baggy portion must be free from cuts. The oil seal in which the shaft rotates must be in good condition.

6 New rubber boots should be fitted to the inner ends of the shafts whenever the transmission is dismantled. Fitting them is also advisable whenever the drive shafts are removed, and there is the slightest suspicion that the boots are near the end of their life, otherwise the great labour of removing the shafts may soon have to be repeated.

FIG.7.4 REMOVING THE INTEGRAL SHAFTS FROM THE CONSTANT VELOCITY JOINTS WITHOUT DISMANTLING THE SUSPENSION.

1 CV joint   3 Drive shaft
2 Circlip   4 Boot pulled back

Chapter 8 Brakes

Contents

Specifications

Front brakes

discs:

— diameter	8.937 in	(227 mm)
— nominal thickness	.392 to .400 in	(9,95 to 10.15 mm)
— minimum allowable thickness after refacing	.368 in	(9.35 mm)
— minimum allowable thickness from wear	.354 in	(9 mm)
— maximum allowable run-out	.006 in	(0.15 mm)

Brake calipers	Floating, single cylinder type	
Minimum allowable thickness of brake linings	.06 in	(1.5 mm)
Caliper cylinder bore	1.890 in	(48 mm)
Brake lining clearance	Automatic adjustment	

Rear brakes

Drum diameter	7.2930 to 7.304 in	(185.24 to 185.53 mm)
Refacing drums: maximum depth of machining	.03 in	(0.8 mm)
Maximum allowable diameter from wear	7.355 in	(186.83 mm)

Brake linings:

— length (developed)	7.086 in	(180 mm)
— width	1.181 in	(30 mm)
— thickness (New	.165 to .177 in	(4.2 to 4.5 mm)
(Minimum allowable	.06 in	(1.5 mm)

Wheel cylinder bore	3/4 in	(19.05 mm)
Master cylinder bore	3/4 in	(19.05 mm)
Manual parking brake	Acting mechanically on rear brake shoes	
Brake pressure regulator	Acting on rear wheels - For settings see text.	

Brake fluid	FIAT ASSURVA (Blue) or Castrol Girling Universal Brake and Clutch Fluid to specification FMVSS 116 DOT 3; SAE J1703
Capacity	½ Imp. pint (0.315 litre) 2/3 U.S. pint

1 General description

1   The brakes use discs at the front and drums at the rear. The hydraulic system is dual, a tandem master cylinder working separated circuits for the front and rear brakes. A pressure regulator valve at the rear is connected to the rear suspension, and limits the braking effort at the rear when the back of the car is high, either due to light load, or heavy braking. This ensures maximum retardation and control by preventing the rear wheels locking under hard braking.

2   A brake servo is now standard on all cars. Originally it was only fitted to the Rally and Coupe. On right hand drive cars the unassisted master cylinder was on the right. Now with the servo the master cylinder is on the left, as for left hand drive cars, and the pedal has a cross rod inside the body. This improves accessibility for right hand drive cars both to the master cylinder, and other components such as the generator.

3   The brakes do not call for much actual work, but there are a number of important checks. If these checks are made any deterioration of the brakes can be noted before danger is caused. Maybe it is because the brakes are so reliable, but it is a sobering fact that many apparently enthusuastic owners allow the brakes to get in an unsafe condition.

4   Checking the hydraulic fluid is a 300 mile, or weekly, task. The level gradually falls as the brakes wear, and comes sharply up as new pads are fitted. But this is a small variation compared with the size of the reservoir. Normally the level will always be correct: But it must be checked all the same. One day it may be low, indicating a leak.

5   At 3,000 miles (5,000 km) during the check underneath the car, all pipes, particularly the flexible ones, are checked for leaks and damage, and the front pads inspected. At 6,000 miles (10,000 km) the rear drums are removed for a check inside. At such checks the signs to look for are freedom from seepage of hydraulic fluid, enough lining material left to last until the next inspection, and a good rubbing surface on drum or disc. This last is needed for good braking: it is also indicative that the brakes are working properly.

6   Poor braking can grow gradually: the driver must be alert for a fall in performance. Normal braking is quite gentle. At intervals the opportunity must be made to find an empty road, and do a hard brake test.

7   The brake fluid has to stand high temperature, be non-corrosive to the brake metal parts, and not soften those of rubber. It is vital that only fluid to the correct specification is used. Avoid using different makes. Changing the fluid is a 36,000 mile (60,000 km) task. The fluid absorbs damp, so in time its quality deteriorates. Never reuse old fluid. When working on the hydraulics, let all fluid that wants to drip out do so, rather than plugging the system, as this is of additional benefit in keeping the system clean. If it is ever suspected that the wrong type of fluid has been put in, then the whole system must be flushed out, and new rubber parts fitted throughout; master cylinder, all wheel cylinders, the flexible pipes, pressure regulator, and pressure failure warning switch. It is recommended anyway that this is done at 60,000 miles (100,000 km). Never wash brake parts in anything other than brake fluid.

8   If there is an hydraulic failure of one component, then at least the others must be suspect too.

2 Front brake inspection and checks

1   Whilst doing the 3,000 mile (5 000 km) routine maintenance task, the front brakes must be checked.

2   Once familiar with the car this can be done fairly well through the holes in the wheel, but to get a good view these should be removed.

3   Check the thickness of pad lining remaining. If this is 1/16 in or less, the pads must be replaced. See the next Section.

4   It is suggested that a set of pads be bought, so that the change can be made as soon as its need is noticed, which will save bother.

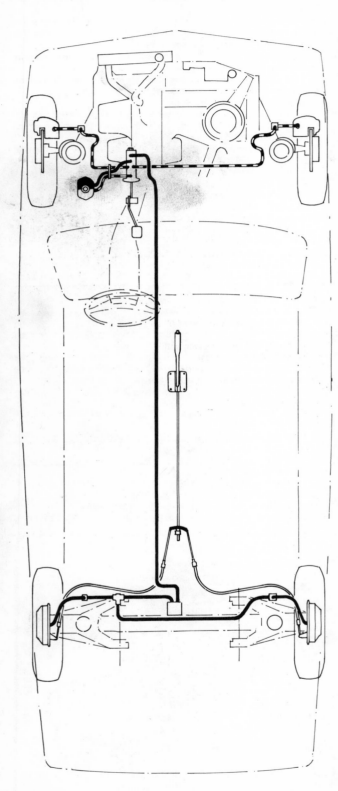

FIG.8.1 THE LAYOUT OF THE BRAKING SYSTEM

The front and rear circuits are independant

5 Check the hydraulic pipes have no seepage of fluid, nor that there are any signs of damage, particularly of rubbing, or weathering of the flexible pipe. Check there are no signs of fluid seeping out of the brake caliper, past the piston.

6 Check the surface of the disc. This should be shiny and smooth. Though other signs of brake inefficiency would have been apparent, if the discs have not been polished up by the pads, then the brakes cannot have been working properly.

3 Changing the front brake pads

1 Jack up and remove the front wheel.

2 Pull out the spring clips that hold the two caliper locking blocks. (See Fig.8.2).

3 Pull out the locking blocks. (photos).

4 Lift off the caliper, and lodge it on the suspension so its weight will not hang on the flexible pipe.

5 Take out the old pads, noting the anti-chatter springs.

6 Wipe the caliper clean, especially the flanks of the piston that are sticking out due to the thinness of the old pads. If very dirty, wash the caliper with ordinary detergent and water, and dry it. Do not use petrol or other solvents, though brake fluid is very satisfactory, if messy.

7 Push the hydraulic piston back into the caliper. Watch the level in the hydraulic reservoir beside the master cylinder. The level will rise: check it does not overflow.

8 If there is risk of the reservoir overflowing, hold the caliper with the bleed nipple uppermost. Slacken the bleed nipple, and push the piston home, expelling the excess fluid out of the nipple. Retighten the nipple whilst it is still awash with escaping fluid, so no air can get in.

9 If the piston is stubborn, push it in by using a carpenter's clamp. Take care the rim of the piston is not burred.

10 Reassemble using the new pads, and checking all the anti-chatter springs are in position.

11 Press the brake pedal to bring the piston and pads up the disc.

12 Check the hydraulic fluid level.

13 Repeat for the other side.

14 Note that the pad lining type used is denoted by colour code daubs of paint. Both pads on both sides must all have the same lining. More than one type is supplied by FIAT Ensure that the lining used is approved by FIAT.

15 Use the brakes gently for at least a dozen applications so the pads can bed in.

4 Removing the front caliper

1 The front caliper will often need to be taken off to clear the suspension or steering for other work.

2 Remove the spring clips and locking blocks as described in the previous Section.

3 Lift off the caliper. Lodge it or tie it up where it cannot strain the hose if there is no need to take it right off, as when working on the front suspension.

4 If the caliper needs to be taken right off, then the flexible hose must be disconnected. As this work is presumably to overhaul the front caliper, refer to the next Section.

5 With the caliper off, remove the pads, and all the anti-chatter springs.

6 Undo the two bolts that hold the caliper support bracket to the steering knuckle. (photo).

7 Once familiar with the car, if removing the caliper and support bracket for work on the suspension, it may be preferred to take off the caliper, pads, and support bracket as an assembly by simply taking out the two bolts at the back.

8 On reassembly, reverse the dismantling procedures. But ensure the mounting surface for the support bracket on the steering knuckle is clean, and if the bolts are rusty, grease them. Note that as the brake pads are normally in light contact with the disc, the caliper must be carefully fitted to slide back in.

5 Overhauling the front brake caliper

1 Jack up and remove the front wheel.

2 Wash thoroughly with water and household detergent the caliper assembly, and the flexible pipe, particularly the fixing bracket and union at the car end of the flexible pipe.

3 Have ready a tin to catch the brake fluid, and sheets of clean newspaper on which to put parts.

4 Take out the spring clips and locking blocks, and take the caliper off the support bracket.

5 Get an assistant to press gently and slowly on the brake pedal, so as to push the piston out of the caliper cylinder.

6 Catch the piston and its dirt shield, and put them on a clean surface (the newspaper).

7 Lodge the caliper back on the support bracket where it cannot get dirty, or strain the flexible pipe.

8 Disconnect the flexible pipe. This is best done at the car, or inboard, end. Undo the union between the two parts of the pipe,

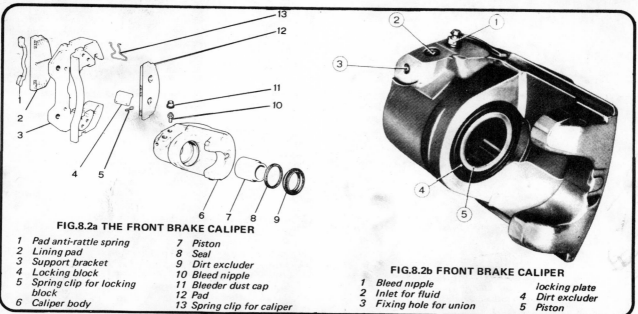

FIG.8.2a THE FRONT BRAKE CALIPER

1 Pad anti-rattle spring	7 Piston
2 Lining pad	8 Seal
3 Support bracket	9 Dirt excluder
4 Locking block	10 Bleed nipple
5 Spring clip for locking block	11 Bleeder dust cap
6 Caliper body	12 Pad
	13 Spring clip for caliper

FIG.8.2b FRONT BRAKE CALIPER

1 Bleed nipple	locking plate
2 Inlet for fluid	4 Dirt excluder
3 Fixing hole for union	5 Piston

and then the flexible one from the bracket. In this way the pipe is firm whilst being undone, and also the flexible pipe can be taken away for inspection with the caliper.

9   Clean all the parts very thoroughly. Do not use solvents other than alcohol (methylated spirits) or brake fluid.

10 Check that the caliper cylinder and the piston are free from scores. If not, they must be replaced.

11 Discard the piston sealing cap, and dirt excluding shield or ring.

12 Examine the flexible pipe (See Section 17). If there is any doubt, fit a new one.

13 As parts are reassembled, lubricate them with brake fluid. Fit the cup to the piston, then the piston into the cylinder, and push it down as far as it will go. Then fit the dirt shield, getting it well seated into its groove.

14 Reassemble the pads and caliper to the support bracket, taking care no dirt is scattered into the pipe unions.

15 Fit the flexible pipe. Make sure it is tightened with the wheel straight without any twists or unfair bends. Check the steering can move from lock to lock without risk of damage to the hose.

16 Fill the master cylinder reservoir, and pump up the fluid. Check for leaks. Bleed the system. (See Section 20).

17 Note that if any of the other wheels need doing, the new fluid should not be put in until all have been done, so the old fluid does not have a chance to mix with it. If wishing to do both calipers at the same time the piston of the second one can be blown out by temporarily closing the pipe to the first with a wooden bung held in by yet another assistant.

6   Removing and replacing a front brake disc

1   If a disc is badly scored, pad wear will be rapid, so the disc should be replaced or resurfaced.

2   If the disc surface is cracked or chipped, then it must be replaced at once, as the braking is liable to be dangerous.

3   Remove the complete brake caliper and support bracket as described in Section 4.

4   Remove the two bolts holding the disc to the hub, one being a long wheel locating bolt. (photo).

5   Take off the flange, followed by the disc.

6   If the disc is not too badly scored, it is possible to machine it smooth, within the limits given in the specification. But the cost may be as much as a new disc.

7   Fit the new disc on the hub, washing off any preservative first.

8   Spin the hub, and measure the run out of the rim of the disc. If it is not true within the specification, take it off and refit it again. In another position the errors of hub and disc should be made to cancel.

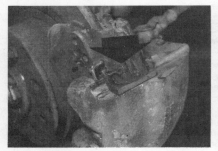
3.2 Pull out the spring clips

3.3 Slide out the locking blocks.

3.4 Then the caliper is free.

3.5a When lifting out the pads,

3.5b Note how the two pad and the two caliper springs that stop rattles and squeaks go,

4.6 The support bracket can be removed from the steering knuckle

4.7 By removing just two bolts. The pads and caliper can be left on it still if convenient.

6.5 With the caliper and support bracket off, just two bolts need to be taken off to remove the disc.

7   Rear brake inspection and checks

1   Item 3.11 of the 6,000 mile (10,000 km) maintenance task is to check inside the rear brake drums. Though later cars do have inspection holes allowing the lining thickness to be seen without removing the drum, this is not thorough enough.

2   Chock the car's other wheels, put it in gear, and release the hand brake.

3   Jack up and remove the rear wheel.

4   Take out the two bolts holding the drum to the hub. One is the long wheel locating bolt.

5   Pull off the brake drum.

6   Check the thickness of lining remaining on the shoes. It will not be the same all round the shoe. The leading shoe also wears faster than the trailing one. If the thickness is less than 1/16 in anywhere, the shoes must be replaced. (See the next Section).

7   If the trailing shoe is still all right, it need not be changed. But what is done to one side of the car must be done to the other, to keep even braking.

8   Blow all dust out from around the hydraulic cylinder, and behind the shoes. Check no hydraulic fluid is seeping from the cylinder. If it is, overhaul the cylinder as described in Section 9. If fluid or hub grease had got onto the brake linings, these must be removed. See the next Section.

9   Wipe all dust out of the brake drum. Check its surface for scoring or cracks. If badly scored lining wear will be rapid. If cracked it should be replaced. If within the limits in the specification, scoring can be removed by machining.

8   Changing the rear brake shoes

1   The rear brake shoes must be replaced when the lining is worn to the limit given in the specification (approxiamtely 1/16 in). They must also be replaced if the lining is badly contaminated with brake fluid or grease. A minor wetting can be washed off with petrol, but if the contamination is deep, it cannot be got out, and will affect the braking characteristics of the lining. The linings are bonded to the shoe. This is a special process out of the scope of an owner. Replacement shoes should be bought from a FIAT agent. Do not get non genuine spares, that might have the lining of the wrong grade. It is recommended that the shoes are bought in advance, so that when the need for them arises during a routine inspection thay can be fitted then, without need to dismantle the car again later.

2   The drum will already have been removed as described in the previous Section.

3   It is possible to remove the shoes with the wheel's hub in place. The flange has semi-circular sectors cut out to give room for the shoes to come off. However, there is a knack in removing the shoes, and it is much easier if the hub is first taken off. So nudo the nut on the end of the stub axle. Pull off the hub. (See Chapter 11/12 for details).

4   Undo the steady springs, by giving their caps a half turn to disengage the slot from the pin (photos).

5   Pull a shoe (if a right handed person, the right shoe)out from its seat on the wheel cylinder, and pivot at the bottom, and work it up the post of the self adjuster.

6   Once off the self adjuster post, the pull-off spring tension is eased, as the shoe can move towards the other, so the springs can be unhooked. Before taking the springs off, note the way they are fitted.

7   Take off the other shoe.

8   The self adjusters must now be transferred to the new shoes. To undo them the spring must be compressed to allow the circlip to be undone. The spring is strong. If possible, get the FIAT agent to make the transfer when buying the new shoes from them. Otherwise a clamp must be organised. A vice, a carpenter's 'G' clamp, or a valve spring compressor are all possibilities.Small

7.5 The rear drums must be taken off regularly to check all is well inside. There are only two bolts to undo.

8.3a The shoes can be taken off with the hub in place.

8.3b But it is easier with it off. Note the way the pull of springs and hand brake linkage fit.

8.4 A quarter turn releases the steady spring.

8.5 The shoe must be worked up the self-adjuster post till it can be turned.

8.8 The self-adjusters must be transferred to the new shoes.

bits of steel must be put between the clamp and the adjuster washer so the circlip is not trapped.

9   After long mileages the self adjusters need replacement. The washers wear, also the hole in the bush gets bigger, so the adjustment provided is not close enough.

10 If the hydraulic cylinder needs overhaul, now is the time with the shoes out of the way.

11 When reassembling the new shoes with the adjusters, and the shoes to the brakes, put a slight smear of grease on all the working surfaces for the adjusters, the bottom shoe pivot, and the steady springs; but not where the shoe sits on the hydraulic cylinder piston.

12 Fit the first shoe (the left one if right handed) into place with the springs fitted. Hook the second shoe onto the springs, and then pull it across until the self adjuster can be fitted over its post. Then wriggle the shoe down into position, and work the ends of the shoe into place. Make sure the hand brake linkage is in place.

13 Fit the pins for the steady springs from behind the back plate, and hold them from there whilst fitting the spring and cap from the front.

14 Some people prefer to take off and fit the pull-off springs by pliers with the brake shoes in place. This demands strong hands. If the pliers slip, the hands can get cut. But if the pliers do not slip, the method is better, and if it can be done this way, then the shoe will slip on and off the self adjuster post much more easily, and all this can be done without removing the hub.

15 When refitting the hub, tighten the nut on the stub axle to 101 lbf ft (14 kg m) and then stake the nut to the axle by hammering its collar into the groove.

9   Overhauling the rear brake wheel cylinder

1   If there is seepage of fluid out of the ends of the wheel cylinder, or if the wrong fluid has been put in the system, or if other rubber components cast suspicion on the state of these ones, the cylinder should be overhauled.

2   Remove the brake shoes as described in the previous Section.

3   Clean all round the wheel cylinder, both on the shoe side, and the outside, of the brake back plate. If there is much dirt, wash with water and household detergent. Do not use petrol or other solvents.

4   Spread a sheet of newspaper beside the car, with the new rubber cups ready. Then the work can go on steadily, even though there may be some seepage of fluid out of the end of the pipe. New cups will definitely be needed. It is pointless reassembling the cylinder with the old cups.

5   Take the rubber boots off both ends of the cylinder.

6   Push the piston in at one end, and expell out of the other the whole train of pistons, rubber cups, spring, and its two backing washers.

7   Discard the rubber parts.

8   Wash the metal parts and cylinder with brake fluid, and wipe them.

9   Examine the pistons and the cylinder bores. They should be free from scores or pitting. If the surface is not perfect then the cylinder must be scrapped.

10 Assuming the cylinder is serviceable, lubricate the cups and pistons with brake fluid, and reassemble, ensuring absolute cleanliness. The sharp edges of the cups must go inwards.

11 Refit the shoes and drum, refill the hydraulic reservoir, and bleed the brakes. (See Section 20.)

12 If the wheel cylinder or piston surfaces are not good, the assembly must be changed. Imperfections will wear the sharp edge of the rubber cup, and allow air into the system, and in due course allow leaks as well.

13 To change the wheel cylinder, disconnect the hydraulic pipe at the rear. Take out the two bolts holding the cylinder to the back plate. Before fitting the new cylinder, clean the seating surfaces on the back plate. Ensure no dirt gets in the pipe union. Reconnect the pipe, fit the brake shoes and drum. Fill the hydraulic reservoir, and bleed the system.

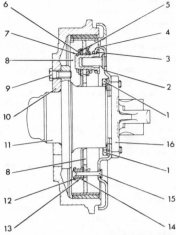

FIG.8.3 REAR BRAKE SECTION

1 Back plate bolts	9 Drum securing bolt
2 Back plate	10 Drum
3 Self adjuster bush	11 Hub
4 Spring	12 Steady spring cap
5 Friction washers	13 Steady spring
6 Washer	14 Inner cup of steady spring
7 Circlip	15 Pin
8 Shoe with lining	16 Axle flange

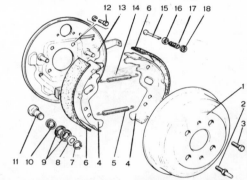

FIG.8.4 EXPLODED VIEW OF THE REAR BRAKE

1 Drum	10 Self adjuster spring
2 Long headed bolt	11 Bush
3 Drum bolt	12 Back plate fixing bolts
4 Brake shoes	13 Back plate
5 Lower pull-off spring	14 Top pull-off spring
6 Inner cup	15 Steady pin
7 Circlip	16 Inner cup
8 Washer	17 Steady spring
9 Self adjuster friction washers	18 Cap

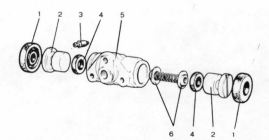

FIG.8.5 REAR WHEEL CYLINDER

1 Dust boots	4 Cups
2 Pistons	5 Cylinder
3 Bleed nipple	6 Washers and spring

10 Handbrake adjustment

1   The handbrake does not normally need adjustment. Normal wear of the rear brake shoes will be taken care of by their self adjusters. However in due course the cable stretches, and there is wear in the handbrake linkage.

2   First ensure the rear brake self adjusters have had a chance to do their work. Drive the car both forwards and in reverse and apply the brakes hard, when going at about 10 mph. This will bring both shoes in turn, when each is acting as the leading shoe, into close contact with the drum.

3   Now apply the handbrake and count the number of clicks of its rachet that it moves. If this is in excess of four, adjust the brake.

4   Jack up both back wheels.

5   Apply the handbrake one click.

6   Under the car locate the adjustment point on the cable immediately behind the lever. (photo). Undo one nut, and tighten the other to shorten the linkage. Do this till brake drag makes it slightly difficult to rotate the back wheels.

7   Check that when the lever is applied three clicks it is impossible to turn the wheels, but that they are still quite free when the lever is released. Check that the linkage system in distributing the effort equally to both wheels.

8   Whilst working on it, oil the pivots of the linings.

9   Lock the adjustment nut again.

10   Road test the car, applying the handbrake hard at about 15 mph. It should be possible to lock both back wheels. If the adjustment is correct, but the brakes do not stop the wheels, then the inside of the drums should be examined as given in Section 7. Drive the car about a mile; stop when going uphill be using the gears. Feel the temperature of the rear brake drums. They should be cold. If hot the handbrake is too tight.

10.6 The adjustment point on the later type of handbrake cable.

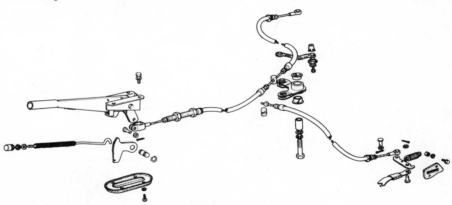

Fig.8.6 Early handbrake mechanism on cars up to spares number 425878

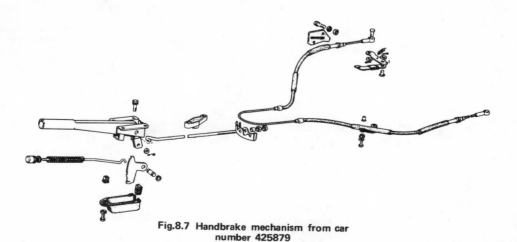

Fig.8.7 Handbrake mechanism from car number 425879

11 Rear brake effort regulator

1 It is important that the brakes do not lock the rear wheels when the brakes are used hard. Sliding tyres do not give such good grip, so the braking distance will be longer. Worse still, if it is the back wheels that lock, the car is unstable, and control may be lost. The braking that can be applied to the rear wheels without them locking depends upon the weight upon them. So a regulator is fitted coupled to the rear suspension, and this limits the hydraulic pressure passed to the rear brakes when the rear of the car is high, either due to being unladen, or if pitching forward under heavy braking.

2 On early cars, up to those with Number for parts 459, 999, the regulator was worked by a rod connected to the centre of the rear spring.

3 For cars with parts Number 460, 000 onwards, the regulator is worked by a rod fixed to the left suspension arm.

4 If the regulator leaks, or fails to work it should be replaced by a new one, though parts may be available locally to overhaul the existing one.

5 Under normal driving, failure of the regulator will be difficult to detect. First test the rear brakes by applying the handbrake at about 15 mph, and check it can lock the rear wheels. This proves the brake shoes are in order.

6 Now test the brakes from about 20 mph on a dry smooth level road. It should be possible to lock the front wheels. Wheel locking is shown by the noise, smoke, and by leaving black tyre marks. If under these conditions the rear brakes lock, particularly if they lock before the front, under less hard pedal pressure, it is indicated that the pressure is not being limited.

7 Now stop from about 50 mph hard, but not as hard as possible. Get out of the car and feel the temperature of the rear brake drums. They should be very hot. If not the regulator is keeping all pressure off them.

8 To change the regulator, first wash with water all dirt from the area, particularly the pipe unions. On cars for some markets, there will also be a shield to come off.

9 Disconnect the link rod from the suspension. (photo).

10 Take off the hydraulic reservoir lid, and put over its mouth a sheet of polythene, then replace the lid. This will restrict the amount of fluid that leaks out.

11 Disconnect the pipes from the regulator, putting a tin of catch fluid drips.

12 Undo the fixing bolts.

13 Fit the new regulator in position. Leave off the unions, and only put the bolts finger tight.

14 Set the link rod in the appropriate position depending on whether it is old or new type. See paragraphs 19 and 20. Get an assistant to hold this.

15 Pull back the rubber cover of the regulator, and turn it about one of its mounting bolts, with the other moving in its slotted hole, till the regulator end of the rod is just touching the end of the regulator piston. Tighten the mounting bolts to a torque of 18 lbf ft (2.5 kg m).

16 Connect the pipes to the unions.

17 Connect the link rod.

18 Refill the hydraulic reservoir, and bleed the system. (See Section 20).

19 The adjustment position for rods of the old type is set as follows. The car should be unladen, but with a full fuel tank. Disconnect the bottom of the link from the fitting on the spring. Lower the rod so the link's eye lower edge is 1¼ ins (31 mm) below the upper edge of the pin on the spring fitting. With the rods far end in this position, its near end should just be contacting the piston in the regulator. (See Fig. 8.8).

20 On the new type, disconnect the outer end of the rod from the left, rear, side of the suspension arm. Pull the end of the rod down until it is $2.126 \pm .197$ in (54 ± 5 mm) below the edge of the bump stop housing on the underneath of the suspension arm. Now adjust the position of the regulator till the inner end of the rod is just touching the piston. (See Fig.8.9).

11.5 The brake regulator should only need adjustment if it has to be removed.

11.9 The outer end of the regulator rod (later type).

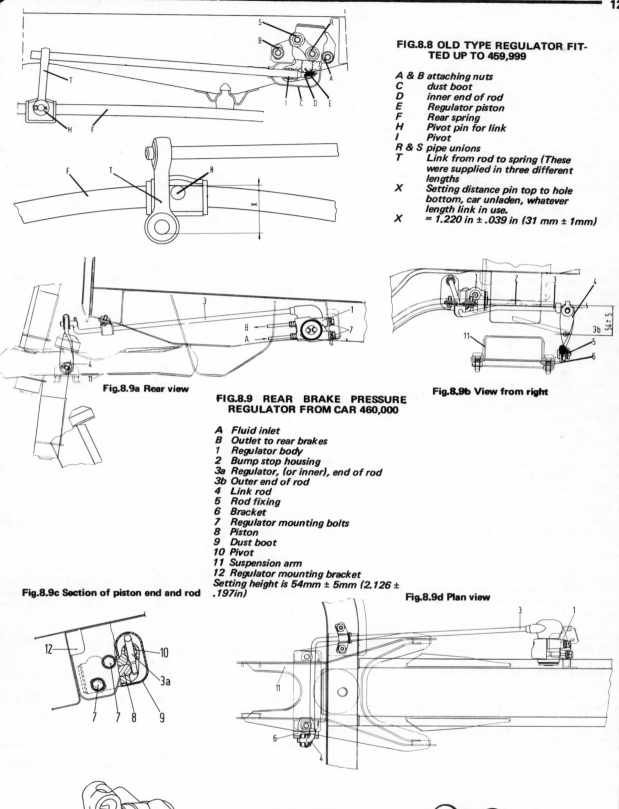

FIG.8.8 OLD TYPE REGULATOR FITTED UP TO 459,999

A & B   attaching nuts
C   dust boot
D   inner end of rod
E   Regulator piston
F   Rear spring
H   Pivot pin for link
I   Pivot
R & S   pipe unions
T   Link from rod to spring (These were supplied in three different lengths
X   Setting distance pin top to hole bottom, car unladen, whatever length link in use.
X   = 1.220 in ± .039 in (31 mm ± 1mm)

Fig.8.9a Rear view

Fig.8.9b View from right

FIG.8.9 REAR BRAKE PRESSURE REGULATOR FROM CAR 460,000

A   Fluid inlet
B   Outlet to rear brakes
1   Regulator body
2   Bump stop housing
3a Regulator, (or inner), end of rod
3b Outer end of rod
4   Link rod
5   Rod fixing
6   Bracket
7   Regulator mounting bolts
8   Piston
9   Dust boot
10 Pivot
11 Suspension arm
12 Regulator mounting bracket
Setting height is 54mm ± 5mm (2.126 ± .197in)

Fig.8.9c Section of piston end and rod

Fig.8.9d Plan view

Fig.8.10 Exploded view of the pressure regulator

12 Master cylinder removal

1   A likely minor defect calling for overhaul of the master cylinder is that air gets into the brakes, calling for frequent bleeding. This could be drawn past the pistons' cups, without there being a leak of fluid. If in slightly worse condition then fluid may leak out, showing at the master cylinder's mounting flange, or on cars without servos, leaking down inside the car. In extreme cases, the piston cups may swell, so the piston is unable to return to the off position, and causes brake binding. The latter situation implies that the wrong fluid has been used, so the overhaul of the master cylinder should be done in conjunction with the complete draining of the fluid and the renewal of all the cups in the wheel cylinders, regulator, pressure warning switch, and all the flexible pipes. The renewal of all such rubber components is recommended anyway as a standard procedure for brakes after 60,000 miles (100,000 km).

2   Remove the spare wheel. On right hand drive cars, without brake servos, that is those cars with the master cylinder on the right, remove the air cleaner.

3   Disconnect the two pipes from the reservoir to the master cylinder. Use a small jar to catch the fluid after the pipes are taken off the fittings on the master cylinder.

4   Have plenty of rag below the pipes to catch any drips of fluid, as it will ruin the paint.

5   Undo the two unions for the delivery pipes to front and rear brakes. (photo).

6   Undo the two nuts, with spring washers holding the master cylinder in place.

7   Pull the master cylinder forward to disengage the studs and the actuating plunger, and take it off, in the case of early cars, the dash, and on later ones, the brake servo.

8   Refitting the master cylinder is the reverse process.

9   After refitting, bleed the brakes. (Section 20).

10 Then get an assistant to hold the pedal on whilst checking for leaks. Check visually, and also check that the pedal does not gradually go down under sustained pressure. Such movement could be allowed either by an external leak, or an internal one past the pistons.

13 Overhauling the master cylinder

1   Clean the outside of the master cylinder, but only use brake fluid or alcohol (methylated spirits). If other solvents such as petrol are used, traces will remain afterwards, and could degrade the rubber cups.

2   Refer to Fig.8.11.

3   Remove the rubber boot from the cylinder end.

4   Remove the two piston stop screws (16 and 21) from the underneath of the cylinder.

5   Take out of the open end of the cylinder such pistons, cups etc as are willing to come out easily at this instance, laying them out in the order in which they were fitted, so nothing can get muddled up.

6   Take out the plug (24) from the other end of the cylinder.

7   With a pencil push the remaining components out.

8   Discard all the rubber parts.

9   Examine the cylinder bore and the pistons for scratches or pitting. They must have a smooth surface, otherwise there will be seepage of fluid past the cups, and the latters' lips will wear rapidly. If the surface is not good, then a new cylinder is needed. In some cases it may be possible to polish out the scratches, but the clearance between bore and pistons should not exceed 0.006 in (0.15 mm).

10 On reassembly wet all parts liberally with brake fluid.

11 Fit all the cups into place using the fingers only to push them gently into place. Cups with lips must have the lips towards the high pressure side, away from the actuating rod. Push the secondary piston down with a pencil, then fit its stop screw. Check it moves freely. Then fit all the primary piston parts.

12 If the car has a servo, before refitting the master cylinder check that the servo rod sticks out beyond the mating face 0.049

to .073 in (1.26 to 1.85 mm).

13 On cars without servos, check after fitting that there is a little free play between the pedal's push rod and the rear end of the piston. Otherwise the pushrod cannot return to the end of its stroke, to recoup fluid through the ports.

14 Checking the brake servo action

1   Poor braking can come on gradually so escape notice. If the pedal pressure seems high the servo action should be checked as follows.

2   Do a brake test from about 25 mph, on a smooth, level, and traffic free road. The car should pull on straight, and it should be possible to lock the wheels, leaving black tyre marks.

3   Switch off the engine. Apply the brakes about six times to deplete the vacuum reserve.

4   Press the pedal down, and hold the brakes on lightly. Start the engine; the pedal will tend to fall away from the foot: less pressure will be needed to hold the brakes applied. If this effect is not felt the servo is not giving assistance.

5   Start up. Run the engine at medium speed, to build up depression Switch off the engine and close the throttle. Wait for 90 seconds. Then try the brakes. There should be enough vacuum for two or three applications of the brakes. If the depression has been lost either the check valve is faulty, or there is a leak.

15 Removing the brake servo power unit

1   If the checks in Section 14 show the power unit to be faulty, it is quite easy to remove it, but its overhaul is delicate. It is recommended that if possible a reconditioned unit is fitted. If it has to be overhauled, then a set of new washers, seals and gaskets, and special lubricant will be essential. Such parts may not be available from the FIAT agent, as most probably they only stock complete servos. However specialist brake firms do hold such items.

2   The master cylinder is removed with the servo, then the two separated.

3   Have a container ready; then remove the pipes to the master cylinder from the reservoir. Do not let any fluid drip on the car, as it will ruin the paint. (See Section 12:3).

4   Undo the pipes from the master cylinder to the front and rear brakes.

5   Disconnect the suction pipe from the manifold at the servo.

6   Disconnect the push rod at the brake pedal by removing the split pin.

7   Undo the nuts that hold the servo unit to the bracket on the dash.

8   Lift off the assembly of master cylinder and servo, unhooking the push rod from the pedal. Take care the hydraulic fluid does not drip on the paint.

9   Clean the outside with alcohol or brake fluid.

10 Undo the nuts securing the master cylinder to the servo, and separate the two.

11 If fitting a new servo, refer to paragraphs 28 to 32 of the next Section.

16 Overhauling the brake servo power unit

1   Remove the check valve for the suction on the servo front shell.

2   Mount the servo in a vice, pedal push rod end up, using padded jaws on the mounting studs for the master cylinder.

3   Scribe a mark so that the front and rear parts of the shell of the vacuum cylinder will be reassembled in the same orientation.

4   Remove the boot.

5   Arrange a pair of long levers on the servo's studs that secured it to the dash. Rotate the rear shell clockwise to disengage its lips

12.3 Drain old brake fluid into a tin, and do not reuse it.

12.5 The master cylinder on the end of the servo is very easy to reach.

15.2 If the servo needs to come off, it and the master cylinder can come off together.

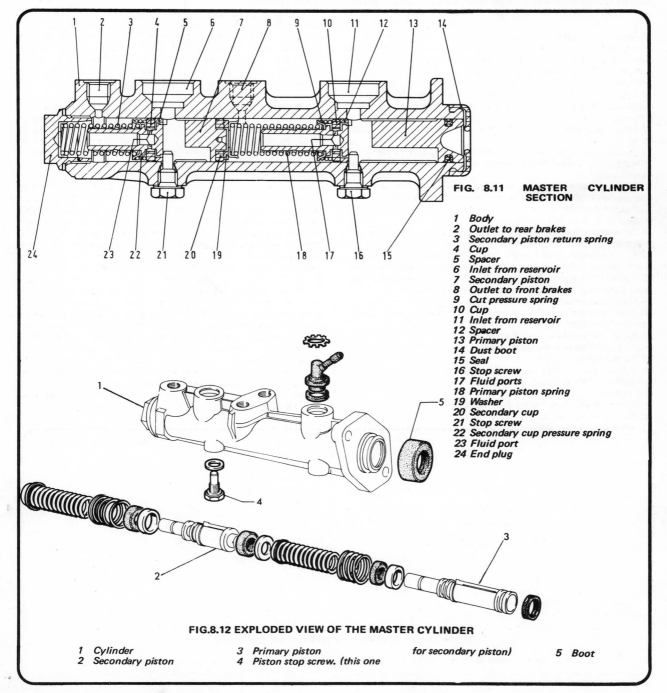

FIG. 8.11 MASTER CYLINDER SECTION

1 Body
2 Outlet to rear brakes
3 Secondary piston return spring
4 Cup
5 Spacer
6 Inlet from reservoir
7 Secondary piston
8 Outlet to front brakes
9 Cut pressure spring
10 Cup
11 Inlet from reservoir
12 Spacer
13 Primary piston
14 Dust boot
15 Seal
16 Stop screw
17 Fluid ports
18 Primary piston spring
19 Washer
20 Secondary cup
21 Stop screw
22 Secondary cup pressure spring
23 Fluid port
24 End plug

FIG.8.12 EXPLODED VIEW OF THE MASTER CYLINDER

1 Cylinder
2 Secondary piston
3 Primary piston
4 Piston stop screw. (this one for secondary piston)
5 Boot

from those on the front shell. Hold it down whilst turning, to hold the rear shell down against the power piston's return spring.

6   Lift the components out of the front shell.

7   Remove the rear shell from the valve body.

8   Remove the diaphragm from the plate/valve body.

9   Remove the air silencer with the air filter that is around the valve rod, from the valve body, being careful not to chip the plastics.

10 Press in the valve rod, and remove the valve retainer key. Remove the valve rod and plunger assembly.

11 Note that the valve rod and plunger are serviced as an assembly only.

12 Press the reaction disc out of the valve body.

13 Remove the push rod.

14 Remove the front seal from the front shell if it needs replacement; replacement is recommended. The same applies to the rear seal.

15 Examine all parts for distortion, cracks, scratches etc. It is recommended that unless some particular defect has occurred after a short mileage, all flexible parts, such as the diaphragm, seals etc, are all replaced, as having been disturbed they are unlikely to be reliable for long.

16 Apply the special power brake lubricant to the cylinder surface of the plate/valve body and to the surfaces of the valve rod and plunger.

17 Insert the valve rod and plunger assembly into the valve body.

18 Press down on the valve rod and align the groove in the valve plunger with the slot in the valve body, and insert the retainer key.

19 Fit the diaphragm over the plate part of the valve body making certain the diaphragm is seated in the groove.

20 Put the air filter and silencer over the rod and into the valve body.

21 Lubricate the entire surface of the reaction disc liberally with power brake lubricant, and put it in the valve body.

22 Lubricate with power brake lubricant the outer bead of the diaphragm, and the part that touches the shell, to help assembly.

23 Fit the new seal to the rear shell. Lubricate it with the power brake lubricant, and then fit it carefully to the valve body.

24 Fit the new seal to the front shell.

25 Put in the return spring, and then reassemble the components into the front shell.

26 Close the two halves of the shell of the vacuum cylinder by rotating them anti-clockwise to engage the lips.

27 Fit the boot.

28 Adjust the acuating rod for the master cylinder so it protrudes 0.049 to 0.073 in (1.26 to 1.85 mm) beyond their mating face.

29 Put the master cylinder back on the servo.

30 Refit the assembly to the car.

31 Bleed the brakes.

32 Test the brakes and check the servo action as given in Section 14.

17 Hydraulic pipes and hoses

1   Periodically all brake pipes, pipe connections and unions should be completely and carefully examined.

2   First examine for signs of leakage where the pipe unions occur. Then examine the flexible hoses for signs of chafing and fraying and, of course, leakage. This is only a preliminary part of the flexible hose inspection, as exterior condition does not necessarily indicate the interior condition, which will be considered later.

3   The steel pipes must be examined equally carefully. They must be cleaned off and examined for any signs of dents, or other percussive damage and rust and corrosion. Rust and corrosion should be scraped off and, if the depth of pitting in the pipes is significant, they will need replacement. This is particularly likely in those areas underneath the car body and along the rear axle where the pipes are exposed to full force of road and weather conditions.

4   If any section of pipe is to be taken off, first of all drain the fluid, or remove the fluid reservoir cap and line it with a piece of polythene film to make it air tight, and replace it. This will minimise the amount of fluid dripping out of the system, when pipes are removed. It is normally best to drain all the fluid, as a change is probably due anyway.

5   Rigid pipe removal is usually quite straightforward. The unions at each end are undone, the pipe and union pulled out, and the centre sections of the pipe removed from the body clips where necessary. Underneath the car, exposed unions can sometimes be very tight. As one can use only an open ended spanner and the unions are not large burring of the flats is not uncommon when attempting to undo them. For this reason a self- locking grip wrench (Mole) is often the only way to remove a stubborn union.

6   Flexible hoses are always mounted at both ends in a rigid bracket attached to the body or a sub-assembly. To remove them it is necessary first of all to unscrew the pipe unions of the rigid pipes which go into them. The hose ends can then be unclipped from the brackets. The mounting brackets, particularly on the body frame, are not very heavy gauge and care must be taken not to wrench them off.

7   With the flexible hose removed, examine the internal bore. If it is blown through first, it should be possible to see through it. Any specks of rubber which come out, or signs of restriction in the bore, mean that the inner lining is breaking up and the pipe must be replaced.

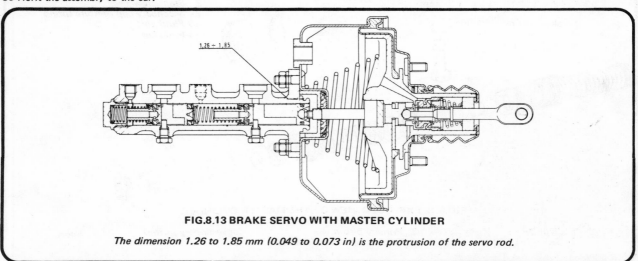

1,26 ÷ 1,85

FIG.8.13 BRAKE SERVO WITH MASTER CYLINDER

The dimension 1.26 to 1.85 mm (0.049 to 0.073 in) is the protrusion of the servo rod.

8 Rigid pipes which need replacement can usually be purchased at any garage where they have the pipe, unions and special tools to make them up. All they need to know is the total length of the pipe, the type of flare used at each end with the union, and the length and thread of the union. Fiat is metric remember.

9 Replacement of pipes is a straightforward reversal of the removal procedure. If the rigid pipes have been made up it is best to get all the sets (bends) in them before trying to install them. Also if there are any acute bends, ask your supplier to put these in for you on a tube bender. Otherwise you may kink the pipe and thereby restrict the bore area and fluid flow.

10 When refitting the flexible pipes check they cannot be under tension, or rub, when the wheels are at the full range of suspension or steering movement.

18 Brake pressure warning switch

1 On cars for certain markets, including North America, switches are fitted to light a lamp on the dash if one of the circuits in the dual system fails.

2 The two systems are piped through a shuttle valve mounted on the dash. (photo). If the pressure is different between the two halves of the system, the valve will be pushed over one way.

3 When bleeding the brakes, the ignition should be switched on and the handbrake off, then the function of this switch can be watched, and also when bleeding is finished, it will show if the switch is jammed over one way. Should this happen, get an assistant to hold the brake pedal down, and slacken a nipple on the circuit that was not bled last, and allow a very small amount of fluid to escape to let the differential shuttle of the switch move over. This must be done carefully, or it will overshoot.

4 Before assuming the switch has failed, test the wiring to the warning light.

5 If the switch fails, it should be replaced as a unit. Fit a sheet of this plastic over the mouth of the hydraulic reservoir and replace the lid. Put rag around the switch to absorb the drips of fluid which will otherwise take off the paint. Undo all the unions. Do not pull the pipes at all far away from their unions lest they be flattened by bends. Disconnect the switch wires. Undo the bolt fixing the switch.

6 Fit the new switch. Bleed the brakes, and whilst doing so check the operation of the warning light.

19 Removal of the brake (and clutch) pedals

1 The pedals share the pivot for the clutch pedal, so must be removed as a pair.

2 Inside the car take out the split pin from its pivot, and unhook the clutch cable. Do the same for the brake push rod if the car has a servo.

3 Unhook the brake pedal return spring.

4 Take off the nut and washers on the right end of the pedal pivot (part of the clutch pedal).

5 Remove the screw and take off the tab holding the pedal spacer.

18.2 The switch for brake pressure failure warning is just above the master cylinder. (Left hand drive).

6 Try and withdraw the clutch pedal. It will probably be necessary to undo the electric harness bracket so the wires can be pushed out of the way.

7 Take out the clutch pedal, and then lower the brake pedal and spacer.

8 Before reassembly smear grease on the pedal pivots and the spacer.

20 Bleeding the brakes

1 If the hydraulic system has air in it, operation will be spongy and imprecise. Air will get in whenever the system is dismantled, or if it runs low. The latter is likely to happen as the brakes wear, and the pistons move further out in the wheel cylinders. Air can leak into the system, sometimes through a fault too slight to let fluid out. In this latter case it indicates a general overhaul of the system is needed. Bleeding is also used at the 36,000 miles task, to change the brake fluid.

2 You will need:
a) An assistant to pump the pedal.
b) A good supply of new hydraulic fluid.
c) An empty glass jar.
d) A plastic or rubber pipe to fit the bleed nipple.
e) A spanner for the nipple.

3 Top up the master cylinder, and put fluid in the bleed jar to a depth of about ½ in.

4 Start at the nipple furthest away from the master cylinder; ie rear brake, passenger side, and work nearer.

5 Clean the nipple and put the pipe on it.

6 Tell your assistant to give a few quick strokes to pump up pressure, and then hold the pedal down.

7 Slacken the nipple, about ½ or 1 turn, till the fluid or air begins to come out. This is usually quite apparent either as bubbles or dirt in the clean fluid in the jar.

8 As soon as the flow starts, tell the assistant to keep pumping the pedal everytime it gets to the end of its travel, and tell you all the timeswhere the pedal is; 'down, up' etc. The pedal should be pushed down hard, but released slowly.

9 As soon as air has stopped coming out shut the bleed nipple; do so as the assistant is pushing the pedal down. Do not go on too long, lest the reservoir be emptied, and more air pumped in. About 15 pedal pumps is safe.

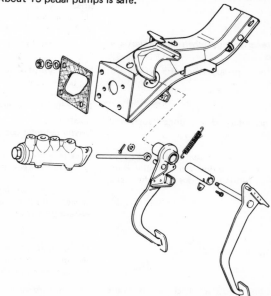

FIG.8.14 PEDAL PARTS, FOR A CAR WITHOUT SERVO

10 Refill the reservoir, and repeat at the other wheels. Also keep going on the original wheel after refilling the reservoir if dirty fluid is still coming out, to get rid of all the old.
11 Bleeding is greatly speeded, and can be done by one person, if spring loaded valves are fitted to the nipples. These are available from accessory shops.
12 Keep hydraulic fluid clear of the car's paint. It ruins it. Throw old fluid away. It attracts damp, so deteriorates in use.
13 If there is difficulty in getting air out of the system, then each time the assistant releases the pedal, close the nipple, so no back flow can take place.
14 On cars with pressure differential switches to give warning when pressure fails in one of the brake lines, the valve may stay over to one side after bleeding. If this occurs, bleed a very small amount out of the other, to allow the valve to centralise.
15 If bleeding is needed frequently, this indicates an overhaul of the master cylinder, and maybe the wheel cylinders too, is needed.

21 Fault diagnosis and remedies

Before diagnosing faults in the brake system
check that any irregularities are not caused by:

1 Uneven and incorrect tyre pressures
2 Incorrect 'mix' of radial and cross-ply tyres
3 Wear in the steering mechanism
4 Defects in the suspension and dampers
5 Misalignment of the bodyframe

Symptom	Reason/s	Remedy
Pedal travels a long way before the brakes operate	Rear brake shoes set too far from the drums	Check self adjusters.
	Failure of half the hydraulic system	Check for leaks.
Stopping ability poor, even though pedal pressure is firm	Linings and/or drums badly worn or scored	Dismantle, inspect and renew as required.
	One or more wheel hydraulic cylinders seized, resulting in some brake shoes not pressing against the drums or pads against discs	Dismantle and inspect wheel cylinders. Renew as necessary.
	Failure of half of the system	Check for leaks.
	Brake linings contaminated with oil	Renew linings and repair source of oil contamination.
	Wrong type of linings fitted	Verify type of material which is correct for the car and fit it.
	Rear brake shoes wrongly assembled	Check for correct assembly.
	Servo unit not working	Check suction hose. Check servo
Car veers to one side when the brakes are applied	Brake linings on one side are contaminated with oil	Renew linings and stop oil leak.
	Hydraulic wheel cylinder(s) on one side partially or fully seized	Inspect wheel cylinders for correct operation and renew as necessary.
	A mixture of lining materials fitted between sides	Standardise on types of linings fitted.
	Unequal wear between sides caused by partially seized wheel cylinders	Check wheel cylinders and renew linings and drums as required.
Pedal feels spongy when the brakes applied	Air is present in the hydraulic system	Bleed the hydraulic system and check for any signs of leakage.
Pedal feels springy when the brakes are applied	Master cylinder or brake backplate mounting bolts loose	Retighten mounting bolts.
	Severe wear in brake drums causing distortion when brakes are applied	Renew drums and linings.
Pedal gradually down under sustained pressure	Small leak	Trace leak.
	Master cylinder cups failed, being bye-passed	If none visible, suspect master cylinder, and overhaul it.
Pedal travels right down with little or no resistance and brakes are virtually non-operative (unlikely: due to the dual system)	Leak in hydraulic system resulting in lack of pressure for operating wheel cylinders	Examine the whole of the hydraulic system and locate and repair source of leaks. Test after repairing each and every leak source.
	If no signs of leakage are apparent the master cylinder internal seals are failing to sustain pressure	Overhaul master cylinder. If indications are that seals have failed for reasons other than wear all the wheel cylinder seals should be checked also and the system completely replenished with the correct fluid.
Binding, overheating	Master cylinder faulty cups	Overhaul master cylinder.
	Master cylinder no free play	Check pedal clearance.
	Handbrake too tight	Readjust.
Vibration, pedal pushed up in phase with slow vibration	Discs/drums worn	Have drums skimmed. Renew discs.
Juddering	Loose back plate	Tighten.
	Dust in rear drums, or oily linings/pads or front or rear	Clean and/or reline.

Chapter 9 Electrical system

Contents

Specifications

Voltage	12 volts
Polarity	Negative earth

Battery (Hot or temperate climate)		34 Amp. hour
Specific gravity: at 60°F (150°C)	Fully charged	1.28
	Half charged	1.22
	Nearly discharged	1.16
	Flat	1.11

Generator:
Dynamo (early cars)

Type	D90/12/16/3 E
Maximum continuous output	16 amps (230 watts)
Maximum peak output	22 amps (320 watts)
Cut-in speed (12 v) (68°F - 20°C)	1710 - 1790 rpm
Speed for maximum continuous output	2550 - 2700 rpm
Speed for peak output	3050 - 3200 rpm
Maximum speed	9000 rpm
Rotation of drive	Clockwise
Poles	2
Field	Shunt
Engine to dynamo speed	1 : 1.86 (new belt)
Minimum engine speed for charge	940 rpm (approx)
Field winding resistance	8 ohms at 20°C
Armature winding resistance	0.145 ohms at 20°C

Dynamo Regulator

Type	GN 2/12/16	
Cut out closing voltage	12.2 - 13.0 volts	
Reverse current maximum	16 amps	
Air gap, contacts closed	.014 in	(0.35 mm)
Points gap	.016 - .020 in	(0.39 - 0.51 mm)
Regulator air gaps	.039 - .044 in	(0.99 - 1.11 mm)

Setting voltage at 8 amps, warm	13.9 - 14.5 volts
Setting current at 13 volts, warm	15 - 17 amps
Regulating resistance	80 - 90 ohms
Voltage regulating resistance	16 - 18 ohms

Alternator (later cars)

Type	Bosch G1 - 14V 33A 27
Maximum output about	38 amps
Output at 14 volts and 5,000 rpm	29 amps at least
Cut-in speed (12 v) (77°F, 25°C)	1,050 - 1.150 rpm
Maximum speed	14,000 rpm
Drive rotation	Clockwise
Engine to alternator speed	1 : 2
Field winding resistance	4 ohms

Alternator Regulator

Type	Bosch AD 1/14V

Starter motor

Type	Pre-engaged by solenoid
Model	FIAT E84 - 0.8/12
Power	0.8 KW
Poles	4
Field	Series
No load test: 11.9 volts	30 amps or less; 6,000 - 8,000 rpm
Solenoid winding resistance	0.37 - 0.41 ohms
Lubrication - Armature bushes	Engine oil
Armature spiral grooves	SAE 10(W) oil
Free wheel splines	Castrol LM Grease

Heater fan

Heater fan	20 watts

Lamps

Headlamps	Dependant on market and model
Turn indicators	21 watt
Side turn repeaters (Europe)	4 watt
Parking lights	5 watt
Licence number plate	5 watt
Interior lights	5 watt festoon type
Instrument lights	3 watt

Fuses

Fuses	9
Fuse rating	Engine fan 16 amp
	Remainder 8 amp
Optional - Heated rear window	16 amp

1 General description

1 The electrical system is 12 volt, negative earth. On early cars the generator was DC, that is, a dynamo. Later cars have alternators. The fan is electrical. The 'V' belt that would normally be called a 'fan belt' is at the right end of the engine, and drives the water pump and generator. It is tensioned by moving the generator on its mountings in the normal way.

2 Cars built to specifications to suit various markets vary in minor detail, such as lamps, and the addition of things like 'Fasten seat belts' warnings.

3 The wiring diagrams in this book show the basic wiring for Europe. Special wiring for particular countries is shown in the special drivers handbook supplied with the car. These books prepared by FIAT to suit local variations are available from the local agent if the car's original one has been lost.

2 The battery: general maintenance

1 Topping up the electrolyte is a weekly task, though it may need doing daily when on long journeys.

2 When inspecting the engine compartment the battery should be checked for leaks, security, and corrosion. The terminals should not corrode if properly protected. To do so, disconnect them, and take out the terminal bolt. Clean all very thoroughly. Smear liberally · with vaseline (petroleum jelly), not grease. Reassemble, and wipe off the surplus vaseline. If the area near the battery corrodes, treat it as described in Section 5.

3 Electrolyte

1 The liquid in the battery is sulphuric acid. It is highly corrosive to the car, you, and your clothes.

2 It should be kept topped up with pure water. The acid itself does not get used up. The water bubbles off as gas as the battery charges. The water is normally got in the form of distilled water. It is better to top it up with drinking water than to let the level get low for lack of the distilled water.

3 Due to chemical reactions inside, the electrolyte specific gravity (sp gr) falls as the battery discharges. This can be measured with a hydrometer.

4 If the battery acid is spilled the lost electrolyte must be replaced with acid. This must be mixed to the correct sp gr. If diluting concentrated acid, pour the acid into the water. NEVER add water to acid: It will explode. First dilute with 1 part acid to 2½ parts water. Then continue till the required sp gr. is achieved as appropriate for that temperature.

5 On old batteries the sp gr. cannot be got back to that of a new one due to permanent chemical changes.

4 Charging

1 If the car is used frequently, on good journeys, and has a young battery, the generator will keep the battery fully charged.

2 Old batteries do not hold their charge.

3 Town journeys do not give good charges due to idling at

traffic halts, particularly on early cars with dynamos.

4 If the battery is not kept fully charged its plates deteriorate faster than normal.

5 In winter the battery may well not be kept properly charged. It should therefore be recharged from an outside source at least once in the winter.

6 Charge at a rate not exceeding 3½ amps. When fully charged the battery gasses move freely, and the sp gr. reaches a maximum. Continue to charge for about 2 hours after this.

7 Do not have a so called 'boost charge', which takes only about 1—2 hours This will shorten the life of the battery by a factor of many years.

8 An old battery can often be revived by 'cycling' it once or twice. Let it discharge fully, slowly, by leaving the parking lamps on. Then charge it at only 1½—2 amps, till fully charged.

5 Battery leaks and corrosion

1 If the battery leaks, remove it immediately before the acid can do any more damage.

2 If the casing is cracked, take it to an expert to mend. It is not at all easy to get a repair to last. The corrosion from a leak is so severe that it is not a good risk to have an unreliable repair. Leaks in the joint round the top are more easily dealt with. A small one can be filled with a household sealant, but for larger cracks melt some pitch.

3 Halt any corrosion in the car by washing out the area with plenty water.

4 Once thoroughly dry, paint with a zinc based rust preventer, followed by the normal undercoat and top coats of paint.

6 The charging system

1 The charging system consists of a generator and control circuit to suit its output to the state of charge of the battery and the electrical equipment in use. It must also prevent the generator being driven as a motor by the battery when the engine is not running.

2 Early cars had a direct current (DC) system using a dynamo, and output regulator with cut out. Later cars use alternating current (AC). The output of the alternator is rectified to DC, and these rectifiers obviate the need for a cut out to prevent the battery discharging through the generator. The alternator also has a regulator to control the output, but it is much smaller than the dynamo's. The regulator is in the right hand part of the engine compartment on the mudguard beside the heater.

3 Routine maintenance consists of checking the 'V' belt tension, and fitting new belts, and of cleaning the brushes on dynamo or alternator. The mileages are given in Sections 2,5 and 6 of the Routine Maintenance.

4 Faults in the system may be due to the generator or its regulator. There can be two types of generator fault. The charging rate may become low, or the output may stop completely. A low output is difficult to detect unless an ammeter is fitted. The first symptoms are likely to be a flat battery. But a comlete failure will be shown by the so called ignition warning light. This is a misnomer. Like the oil warning light it comes on when the ignition is switched on. It stays on until the generator is charged.

7 Removing the generator

1 The generator will need to be removed for routine cleaning of the brushes, be it dynamo or alternator, or after the tests done in position with the engine running as described in subsequent Section indicate an internal fault.

2 Remove the air cleaner complete, and cover over the carburettor air intake.

3 Disconnect the leads from the generator. The two terminals of a dynamo are different sizes, so cannot be muddled. On alternators note that one of the leads to the alternator plug is live.

4 Slacken the pivot bolts underneath the generator, and the adjuster bolt working in the slotted bracket on top. Move the generator to slacken the 'V' belt, and take that off. (photos).

5 Now completely undo and take off the adjustment and pivot bolts, supporting the generator with a hand underneath. This is not as easy as it sounds, as access is difficult, particularly on cars with fuel evaporation absorption canisters and the attendant pipes. An assistant who can reach across the car from the left is a great help: otherwise it is probably worth removing the front grille and taking off the bonnet so that it is possible to lean over the engine from in front.

6 Replace the generator in reverse sequence. If the belt is not nearly new, fit a new one, and adjust it to give ½ in (12 mm) sag between pulleys when pushed hard by one finger.

8 Dynamo tests

1 The dynamo consists of an armature rotating in a magnet. The magnetism of this is provided by the field coils. These are wound on poles on the body or yoke. The current is generated in the rotating armature, and because it is tapped off at the brushes running on the commutator, the output is DC.

2 If, with the engine running, no charge comes from the dynamo, or the charge is very low, first check that the drive belt is in place and is not slipping. Then check that the leads from the control box to the dynamo are firmly attached and that one has not come loose from its terminal.

3 If wiring has recently been disconnected check that the leads have not been incorrectly fitted.

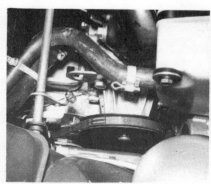

6.2 The generator is difficult to get at beneath the water pump and manifolds.

7.4a The adjuster works in a bracket on the water pump. In this case a dynamo is shown.

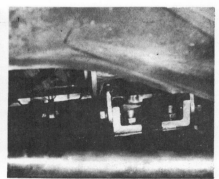

7.4b The pivot bolts underneath, seen from below the car.

4 Make sure none of the electrical equipment such as the lights or radio, is on, and then take the leads off the dynamo terminals. Join the terminals together with a short length of wire.

5 Attach to the centre of this length of wire the positive clip of a 0-20 volts voltmeter and run the other clip to earth on the dynamo yoke. Start the engine and allow it to run approximately 1,500 rpm. At this speed the dynamo should give a reading of about 15 volts on the voltmeter. This speed is a fast idle: do not run the engine faster or the field winding may be overloaded.

6 If no reading is recorded then remove the dynamo and check the brushes and brush connections. If a very low reading of approximately 1 volt is observed then the field winding may be suspect.

7 If a reading of between 4 to 6 volts is recorded it is likely that the armature winding is at fault.

8 If a satisfactory reading is obtained, then the fault is either in the wiring or the control box. Reconnect the two wires onto the generator. They have different sized terminals, so cannot be muddled.

9 Take off the leads on terminals 51 and 67, the front two, on the regulator. These can be muddled, so make sure they are marked to prevent this.

10 Again join the two leads together and repeat the same test. If again it is successful, and there is full generator voltage, then those leads must be alright, and the fault is in the control box or the wiring beyond. Refit the leads and refer to Section 13.

11 If the first test proved the generator faulty it must be removed for further testing. Remove it as described in Section 7, and dismantle it as described in Section 9.

12 Check the resistance of the field windings. This is easier done on the bench, as an accurate ohmmeter or Wheatstone bridge must be used. See the specification. If the reading is very high there is an open circuit. If the reading is below the specification then a short circuit is indicated. If the field windings have gone, unless a visual inspection discloses an easily mended defect, a reconditioned unit will probably be needed. Replacement windings are unlikely to be available quickly, and are difficult to fit. It may be possible to get a serviceable body complete at a breakers, and put your armature into the other body.

13 If the field winding seems all right then the fault must be deeper in.

14 The brushes could well be at fault. They should be checked now anyway and the commutator cleaned as in Section 9. Assuming all is in order continue with the fault finding as follows.

15 Examine the commutator segments. If the armature has some burned out windings with short circuits there will be burns on the commutator, and the windings may show signs of over heating.

16 Test the resistance of the windings by checking the resistance from one segment to the segment at 180°. This is very low, so needs accurate measurement. If facilities are not available this is where you give up. But the point is to be able to prove that it is the armature at fault or not, so you know what to do. Again, a replacement armature may be difficult to get, and one from a breakers may have a bad commutator, so you may be forced to get a reconditioned one.

17 If you do decide to measure the resistance of the armature then one method is to feed a low voltage of 1 to 2 volts in and measure the current. R=V/A.

9 Stripping and reassembling the dynamo

1 Take the nuts off the two long bolts clamping the whole dynamo end to end.

2 Pull off the brush-end end plate. Do this gently so the brushes slide off the end of the armature without risk of breakage. (photos).

3 Pull the yoke (the main body) off the armature (the heavy central part that rotates). Leave the pulley and pulley-end plate on the armature.

4 Clean all the parts. Do not immerse the end plates in any cleaning fluid, as this will get into the sealed bearings.

5 Before reassembly fit the new brush tails to their terminals. Slide the brushes into their holders, and hook the springs back so the brushes lodge held back in the mountings, so that when fitted they will clear the commutator. The springs can be hooked into position after the generator has been reassembled, with a small screw driver through the holes in the end plate.

10 Dynamo overhaul

1 It is assumed that the dynamo has not been stripped for some time. It will therefore need cleaning, relubrication of the bearings, and new brushes.

2 All this is part of its 18,000 mile maintenance task.

3 New brushes should be bought before starting work, as the need for them is a certainty. They should be fitted unless the existing ones are worn less than 1/8 in (3 mm).

4 Note the way the brushes and springs are fitted. Then remove them. Clean out the brush holders.

5 Do not immerse the generator end plates with the bearings in cleaning liquid, as dirt and liquid will not be fully removed. But wipe off the outside dirt. The design of the bearing houses varies. Unbolt or lift off one of the dirt shields: wipe away the old grease on the outside of the bearing, and push in some new grease. Check the bearings run smoothly and have no more than a trace of free movement.

6 The armature should be wiped clean. Take care the rag does not catch in and damage the windings.

7 Next check the condition of the commutator. If it is dirty and blackened, clean it with a rag just damped with petrol. If the commutator is in good condition the surface will be smooth and

9.2 Having taken off the two nuts the end plate just lifts off.

9.3 Then the yoke can be lifted off the armature and drive end plate.

9.5 To put the end plate back on hook the brush springs up so they hold back the brushes.

free from pits or burnt areas, and the insulated segments clearly defined.

8   Scrape the dirt out of the undercut gaps of insulator between the metal segments with a narrow screwdriver.

9   If, after the commutator has been cleaned, pits and burnt spots are still present, wrap a strip of fine glass paper round the commutator. Rub the patches off. Keep moving the paper along and turning the armature so that the rubbing is spread evenly all over. Finally repolish the commutator with metal polish such as Brasso. Then reclean the gaps.

10   In extreme cases of wear the commutator can be mounted in a lathe. With the lathe burning fast, take a very fine cut. Then

polish with fine glass paper, followed by metal polish.

11   If the commutator is badly worn or has been skimmed the segment may be worn till level with the insulator in between. In this case the insulator must be undercut. This is done to a depth of 0.040 in (1.0 mm). The best tool is a hacksaw blade, if necessary ground down to make it thinner. The under cutting must take the full width of the insulator away, right out to the metal segments on each side.

12   Again clean all thoroughly when finished, and ensure no rough edges are left. Any roughness will cause bad brush wear. In all this work it must also be remembered that the commutator is not very strong.

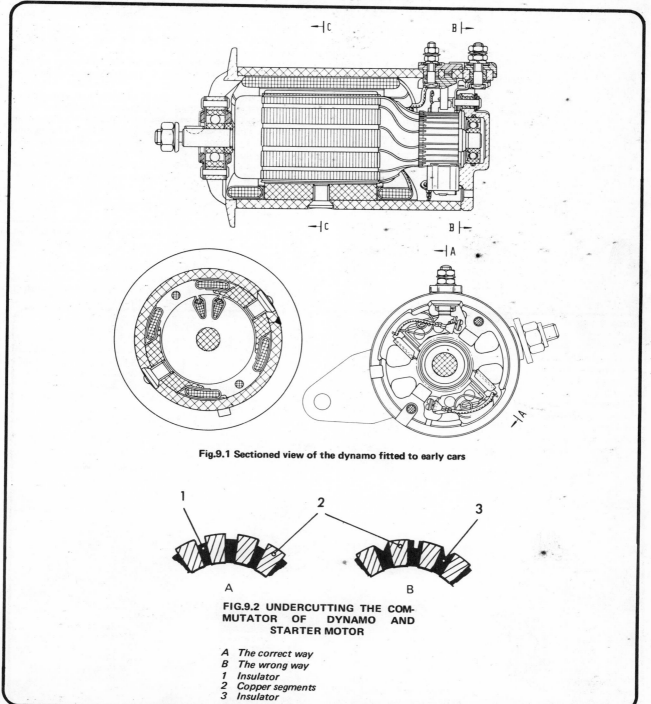

Fig.9.1 Sectioned view of the dynamo fitted to early cars

FIG.9.2 UNDERCUTTING THE COM-
MUTATOR OF DYNAMO AND
STARTER MOTOR

A   The correct way
B   The wrong way
1   Insulator
2   Copper segments
3   Insulator

11 Alternator description and tests

1   The alternator develops its current in the stationary windings, the rotor carrying the field. The brushes therefore carry only a small current, so they last a long time, and only simple slip rings are needed instead of a commutator.

2   The AC voltage is rectified by a bank of diodes. These also prevent battery discharge through the alternator.

3   Very little servicing is needed. Every 36,000 miles the alternator should be stripped and the brushes cleaned and checked.

4   Fault-finding is more a matter of confirming the fault is in the alternator, and it is probable then that a new unit will have to be fitted. However, if parts are available, component repair is possible. To fit new rectifiers or stator windings requires experience with a soldering iron, and should not be done by someone completely inexperienced.

5   The adjustment of the alternator drive belt is a 3,000 mile (5,000 km) task, and was detailed in task 2.1 of the Routine Maintenance.

6   To prevent damage to the rectifying diodes, the alternator leads should be disconnected whenever electric welding is being done on the car, or the battery being charged from an external charger.

7   The alternator should be tested on the car, as then it can be run up to speed by the engine, whilst under load from the car's electrical equipment.

8   Locate the alternator's output wire. This is the B+ terminal, which has a brown wire. It is difficult to pick it up at the alternator plug itself, but it goes to a junction point for brown wires and a red one where the leads from the battery and the main switches join. Put an ammeter in this lead. That the correct brown lead is being used can be confirmed by turning on lights, ignition etc. The ammeter should show no current at this time. Also connect a voltmeter from this point to earth.

9   Start up the engine, and set it to run at 2,000 rpm. Turn on the headlights and heater fan to load the alternator. The voltage should be about 14 and the amperage about 29.

10 Note that a normal car type ammeter is fitted in the brown lead to the battery, so under such test it will show quite a low current, as the load is being born by the alternator.

11 If the current is low the alternator appears to be faulty. If the voltage is low, then the regulator is probably wrong.

12 Stripping and examining the alternator

1   It is assumed at this stage that the alternator is only being stripped either to clean and check the brushes, or to trace a fault. So only partial dismantling is necessary. Fault-finding and repair should be left to the official agent if you have no experience of electricity and electronics.

2   Undo the long bolts clamping the two parts of the body together. Prise them apart, keeping the two straight. Pull the front part away, with the rotor still inside.

3   Clean all the parts, but do not dip them in any liquid. Check the condition of the slip rings, which should be smooth and shiny. The brushes' minimum length is 2/3 of their original.

4   If the alternator has failed, it is now stripped enough to check the field windings on the rotor, and the stator windings. As a repair will need knowledge of radio techniques, such as soldering without overheating the diodes; some knowledge is assumed here. Check the windings are neither open circuit, or shorted to their rotor/stator. The resistance of the field windings on the rotor should be about 4 ohms. Check the diodes only allow current in one direction.

5   If the diodes or stator coils need replacement they must be unsoldered and removed from the brush-end of the body. Note all leads so that they can be reconnected correctly.

6   If the rotor or the bearings need replacement the drive-end must be dismantled. Undo the nut on the end of the shaft holding on the pulley. Pad the rotor, and put it in a vice with soft jaws, and then undo the nut. Press the drive-end bracket with the bearing off the shaft. The brush-end bearing can be pulled off the other end of the shaft.

7   The bearings are lubricated and then sealed on assembly. If they feel dry or rough, they should be replaced.

8   When reassembling, the brushes have to be fitted into their holders, and put into position after fitting the rotor.

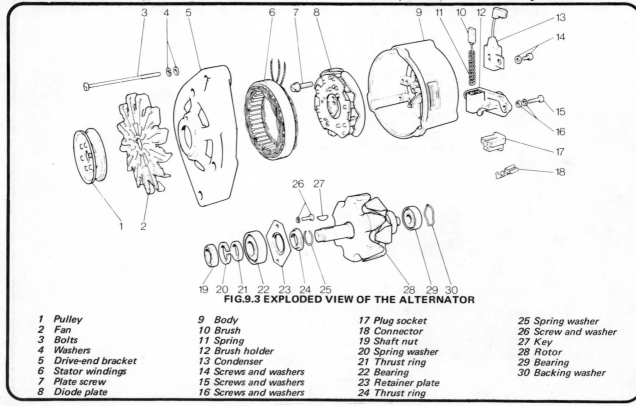

FIG.9.3 EXPLODED VIEW OF THE ALTERNATOR

1 Pulley	9 Body	17 Plug socket	25 Spring washer
2 Fan	10 Brush	18 Connector	26 Screw and washer
3 Bolts	11 Spring	19 Shaft nut	27 Key
4 Washers	12 Brush holder	20 Spring washer	28 Rotor
5 Drive-end bracket	13 Condenser	21 Thrust ring	29 Bearing
6 Stator windings	14 Screws and washers	22 Bearing	30 Backing washer
7 Plate screw	15 Screws and washers	23 Retainer plate	
8 Diode plate	16 Screws and washers	24 Thrust ring	

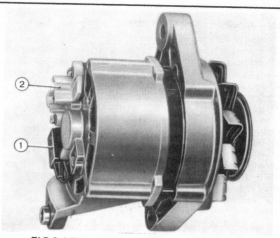

FIG.9.4 THE ALTERNATOR, BRUSH END VIEW

1 Condenser   *2 Brush holder assembly*

13.1 The control box is on the right mudguard: in this case one for a dynamo.

13.2 Looking across the car at the control box. The cut out is the right hand armature.

13 Dynamo control box function and faults

1 The control box has three relays. One is the cut out, another limits the dynamo voltage generated, and the third its current. (photos).

2 The cut out disconnects the dynamo from the battery when it is no longer charging, otherwise it could run off the battery as a motor.

3 The two regulator relays by their combination of voltage and current control regulate the output to suit the electrical load such as lights that might be switched on, and to suit the state of charge of the battery.

4 The current control is set to the maximum safe limit for the dynamo. The voltage regulator is set to a potential that will limit the charge given a full battery to a mere trickle.

5 If the control box has a complete failure the ignition warning light will come on. If there is a partial failure, unless an ammeter is fitted, there will be no warning. Undercharging may become apparent as a flat battery. Minor overcharging will give the need for frequent topping up of the battery. Gross over charging may blow light bulbs, and perhaps result in a smell of burning from the overloaded dynamo.

6 Major defects are likely to be the burning of the points on the relays, so that they never make contact: So no regulation takes place; or the wiring may burn out.

7 Minor defects occur due to wear and general ageing altering the voltage/current at which the cut out or regulators work.

8 A car-type ammeter will show these aberrations, and is a useful fitting for the long term. But for fault-finding more accurate instruments are needed. Unless you have some experience of such things, and of the instruments, it is suggested you do not tamper with the control box. If done incorrectly a new control box and a new dynamo may be needed.

9 In any work on the control box it is important that the leads are not fitted to wrong terminals or the unit will be ruined. It may still work when wrongly wired. But full dynamo current will pass through the regulator contacts. These will eventually weld together. Even if run only a short time wired thus, their life will have been drastically shortened.

14 Cutout checks

1 The cutout is the relay on the right as you look at them with the terminals at the bottom: looking across the car: the only one of the three with points open when the engine is switched off.

2 The dynamo will have been proved satisfactory by earlier fault-finding.

3 Take off the control box cover.

4 Check the voltage at the terminal from the dynamo, number 51, and the output from the cutout, number 30. This will prove that the defect is at the cutout.

5 Assuming there is 12/15 volts at the terminal 51, but none at 30, check the operation of the relay of the cutout. With the engine running fast enough to charge, try pushing it with a finger.

6 If the relay does not hold down there is a fault in the wiring.

7 If it stays down but there is still no voltage at the output terminal 30 points appear to need cleaning. If the push made it work it may need resetting.

8 To reset the cut out wire a voltmeter from terminal 51 (the dynamo connection) to earth. Start up: Warm up for 15 minutes. Increase engine speed gradually, watching both the voltmeter and the cutout. Note the voltage at which the cutout closes: there will be a little kick of the voltmeter. It should close at 12.6 volts. This voltage should be set after the cutout is warmed up by about 15 minutes running.

9 Adjust by bending the arm on which the spring of the contacts rests, increasing the spring tension to raise the operating voltage.

10 On slowing down the cutout should "drop-off", that is cut out, when the dynamo stops charging. The reverse current

should never be high: The official maximum is 16 amps, which is high as such things go. To improve drop-off bend the fixed contacts so that the moving one cannot be drawn so close to the armature. A car ammeter will show this negative current before "drop-off".

15 Voltage regulator checks

1   The circuit needed for testing must not have any current flow through the regulator. See Fig.9.7.
2   Slide a piece of paper in between the cutout points, and connect the voltmeter from the dynamo connection terminal 51 on the left of the control box and to earth. This must be an instrument accurate to 0.3 volt.
3   Start up, and run the engine fast: at 3,000 rpm. The regulator should limit the voltage to 15.5 volts. It is important to take the reading quickly to avoid temperature effects.
4   The reading should be steady. Fluctuations imply the contact points need cleaning. This should be done with fine glass paper, and all dust removed.
5   If adjustment, is needed bend the arm onto which the spring blade rests, increasing the spring tension to raise the regulated voltage. The voltage regulator is the one farthest from the cutout. (Nearest the front of the car), (photo).
6   The FIAT setting procedure is involved. The setting figure of 15.5 volts quoted is a compromise. It is valid at an ambient temperature of 10°C. At 20°C set to 15 volts. These voltages are the maximum. Do not exceed this. If the car is used extensively on long journeys a voltage lower by 0.5 volts should be used.

16 Current regulator checks

1   The current control is set using an ammeter accurate to 0.5 amp. See Fig.9.7. The ammeter is wired between the control box output terminal number 30 and the leads that are normally connected to it.
2   Wedge cardboard between the voltage regulator armature (the one furthest from the cutout) and its arm to hold the contacts closed, so no voltage regulation can take place.
3   Start up the engine.
4   Turn on the headlamps to load the dynamo.
5   Speed up the engine to a fast speed of about 3,000 rpm.
6   The maximum current should be 16 amps.
7   The current should be steady. Fluctuations imply the contacts need cleaning: do this with fine glass paper, and remove all dust.
8   If adjustment is needed bend the arm onto which the spring blade rests, increasing the spring tension to raise the controlled current. The current regulator is the centre one.

17 Alternator regulator

1   Because the alternator starts to charge at 1,100 rpm, which is an engine speed of 550 rpm, it charges even when the engine is idling. Also its output is much higher than the dynamo's. So setting of the regulator is not so critical, and it is not likely to need resetting. This is fortunate, as adjustments are much more likely to give an opportunity for the unwary to damage the alternator.
2   If the tests given in Section 11 indicate that the regulator is at fault, this could be confirmed by a car electrician. In this case a specialist can be just as helpful as the FIAT agent, as the alternator is made by Bosch, and it and the regulator are conventional. Fitting a new regulator is quite simple, but then it ought to be checked for adjustment after fitting.
3   When fitting a new regulator, it is important that the leads are fitted correctly.

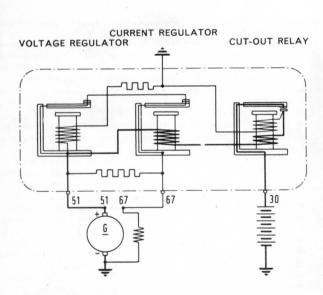

Fig.9.5 Schematic layout of dynamo control systems

15.5 Adjusting the voltage regulator.

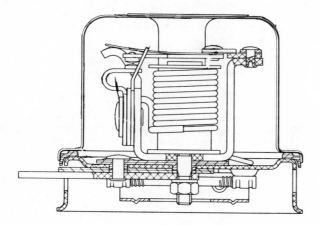

Fig.9.6 Dynamo cut out

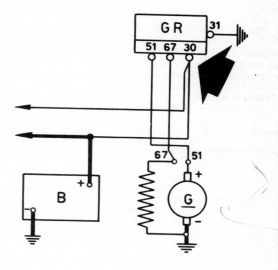

Fig.9.7 Adjusting the regulator. The broad arrow shows where the ammeter must be inserted for setting the current. When setting the voltage, inserting paper in the cut out points has the same effect as cutting the circuit at that point

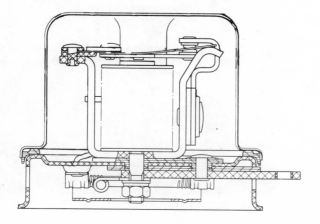

Fig.9.8 Section of the voltage or current regulators

18 The starter motor : description and checks

1 The starter is of the pre-engaged type. When the ignition switch is turned through to the starter position, the solenoid on the top of the starter is switched on, by the thin red wire. The solenoid slides along, pulling on the starter's gear lever. This slides the starter's gear into mesh with the starter ring on the flywheel. Having done this, the solenoid comes to the end of its travel, when a button on it switches the heavy cable direct from the battery to the starter motor itself. The starter now cranks the engine. Should the teeth of the starter and the flywheel have been out of alignment, the starter gear is spring loaded, so will actually mesh as soon as they come in line. This is helped by the spiral splines. Once the engine fires, it would run up to speed very quickly taking the starter with it, and the latter would turn so fast its windings would be damaged. In the drive is a freewheel to prevent this over speeding.

2 If the starter fails some fault-finding can be done with it still on the car. Check the ignition warning light comes on, and does not go out when the starter is switched on. If it goes out then the fault is probably in the battery. If it stays bright, get an assistant to work the switch, whilst listening to the starter. Listen to find out if the solenoid clicks into position. If it does not, pull out the red solenoid wire, and check it with a test bulb. If the wire does live when the key is turned, but the solenoid does not move, then take off the starter to work more comfortably on the bench.

19 Removing the starter motor

1 Take off the positive battery terminal.
2 Take off at the starter the small red wire from the solenoid, and the heavy cable from the battery. (photos).
3 Take out the three bolts through the clutch housing that hold the starter to the engine.
4 Lift out the starter.

20 Overhauling the starter

1 Having removed the starter from the engine, first clean the outside.
2 If the starter has been removed because it will not work, before stripping it, test to see where the defect is, and decide if to try repairing it, or whether it is better to get a replacement one. Connect a lead from the battery negative terminal to the starter body, using one of the bolts that held it to the engine. Connect the positive battery terminal to the little solenoid terminal. The solenoid should slide the starter's gear along the shaft, but the starter will not turn because at present no wire is on the starter's motor terminal. Now add another wire to that terminal. With the solenoid live, the starter should turn after the gear has slid into engagement. If it does not, try the wire direct to the motor's lead on the solenoid terminal nearer the motor main body, on which is the lead into the motor. If the motor now turns it shows that the switch part of the solenoid is faulty.
3 The starter should be dismantled for cleaning and renewing of the brushes every 18,000 miles (30,000 km).
4 Take off the nut on the solenoid, and disconnect the cable from the solenoid into the motor, the field connection. (photo).
5 Remove the nuts and washers on the long studs holding the solenoid to the end frame. Lift off the solenoid, unhooking it from the gear lever.
6 Slacken and slide off the dust cover on the end of the yoke, to uncover the brushes.
7 Disconnect the wire from the field winding to its brush.
8 Hook up the brush springs on the sides of the brush holders, so the load is taken off them.
9 Undo the nuts on the long through bolts holding the whole motor together.
10 Take off the brush-end end plate, and retrieve the one fibre

19.2 Disconnect the battery before taking the heavy cable off the starter, as its bare end would be live.

19.3 The starter motor is held on by three bolts

20.3 It is no use just replacing the brushes through the windows, as the commutator will need cleaning.

20.4 The solenoid is removed by disconnecting the cable into the motor, and then undoing the three nuts.

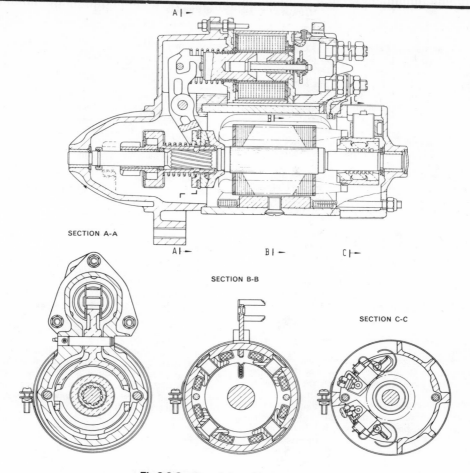

SECTION A-A

SECTION B-B

SECTION C-C

Fig.9.9 Section of the self-starter motor

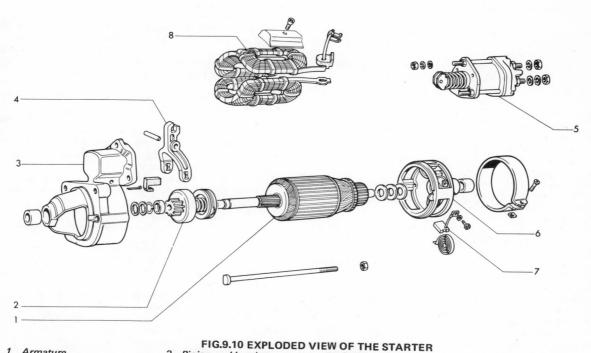

FIG.9.10 EXPLODED VIEW OF THE STARTER

| 1 | Armature | 3 | Pinion end bracket | 5 | Solenoid | 7 | Brush |
| 2 | Pinion with free wheel | 4 | Gear lever | 6 | Brush end plate | 8 | Field windings |

and two steel washers from the end of the armature shaft.

11 Tip the motor pinion end down, and lift the yoke off the armature and pinion end frame.

12 Take out its split pin, and remove the pivot pin for the gear lever from the 'waist' of the pinion housing.

13 Take the pinion housing off the assembly of armature, pinion and gear lever.

14 Clean all the parts by wiping. Do not immerse in cleaning liquid, especially the free wheel and the armature bushes in the end frames, as the liquid will get into the free wheel race and the pores of the bushes.

15 Fit the new brushes. Refer to Section 10 paragraphs 6 to 12 for the action needed on the commutator, which should be dealt with in the same way as the dynamo's. Note FIAT do recommend undercutting the commutator, unlike other manufacturerers of starter motors who do not.

16 Before reassembly lubricate the splines of the free wheel with Castrol LM Grease. Put thin oil on the spiral splines. Put engine oil in the armature bushes, allowing it time to soak in before assembly.

17 Put the brushes in their guides, but clip them back so they will clear the commutator by putting the springs on their side. The springs can be hooked into place after the brush-end plate has been fitted.

21 Engine cooling fan

1 The fan was discussed in Chapter 2/7. As part of the cooling system, in Chapter 2 the main emphasis was on the possibility that it should not work.

2 If it is being worked hard then some allowance may have to be made for the current the fan will draw, particularly under extreme conditions. If for instance the engine is left running in extended traffic delays, the fan could run for long periods. If the headlamps are on too, the load on the electrical system will be high. At idling speed, a dynamo will not be charging at all, and even an alternator will only have a limited output.

22 Windscreen wiper motor

1 Fault finding is complicated by the complex wiring due to the intermittent wiper operation, and the self parking arrangements. Fault finding will need reference to the wiring diagram for the colours of the wires from switch to the timing device, and on to the motor. If the wiper does not work either intermittently or continuously then there is a strong chance that the defect is in the motor. The wiper shares the fuse of the heater fan, so this is easily checked, and eliminated before tackling the wiring.

2 Unplug the wires near the motor, and using a test bulb or volt meter with probes to reach into the terminals, test the circuit with the switch on the steering column in its three positions. Note that because of the self parking facility, the circuit is always partially live.

3 Once a defect in the motor is suspected, it must be removed with the blade mechanism, all on the mounting plate.

4 Disconnect the plug for the leads.

5 Pull off the wiper arms.

6 Take off the fixtures on the ends of the arms spindles so that these can be withdrawn through the bushes in the body below the windscreen.

7 Undo the two bolts holding the motor mounting frame to the bracket on the bulkhead. (photo).

8 Remove the whole assembly.

9 When refitting, grease the arm spindles in their bushes, and all the other links for the connecting levers.

10 Operate the motor before fitting the blade arms. Once the motor has put the spindles in the parked position, the arms can be fitted in their correct orientation. Make sure the assembly is refitted without distortion which could make the linkage stiff.

11 If the operation of the wiper becomes very sluggish due to the need for lubrication of the interconnecting mechanism, or in heavy snow, there is risk of burning out the motor. Always switch off the wiper if it stalls, and if it cannot get back to the parked position, unplug the motor.

23 Combination headlamp dip, flash, and wiper switch

1 The combination, multi-purpose switch on the steering column works the headlamp dip and flash, the turn indicators, and the wipers, with the three stalk switches.

2 The whole switch is supplied for spares as one.

3 If only one part fails, then there is only small hope that some repair can be made to it. If the switch contacts are bad they can be cleaned by squirting in radio switch cleaner, sold in aerosol form by radio enthusiast shops. Sometimes the switch can be made to work by bending a spring contact. But if any part breaks off it will be almost impossible to mend.

4 To change the switch, first take off the positive battery terminal.

5 Remove the two side covers to the column.

6 Undo the two screws, and remove the horn push button and its spring from the steering wheel.

7 Undo the nut in the centre, and remove the steering wheel. Before pulling it off, put the wheel in the straight ahead position.

8 Undo all the wire connecting plugs, leaving them so they cannot get muddled up.

9 Slacken the switch clamp, and slide it off the column.

10 Fit the new switch, and connect up all the leads.

11 Refit the battery terminal, and check everything works.

12 Fit the steering wheel in the straight position.

13 Check that the indicator self cancelling mechanism works.

14 Refit the horn button and side covers.

24 Lighting

1 Many cars are to be seen driving with some lamps inoperative.

2 As bulbs blow without warning and at inconvenient times always carry spare ones on the car. When going to buy a new bulb, or light unit, take the old one with you to be sure of getting the right type.

3 It is possible to check bulbs on the move by reflections in the body panels of vans or in shop windows. But the surest way to check the tail lamps is to walk around and look at them. The small lights at the front are parking lights only, so these will be checked on leaving the car. They are of no use when driving, being too dim to be used in fog in daylight or under any dark conditions.

4 If an indicator flashing light bulb fails, it will give a different flashing speed to the winkers.

5 Except for the headlamps, which have individual fuses, the failure of one lamp only is usually the bulb. Only very occasionally is it a wiring failure, as these failures are usually short circuit rather than an open one. But failure of the earth contact at the light afflicts cars as they get old.

6 Remember in checking the brake lights the ignition must be on. These bulbs are a common failure; they can be checked by reversing close to a wall.

25 Headlight aiming

1 The aim of the headlights is set by the mounting screws on the back. There is also a quick change lever for laden and unladen conditions.

2 When making any changes count how many part turns the screws are moved. The top screw does vertical adjustment, and the side one horizontal. Make sure the laden/unladen lever is in the appropriate position (unladen: to the car's right).

3 In the diagram is the layout for using a wall to set the lights on low beam. (See Fig.9.11).

4 The setting can also be seen well in mist. If on coming traffic flashes at you it is a sure sign the lights are set badly.

26 Special lamps and warnings for North America

1   Cars going to the USA and neighbouring countries have a number of special electrical items.
2   A buzzer warns if the door is opened, but the ignition key is still in the switch steering lock. The same buzzer is used for the seat belt warning system.
3   Instead of the convenient European combined lap and shoulder belt, the seat belts are in separate parts. The warning system to remind the driver and front passenger to do them up operates the buzzer and a warning light on the dash. The system is triggered by the ignition switch, the gear lever, and for the passenger a pad in the seat. The system is switched off by a contact in the lap strap belt reel each side.
4   There is the emissions control circuit for the fast idle described in Chapter 3.
5   Instead of the turn indicators having side repeaters, there are side position lights. The turn indicators themselves, instead of being clearly defined as separate yellow lights front and rear, are red to the rear.
6   Hazard flashers are fitted.

27 Horns

1   The use of twin horns makes fault-finding simple. If only one sounds, then the fault is particular to the one that is silent. If both are silent, then it is a wiring or horn button defect.
2   If a horn fails, it can be adjusted by a screw on the back. Try screwing the screw in first: only a turn or so. Once the horn works again, adjust the screw in or out for the best note. Afterwards put some paint on the screw to seal out water, and to lock it.
3   The fuse is easily checked as it is shared with the interior light.
4   The horn button is the earth return, the black wire. Join a short length of wire from that terminal on one of the horns to a bright metal part and see if that makes the horn work. Check the

live side, the violet wires, with a test bulb.
5   The horn button can be removed from the steering wheel by undoing the two screws. Try earthing the wire to the steering column if the contacts are suspect.

28 Turn indicator flashers

Failure of a bulb will be shown by a change in the speed of flashing, and the note of the clicking. Failure of the flasher itself is usually complete, sticking with the lamp unlit or lit.

29 Instruments

1   Access to the instruments is gained by removing the dashboard as described in Chapter 12.
2   The fuel oil pressure temperature gauges and lights have their senders whose electric resistance varies according to the circumstances they are recording. The temperature, and oil pressure senders are both on the front of the engine. The fuel gauge sender is mounted in the top of the tank, with access only by removing the tank. To check the function of the actual instrument, remove the wire from the sender. Turn on the ignition. Note the reading with the lead off. Then put the lead direct to a good earth. These two tests should give full scale deflections in the two directions. Warning lights should come on when the lead is earthed. If this is successful, then the fault is in the sender. If unsuccessful, the same test should be done at the instrument, first establishing which is the live wire from the ignition switch with a test lamp. This will then show whether the fault is in the wiring to the sender or the instrument itself.

30 Fuses

1   The fuse box is below the dashboard, on the driver's side, covered by a plastic lid. The fuse functions are given in the tables.

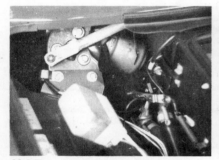

22.7 The wiper motor on right hand drive cars is difficult to get out because the heater is in the way.

22.8 With left hand drive there is much more room.

24.2 The double headlamps of the Coupe have a mounting held under the central grille.

FIG.9.11 HEADLAMP AIMING DIAGRAM, LEFT HAND DRIVE. FOR COUNTRIES DRIVING ON THE LEFT OF THE ROAD THE DIAGRAM IS A MIRROR IMAGE

A   = headlamp centre to centre 40½ in (103 cm)
B   = C – 4.1 in (10.5 cm) new car,
B   = C – 3.5 in (9 cm) car with settled springs.
C   = Height above ground of headlamps.

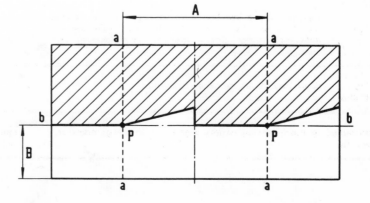

26.5 The inside view of the side marker lights fitted to cars going to North America.

29.2 The oil pressure warning sender and above it the one for excessive water temperature.

31.3 Wire accessories using proper terminals, so they cannot be a source of unreliability.

FIG.9.12 PROTECTED CIRCUITS

FUSE NUMBER	Up to car No. 557999 approximately the electric system is protected by nine 8-Amp. fuses and one 16-Amp. fuse.	From car No. 558000 approximately electric system is protected by seven 8-Amp. fuses and one 16-Amp. fuse.
1 (on right)	(16-Ampere) Horns. Engine cooling fan. - Interior lights.	Direction signals and repeater light. - Stop lights. - Heat indicator. - Fuel gauge and low fuel warning light. - Heater fan motor. - Low oil pressure indicator. - Wiper.
2	Windscreen wiper. - Heater fan.	(16-Ampere) - Horns. - Engine cooling fan motor and relay switch. - Interior lights.
3	High beam, L.H. - High beam indicator	High beam, L.H. - High beam indicator.
4	High beam, R.H.	High beam, R.H.
5	Low beam, L.H.	Low beam, L.H.
6	Low beam, R.H.	Low beam, R.H.
7	Front left parking light. - Parking light indicator. - Rear parking light, R.H. - License plate light, L.H. - Boot light. - Instrument lights.	Front left parking light. - Parking light indicator. - Rear parking light, R.H. - License plate light, L.H. - Instrument lights.
8	Front parking light, R.H. - Rear parking light, L.H. - License plate light, R.H. - Engine compartment light.	Front parking light, R.H. - Rear parking light, L.H. - License plate light, R.H. - Engine compartment light.
9	Fuel gauge and low fuel warning light. - Engine cooling fan relay winding. - Heat indicator. - Low oil pressure indicator. - Stop lights. - Direction signals and repeater light.	**Loose fuse** (16-Ampere,) (optional). - Rear window demister.
10 (Left end)	Spare fuse for additional electric units.	
Unprotected circuits	Ignition, starting, battery charge and no-charge indicator.	Ignition, starting, battery charge (voltage regulator excepted), engine fan relay field winding.

2 Fuses normally seldom blow. Sometimes when a lamp bulb fails it may blow the fuse as it goes, which can cause confusion in the fault-finding. Tracing the fault is easiest on those fuses that serve more than one component.

3 If a fuse consistently blows, it is indicating a short in that circuit, usually intermittent. Do not be tempted to replace the fuse by one thicker than standard. The result will be that as the short gets worse, the wiring of the car will overheat, causing widespread harm, and even the risk of burning the whole car.

4 Whilst searching for the cause of blowing fuses it is economical to use household fusewire laid in the clips and held by the burned out fuse cartridge. The cause of the trouble is likely to be frayed wire, chafing where it passes through a hole in the sheet metal.

5 In addition to the fuse box for individual circuits there is a fuse in the lead to heated rear windows. Most makers of radios have a fuse in the lead.

31 Wiring accessories

1 The most useful accessory would be an ammeter. This should be connected into the brown lead between the battery and all other circuits other than the starter motor. Having mounted the dial on the dash board, lead a pair of wires to the junction of brown and red wires for the alternator and other main circuits.

2 Other items should be wired in from a fused circuit as appropriate. For instance a bright red rear fog light should be wired in from fuse 8. If forgotten, it will be switched off then when the lights are switched off.

3 Connect all wires firmly. Ideally use proper car type connectors, or else terminal blocks as sold for household or radio fittings. Where wires pass through holes in sheet metal such as the bodywork, fit a grommet to prevent chafe. Strap the wires to the existing harness.

32 Fault-finding principles

1 Tracing an electrical fault follows the usual principle of the methodical check along the system.

2 First check for foolish errors, such as the wrong switch turned on, or for such things as an over-riding control like the accessory position of the ignition/steering lock. Also, if other components have failed simultaneously, then a fuse appears to be the fault.

3 If the faulty component is a light, the next assumption to make is that a bulb has blown, and try changing that.

4 If there is still no cure have a brief glance for obvious faults such as a loose wire. On an old car used much in the wet, with salty roads in winter, it is regretted that a good kick or a judicious blow is needed next. If the earth return of a component is poor this will strike a contact. If it does, then strip the component and derust it.

5 The proper systematic tracing of a more elusive fault requires a voltmeter or a test lamp. The latter is a small 12 volt bulb with two wires fitted to it; either using a bulb holder, or soldered direct. To test a circuit one wire is put to earth, and the other used to test the live side of a component. Work back from the component till the point is found where the bulb lights, indicating that the circuit is live until then. To test the earth side, the test bulb is wired to a live source, such as the starter solenoid. Then if the other wire is put to a component properly earthed it will light the bulb.

6 Trace methodically back until a correct result is got. Inaccessible circuits can be bridged with a temporary wire to see if it effects a cure.

7 With the wiring in a loom, defective wiring must be replaced with a separate wire. This must be securely fixed so it cannot chafe.

33 Fault diagnosis

Symptom	Reason/s	Remedy
STARTER MOTOR FAILS TO TURN ENGINE		
No electricity at starter motor	Battery discharged	Charge battery.
	Battery defective internally	Fit new battery.
	Battery terminal leads loose or earth lead not securely attached to body	Check and tighten leads.
	Loose or broken connections in starter motor circuit	Check all connections and tighten any that are loose.
	Starter motor switch or solenoid faulty	Test and replace faulty components with new.
Electricity at starter motor: faulty motor	Starter brushes badly worn, sticking, or brush wires loose	Examine brushes, replace as necessary, tighten brush wires.
	Commutator dirty, worn, or burnt	Clean commutator, recut if badly burnt.
	Starter motor armature faulty	Overhaul starter motor, fit new armature.
	Field coils earthed	Overhaul starter motor.
STARTER MOTOR TURNS ENGINE VERY SLOWLY		
Electrical defects	Battery in discharged condition	Charge battery.
	Starter brushes badly worn, sticking, or brush wires loose	Examine brushes, replace as necessary, tighten brush wires.
	Loose wires in starter motor circuit	Check wiring and tighten as necessary.
STARTER MOTOR OPERATES WITHOUT TURNING ENGINE		
Free wheel in drive faulty	Seized or stuck	Remove, examine, replace as necessary.
Mechanical damage	Pinion or ring gear teeth broken or worn	Fit new gear ring, and new pinion to starter motor drive.
STARTER MOTOR NOISY OR EXCESSIVELY ROUGH ENGAGEMENT		
Lack of attention or mechanical damage	Pinion or ring gear teeth broken or worn	Fit new ring gear, or new pinion to starter motor drive.
	Starter motor retaining bolts loose	Tighten starter motor securing bolts. Fit new spring washer if necessary.

BATTERY WILL NOT HOLD CHARGE FOR MORE THAN A FEW DAYS

Wear or damage	Battery defective internally	Remove and fit new battery.
	Electrolyte level too low or electrolyte too weak due to leakage	Top up electrolyte level to just above plates.
	Drive belt slipping	Check belt for wear, replace if necessary, and tighten.
	Short in lighting circuit causing continual battery drain	Trace and rectify.
	Regulator unit not working correctly	Check setting, clean, and replace if defective

GENERATOR SHOWS NO CHARGE: BATTERY RUNS FLAT IN A FEW DAYS

Generator not charging	Drive belt loose and slipping, or broken	Check, replace, and tighten as necessary.
	Brushes worn, sticking, broken or dirty	Examine, clean, or replace brushes as necessary.
	Brush springs weak or broken	Examine and test. Replace as necessary.
	Stator coils faulty	Fit new item or reconditioned generator.
	Rotor windings faulty	Fit new or reconditioned item or generator.
	Regulator faulty	If mechanical fault, readjust if electrical, replace.

WIPERS

Wiper motor fails to work	Blown fuse	Check and replace fuse if necessary.
	Wire connections loose, disconnected, or broken	Check wiper wiring. Tighten loose connections.
	Brushes badly worn	Remove and fit new brushes.
	Armature worn or faulty	Remove and overhaul and fit replacement armature.
	Field coils faulty	Purchase reconditioned wiper motor.
Wiper motor works very slowly and takes excessive current	Commutator dirty, greasy, or burnt	Clean commutator thoroughly.
	Drive linkage bent or unlubricated	Examine drive and straighten out curvature. Lubricate.
	Wiper arm spindle binding or damaged	Remove, overhaul, or fit replacement.
	Armature bearings dry or unaligned	Replace with new bearings correctly aligned.
	Armature badly worn or faulty	Remove, overhaul, or fit replacement armature.
Wiper motor works slowly and takes little current	Brushes badly worn	Remove and fit new brushes.
	Commutator dirty, greasy, or burnt	Clean commutator thoroughly.
	Armature badly worn or faulty	Remove and overhaul armature or fit replacement.
Wiper motor works but wiper blades remain static	Driving linkage disengaged or faulty	Examine and if faulty, replace.
	Wiper motor gearbox parts badly worn	Overhaul or fit new wiper motor.

LIGHTS

Lights do not come on	If engine not running, battery discharged	Charge battery.
	Light bulb filament burnt out or bulbs broken	Test bulbs in live bulb holder.
	Wire connections loose, disconnected or broken	Check all connections for tightness and wire cable for breaks.
	Light switch faulty	By-pass light switch to ascertain if fault is in switch and fit new switch as appropriate.
Lights come on but fade out	If engine not running, battery discharging	Push start car, and charge battery.
Lights give very poor illumination	Lamp glasses dirty	Clean glasses.
	Reflector tarnished or dirty	Fit new light unit.
	Lamps badly out of adjustment	Adjust lamps correctly.
	Incorrect bulb with too low wattage fitted	Remove bulb and replace with correct grade.
	Existing bulbs old and badly discoloured	Renew bulb
	Electrical wiring too thin not allowing full current to pass	Rewire lighting system.

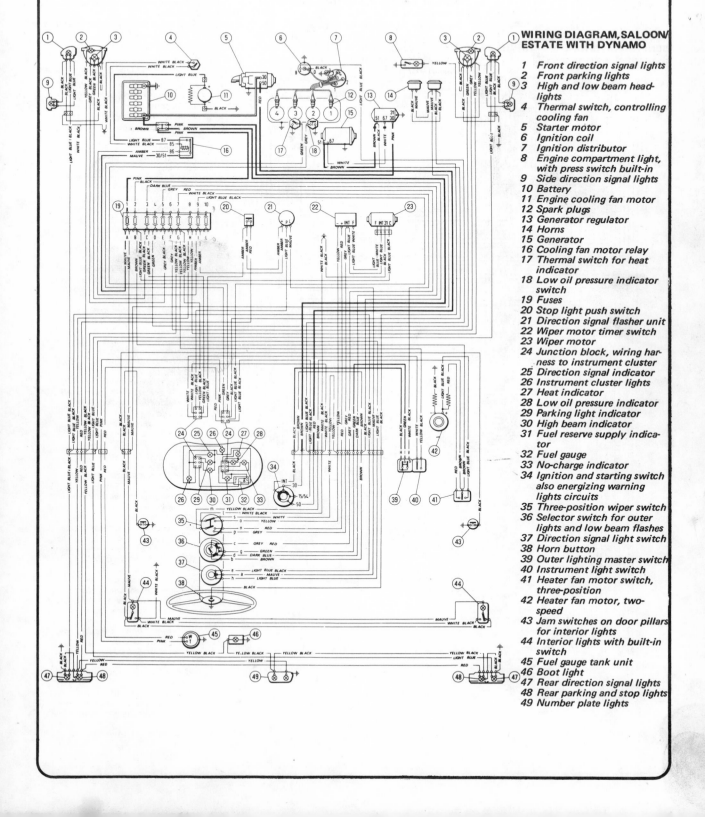

WIRING DIAGRAM, SALOON/ESTATE WITH DYNAMO

1 Front direction signal lights
2 Front parking lights
3 High and low beam head-lights
4 Thermal switch, controlling cooling fan
5 Starter motor
6 Ignition coil
7 Ignition distributor
8 Engine compartment light, with press switch built-in
9 Side direction signal lights
10 Battery
11 Engine cooling fan motor
12 Spark plugs
13 Generator regulator
14 Horns
15 Generator
16 Cooling fan motor relay
17 Thermal switch for heat indicator
18 Low oil pressure indicator switch
19 Fuses
20 Stop light push switch
21 Direction signal flasher unit
22 Wiper motor timer switch
23 Wiper motor
24 Junction block, wiring harness to instrument cluster
25 Direction signal indicator
26 Instrument cluster lights
27 Heat indicator
28 Low oil pressure indicator
29 Parking light indicator
30 High beam indicator
31 Fuel reserve supply indicator
32 Fuel gauge
33 No-charge indicator
34 Ignition and starting switch also energizing warning lights circuits
35 Three-position wiper switch
36 Selector switch for outer lights and low beam flashes
37 Direction signal light switch
38 Horn button
39 Outer lighting master switch
40 Instrument light switch
41 Heater fan motor switch, three-position
42 Heater fan motor, two-speed
43 Jam switches on door pillars for interior lights
44 Interior lights with built-in switch
45 Fuel gauge tank unit
46 Boot light
47 Rear direction signal lights
48 Rear parking and stop lights
49 Number plate lights

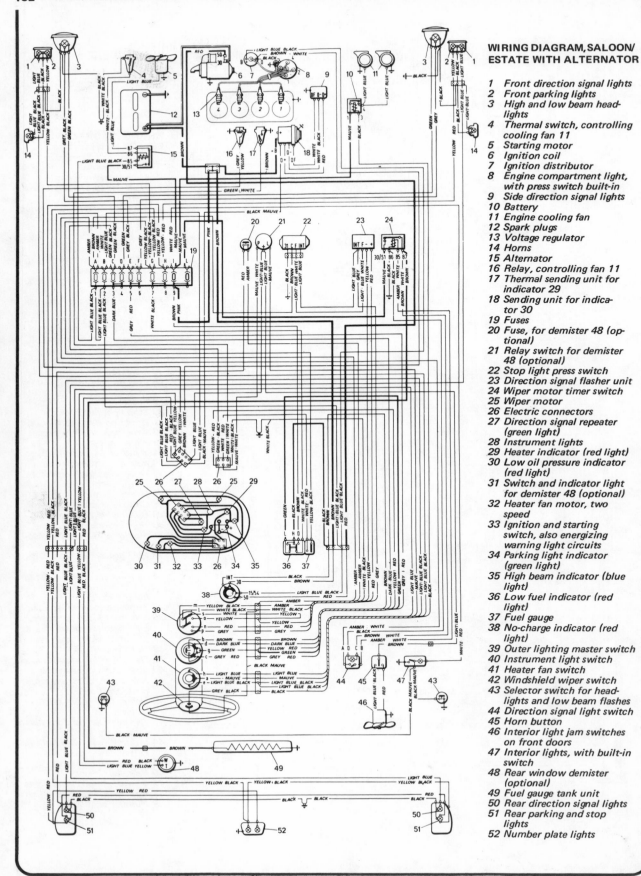

WIRING DIAGRAM, SALOON/ESTATE WITH ALTERNATOR

1 Front direction signal lights
2 Front parking lights
3 High and low beam headlights
4 Thermal switch, controlling cooling fan 11
5 Starting motor
6 Ignition coil
7 Ignition distributor
8 Engine compartment light, with press switch built-in
9 Side direction signal lights
10 Battery
11 Engine cooling fan
12 Spark plugs
13 Voltage regulator
14 Horns
15 Alternator
16 Relay, controlling fan 11
17 Thermal sending unit for indicator 29
18 Sending unit for indicator 30
19 Fuses
20 Fuse, for demister 48 (optional)
21 Relay switch for demister 48 (optional)
22 Stop light press switch
23 Direction signal flasher unit
24 Wiper motor timer switch
25 Wiper motor
26 Electric connectors
27 Direction signal repeater (green light)
28 Instrument lights
29 Heater indicator (red light)
30 Low oil pressure indicator (red light)
31 Switch and indicator light for demister 48 (optional)
32 Heater fan motor, two speed
33 Ignition and starting switch, also energizing warning light circuits
34 Parking light indicator (green light)
35 High beam indicator (blue light)
36 Low fuel indicator (red light)
37 Fuel gauge
38 No-charge indicator (red light)
39 Outer lighting master switch
40 Instrument light switch
41 Heater fan switch
42 Windshield wiper switch
43 Selector switch for headlights and low beam flashes
44 Direction signal light switch
45 Horn button
46 Interior light jam switches on front doors
47 Interior lights, with built-in switch
48 Rear window demister (optional)
49 Fuel gauge tank unit
50 Rear direction signal lights
51 Rear parking and stop lights
52 Number plate lights

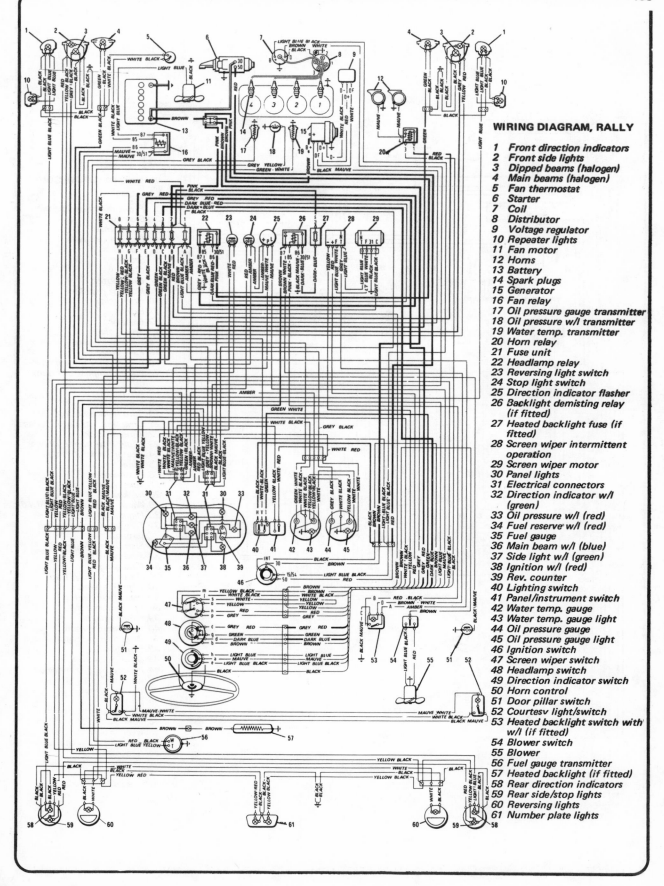

WIRING DIAGRAM, RALLY

1 Front direction indicators
2 Front side lights
3 Dipped beams (halogen)
4 Main beams (halogen)
5 Fan thermostat
6 Starter
7 Coil
8 Distributor
9 Voltage regulator
10 Repeater lights
11 Fan motor
12 Horns
13 Battery
14 Spark plugs
15 Generator
16 Fan relay
17 Oil pressure gauge transmitter
18 Oil pressure w/l transmitter
19 Water temp. transmitter
20 Horn relay
21 Fuse unit
22 Headlamp relay
23 Reversing light switch
24 Stop light switch
25 Direction indicator flasher
26 Backlight demisting relay
  (if fitted)
27 Heated backlight fuse (if
  fitted)
28 Screen wiper intermittent
  operation
29 Screen wiper motor
30 Panel lights
31 Electrical connectors
32 Direction indicator w/l
  (green)
33 Oil pressure w/l (red)
34 Fuel reserve w/l (red)
35 Fuel gauge
36 Main beam w/l (blue)
37 Side light w/l (green)
38 Ignition w/l (red)
39 Rev. counter
40 Lighting switch
41 Panel/instrument switch
42 Water temp. gauge
43 Water temp. gauge light
44 Oil pressure gauge
45 Oil pressure gauge light
46 Ignition switch
47 Screen wiper switch
48 Headlamp switch
49 Direction indicator switch
50 Horn control
51 Door pillar switch
52 Courtesy light/switch
53 Heated backlight switch with
  w/l (if fitted)
54 Blower switch
55 Blower
56 Fuel gauge transmitter
57 Heated backlight (if fitted)
58 Rear direction indicators
59 Rear side/stop lights
60 Reversing lights
61 Number plate lights

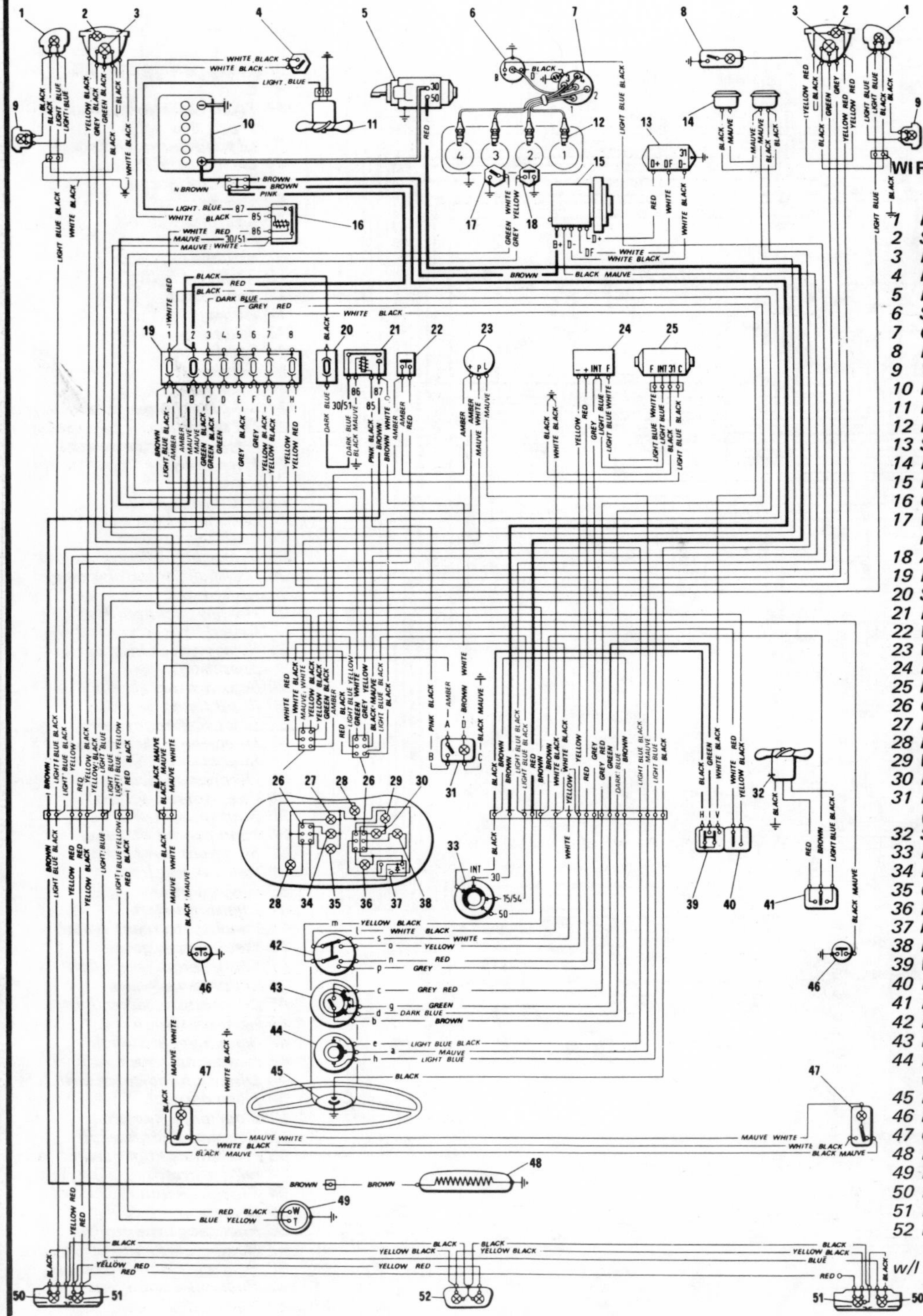

WIRING DIAGRAM, COUPE S

1 Front direction indicators
2 Side lights
3 Headlamps
4 Fan control switch
5 Fan
6 Starter
7 Coil
8 Distributor
9 Voltage regulator
10 Horn relay
11 Horns
12 Battery
13 Spark plugs
14 Repeater lights
15 Fan relay
16 Oil pressure transmitter
17 Water temperature transmitter
18 Alternator
19 Fuse unit
20 Stop light switch
21 Direction indicator flasher
22 Wiper motor
23 Wiper interrupter relay
24 Heater backlight relay
25 Panel lights
26 Connectors
27 Ignition w/l (red)
28 Brake w/l (if fitted)
29 Water temperature w/l(red)
30 Headlamp w/l (blue)
31 Direction indicator w/l
(green)
32 Side light w/l (green)
33 Fuel w/l (red)
34 Fuel gauge
35 Oil pressure w/l (red)
36 Lighting switch
37 Panel light switch
38 Ignition switch
39 Wiper switch
40 Headlamp switch
41 Direction indicator switch
42 Horn switch
43 Door pillar switch
44 Heated backlight switch/
warning light (if fitted)
45 Blower switch
46 Blower
47 Courtesy light/switch
48 Fuel transmitter
49 Heated backlight (if fitted)
50 Rear direction indicators
51 Rear/stop lights
52 Number plate lights

w/l = warning light

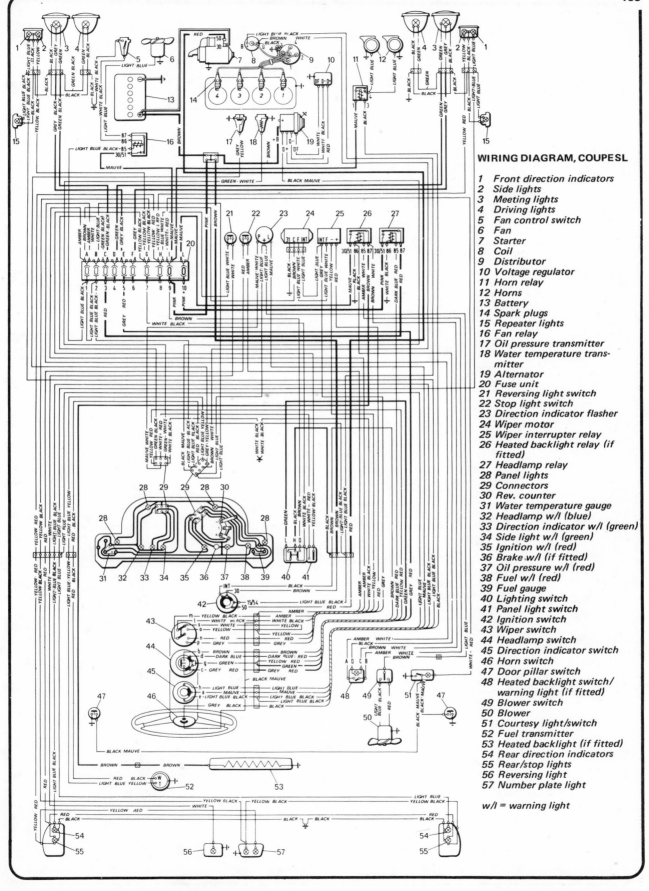

WIRING DIAGRAM, COUPE SL

1 Front direction indicators
2 Side lights
3 Meeting lights
4 Driving lights
5 Fan control switch
6 Fan
7 Starter
8 Coil
9 Distributor
10 Voltage regulator
11 Horn relay
12 Horns
13 Battery
14 Spark plugs
15 Repeater lights
16 Fan relay
17 Oil pressure transmitter
18 Water temperature transmitter
19 Alternator
20 Fuse unit
21 Reversing light switch
22 Stop light switch
23 Direction indicator flasher
24 Wiper motor
25 Wiper interrupter relay
26 Heated backlight relay (if fitted)
27 Headlamp relay
28 Panel lights
29 Connectors
30 Rev. counter
31 Water temperature gauge
32 Headlamp w/l (blue)
33 Direction indicator w/l (green)
34 Side light w/l (green)
35 Ignition w/l (red)
36 Brake w/l (if fitted)
37 Oil pressure w/l (red)
38 Fuel w/l (red)
39 Fuel gauge
40 Lighting switch
41 Panel light switch
42 Ignition switch
43 Wiper switch
44 Headlamp switch
45 Direction indicator switch
46 Horn switch
47 Door pillar switch
48 Heated backlight switch/ warning light (if fitted)
49 Blower switch
50 Blower
51 Courtesy light/switch
52 Fuel transmitter
53 Heated backlight (if fitted)
54 Rear direction indicators
55 Rear/stop lights
56 Reversing light
57 Number plate light

w/l = warning light

Chapter 10 Steering

Contents

Specifications

Steering gear	Rack and pinion
Turns, lock to lock	3½
Adjustment	By shims
Turning circle	33¾ ft (10.3 m)
Steering column	Two part, with two universal joints
Steering box oil	SAE 90 EP
Toe-in (front)	Laden* 0 ± 1/32 in (0 ± 1 mm)
	Unladen: Toe out 3/16 in (5 mm)

*Laden is with 4 occupants and 88 lb (40 kg) luggage.

Caster (loaded)	2¼° ± ¼°
Camber (loaded)	1° ± 20'

Tightening torques:

Track rod ball joint	25.5 lbf. ft	(3.5 kg m)
Knuckle ball joint	58 lb f. ft	(8 kg m)
Nut - steering wheel to column	36 lb f. ft	(5 kg m)
Nut - universal joint on steering column	18 lb f. ft	(2.5 kg m)

1 General description

1 The steering is by rack and pinion. This gives a simple yet rigid layout, ensuring the most precise control, with the minimum of joints to wear.

2 The steering column is articulated, with two universal joints. This allows the steering wheel to be positioned for comfort, despite the rack being very close to the driver. It also "Folds" out of the way in an accident.

3 The rear suspension can have steering effects. The adjustments for the toe-in and camber of this are described in the next chapter.

4 No routine lubrication is needed on the steering. An important item of routine maintenance is the checking and inspection of the steering.

2 Ball joint inspection

1 There are ball joints at the outer ends of the track rods and at the swivels at the bottom of the steering knuckle that carries the hub.

2 In the 3,000 mile (50,000 km) task (item 2.3) of Routine Maintenance is the visual check of the steering. The rubber boots that exclude dirt and water should be inspected to ensure they are properly in position, and not torn. If dirt or water gets into such a joint, it is ruined in a few hundred miles. The joint should be removed, and a new boot fitted without delay.

3 Item 3.15 of the 6,000 mile (10,000 km) Routine Maintenance task is to check the steering for wear. An assistant should wiggle the steering wheel to and fro, just hard enough to make the front wheels move. Watch the ball joints. There should be no visible free movement. Then grasp a front wheel with the hands at 3 and 9 o'clock on the wheel. Work at the wheel hard, to twist it. The rocking should shift the steering wheel. But no lost motion should be felt.

4 There are also ball joints at the inner end of the track rods, where these join to the rack. But these are so well shielded and lubricated that no wear should develop there for considerable mileages.

5 The steering knuckle ball joint is more difficult to check. Again grip the wheel, but this time with both hands at the top. Rock to and fro vigorously, whilst an assistant watches the joint.

6 If any free movement is seen or felt on a ball joint, it must be replaced.

3 Track rod ball joint removal and replacement

1 The ball joints on the outer end of the track rod fit into the steering arm with a tapered pin, held by a nut at the bottom. They have to be removed to disconnect the steering when the suspension is being worked on, as in removing a drive shaft. They have to be taken off the steering arm to fit a new rubber boot. Finally, they have to be taken off for renewal.

2 Jack up the car and remove the front wheel.

3 Undo the self-locking nut on the bottom of the tapered pin under the steering arm (photo).

4 Now extract the taper from the steering arm. This is the difficult bit. It is best to buy a universal steering ball joint separator. This is a small extractor, and over the years will earn its keep, fitting all makes of cars, as ball joints are pretty well standardised. The separator presses the taper out of its seating. Without a separator, the taper must be jumped out by impact. Steady the steering arm with a heavy hammer beside the ball joint. Then hit the steering arm, on the part through which the ball joint taper is fitted. The hit must be a hard blow with a heavy hammer. Note: this hit is from the side. Do not try to drive the ball joint taper out by direct hammer blows, as the threads at the end will be burred over. If the ball joint proves hard to get out either using a separator or a hammer, allow some rust solvent penetrating oil to soak in, then try again.

5 When reconnecting the tapered ball joint pin to the steering arm, grease it.

6 If fitting a new rubber boot to the existing ball joint, wipe away all dirt and old grease. Then smear some molybdenum disulphide grease, such as Castrol MS 3 Grease, over the inside of the joint, fill the rubber boot with it, then fit the boot, squeezing it down tight to force out excess grease and get the boot close in to the joint.

7 If fitting a new ball joint, hold the track rod, undo the locknut, and unscrew the joint from the rod. Grease the track rod threads before fitting the new joint. Check the new joint's rubber boot is properly fitted. Connect the joint to the steering arm. Then check the front wheel toe-in.

4 Steering knuckle ball joint removal and replacement

1 The steering ball joint at the swivel for the steering knuckle on the suspension control arm is an integral part of the latter. If it needs renewal, the whole suspension control arm is replaced. The ball joint need not be removed from the steering knuckle unless it is being renewed. At other times it is easier to remove the suspension arm from the car at its inner end than the knuckle from the ball joint, should it be required to remove the steering knuckle for some other purpose.

2 There is very little room between the ball joint and the drive shaft. Therefore the steering knuckle and suspension arm should be removed from the car still joined by the ball joint, and separated on the bench.

3 Jack up and remove the wheel. The car must be jacked up from the centre point at the front, so both wheels hang free, otherwise the anti-roll bar will be twisted. Support the car securely under the strong points behind the wheel arches.

4 Get an assistant to press hard on the brake pedal, and undo the nuts on the end of the drive shaft, (if no assistant, do this before jacking up).

5 Take the ball joint off the steering arm, as described in the previous section.

6 Undo the nut on the end of the anti-roll bar, and take off the washer on the outside of the rubber bush. On Coupes undo the tie-rod from the suspension arm instead.

7 Take the brake caliper off the knuckle, either by taking out the split pins, wedges, and pads, or direct at the two bolts at the back. Hang the caliper up so the flexible pipe does not get damaged.

8 Take out the pivot bolt at the inner end of the suspension arm, through its bracket on the body.

9 Undo the two bolts at the bottom of the suspension strut, joining it to the steering knuckle.

10 Hold the drive shaft firmly into the transmission, and pull the assembly of steering knuckle and suspension arm off the end. If it proves reluctant to come off, put back temporarily one of the bolts to hang the knuckle on the suspension strut. Squirt penetrating oil into the splined joint of the drive shaft in the hub. Put an old nut on the end of the shaft to protect the threads, and drive it the first part of its movement, to free it. As the arm comes off the anti-roll bar, secure the rubber bush, and note the shims between the second half of the bush and the bar. These must not be changed, as they adjust the caster.

11 Once the suspension arm is off the car, it is easy to get at the ball joint to separate it from the steering knuckle. Undo the nut on the end of its pin.

12 The pin is tapered where it fits into the knuckle, and the problem of removing it is the same as for the track rod ball joints, as described in the previous Section. But in this case the use of a proper separator to extract it is even more strongly recommended. The steering knuckle fitting for this ball joint is much stouter than the one at the end of the steering arm, and jumping it out is going to be very difficult.

13 FIAT supply the complete assembly of suspension arm with the ball joint at the outer end, and the rubber bushes pressed and rivetted into the inner end. So 'overhaul' is simply the matter of buying the new arm.

14 On reassembly make sure the rubber boot on the ball joint is in position. Grease the joint's taper, the splines of the drive shaft, and the pivot bolt at the inner end of the suspension arm, so they all fit easily, and will come off easily another time.

15 Ensure no grease gets on the rubber bushes of the arm and the anti-roll bar. Tighten their nuts after the jack has been lowered, so they are clamped up in the loaded position.

16 Recheck the tightness of all nuts after a road test.

17 Reset the front wheel toe-in.

5 Rack and pinion removal and refitting

1 Inside the car remove the pinch bolt through the bottom end of the steering column, where it joins to the pinion.

2 Jack up the front of the car, and remove both wheels. Make sure the car is secure, as you will be working underneath. Check also there is plenty of room between the car and the garage wall on the right, to bring the rack out sideways.

3 Remove the spare wheel.

4 Remove the shield over the transmission (not fitted to some cars).

5 Undo the ball joints at the ends of the track rods from the steering arms, as described in Section 3.

6 Take out the two bolts from the two 'U' clamps that hold the rack to the car body.

7 Pull the rack towards the engine to disengage the pinion from the steering column. Once it is clear, pass it out to the right side of the car.

8 Before refitting the rack, fill it with oil and check the adjustment of the damping yoke as described in subsequent Sections.

9 Inside the car, turn the steering wheel to the straight ahead position. Get the rack to its midway position by turning it fully one way, then counting the turns of the pinion, wind it fully to the other extreme. Then bring it back half the number of turns. This must be done accurately, counting to about a 1/16th of a turn. The pinion can be turned by padding its splines, and snapping on a selfgrip wrench of the 'Mole' type.

10 Refit the rack from the right hand side, and mount it in the clamps, making sure the rubber packing pads are in good condition. Note the clamps and pads are handed left and right.

11 Before reconnecting the track rods, turn the steering wheel from lock to lock, to recheck the column is correctly aligned. Then put back in the pinch bolt at the bottom of the column.

6 Rack and pinion overhaul

1 The rack and pinion should last for long mileages, particularly if the rubber boots at the end are never damaged. The most likely need is to reset the damping yoke after a long mileage. This is described in the next Section. If the rack and pinion and the ball joints at the inner end all seem worn, then it is worth considering replacing the complete assembly. This is certainly worth while if there is accident damage.

2 Dismantle the rack by first removing the track rods from the inner ball joints rods of the rack. Note that there are flats on the latter so they can be held by an open-jawed spanner.

3 Remove the clamps holding the rubber boots to the rack housing. Early cars also had clamps holding the boot round its narrow end, but these are not necessary on later ones due to ribs in the rubber that ensure a proper seal.

4 Take off the rubber boots.

5 Take off the clamps that held the rack to the car, and their rubber packing.

6 Take off its cover plate, and remove the rack damping yoke with spring, and shims, and oil sealing ring. (See Fig.10.3).

7 Remove the two bolts holding the pinion bearing plate to the housing. Take out the pinion, with oil seal, gasket, shim and top ball bearing.

8 Mount the rack housing in a vice, but be careful not to crush it.

9 Unstake the lock for the lock nuts for the adjustable head for the ball joints at the ends of the rack. The lock nut is the inner one. Undo the lock nuts themselves. (See Fig.10.4).

10 Take off the ends of the rack housing the adjustable heads for the ball joints, bringing with them the ball joints, and their sockets and springs.

11 Slide the rack out of the housing.

12 Take out the lower bearing for the pinion.

13 Check all parts for signs of excessive wear or damage, or

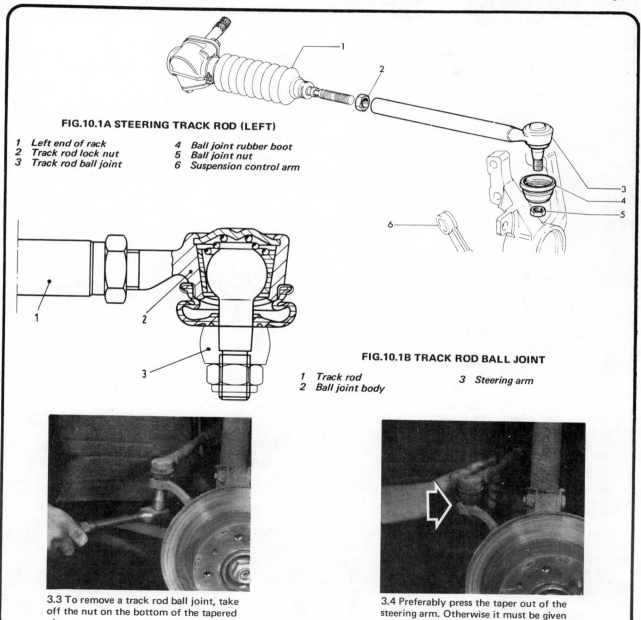

FIG.10.1A STEERING TRACK ROD (LEFT)

1 *Left end of rack*
2 *Track rod lock nut*
3 *Track rod ball joint*
4 *Ball joint rubber boot*
5 *Ball joint nut*
6 *Suspension control arm*

FIG.10.1B TRACK ROD BALL JOINT

1 *Track rod*
2 *Ball joint body*
3 *Steering arm*

3.3 To remove a track rod ball joint, take off the nut on the bottom of the tapered pin.

3.4 Preferably press the taper out of the steering arm. Otherwise it must be given a hard hammer blow on the side.

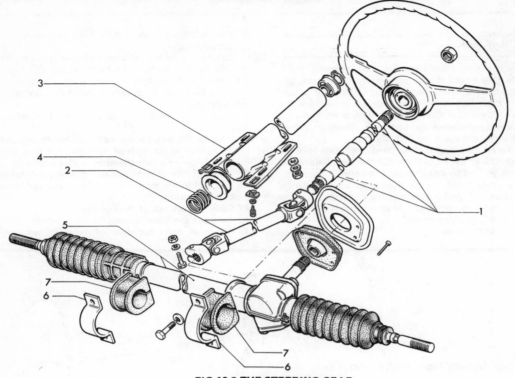

FIG.10.2 THE STEERING GEAR

1 Upper column
2 Lower column
3 Upper column outer tube
4 Bearing spring
5 Rack and pinion

6 Rack mounting clamps left and right
7 Mounting padding, left and right

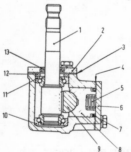

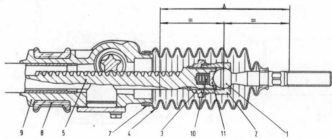

FIG.10.3 SECTION THROUGH STEER-ING RACK AT PINION AND DAMPING YOKE

1 Pinion
2 Cover
3 Gasket
4 Yoke shims
5 Spring
6 Yoke cover
7 Seal
8 Yoke
9 Rack
10 Lower bearing
11 Top bearing
12 Pinion shim
13 Pinion seal

FIG.10.4 SECTIONS OF RACK AND PINION

1 Ball joint rods
2 Adjustable ball joint heads
3 Lock nuts
4 Boots
5 Rack
6 Rack bushes
7 Boot clip

8 Rubber mounting pads
9 Housing
10 Ball joint spring
11 Ball seat. Rack travel = A = 5.118 in (130 mm). Ball joint rod solid angle = 60º

corrosion. New gaskets, a new seal for the pinion shaft, and new rubber boots should be fitted.

14 As all parts are refitted, lubricate them thoroughly with an SAE 90 EP oil. Take care the rack teeth do not scrape the housing bearings as they are slid in.

15 Fit the pinion bearing plate with too many shims, and screw in its bolts gently to settle bearings. Release the bolts until they are finger tight. Measure the gap between the housing and plate. Measure with a micrometer the thickness of the gasket. Calculate the thickness of shims needed. The shims should be thicker than the gap between housing and plate, allowing for the gasket, by 0.001 - 0.005 in. (0.025 - 0.13 mm). Shims are available in four thicknesses from 0.12 - 2.5 mm. The pinion should be able to turn freely, without jerks, and without stiffness exceeding 0.3 lbf. ft (0.04 kg m). There should not be any end float.

16 Reassemble the ball joints to the ends of the rack. Tighten the adjustable heads till a torque of 1½ to 3¼ lbf ft (0.2 to 0.5 kg m) is needed to turn the ball joints in their seats. Check that the track rods can rotate through the solid angle of a cone of 60°. Then lock the heads with the lock nuts, and stake them in position.

17 Adjust the damping yoke, and refill with oil as described in subsequent Sections.

18 If a delicate torque measurer for the small torques mentioned above is not available, one can readily be rigged up using a known weight, such as 1 lb of cheese, on a stick of known length (half being either side of centre to keep it balanced).

7   Steering rack damping yoke adjustment

1   The yoke in the rack housing presses the rack into mesh with the pinion. This cuts out any backlash between the gears. Also due to its pressure it introduces some stiffness into the rack,

which cuts out excessive reaction from the road to the steering wheel.

2   In due course, wear reduces the pressure excerted by the damping yoke. The pressure is controlled by the yoke cover plate and a spring.

3   The yoke setting should be reset if the rack has been dismantled for overhaul.

4   The need for resetting of the yoke if the car has run a long mileage, but the rack is not being dismantled, is not easy to detect. On bumpy roads the shock induced through the steering will give a feeling of play, and sometimes faint clonking can be heard. In extreme cases free play in the steering may be felt, though this is rare. If the steering is compared with that of a new rack on another car, the lack of friction damping is quite apparent in the ease of movement of the steering wheel of the worn one.

5   Access to the yoke with the rack fitted is a little difficult, and if the car is dirty underneath, there is risk of this getting into the rack. So it is much easier done on the bench, removing the race as described in Section 5.

6   Turn the steering to the straight ahead position.

7   Take the cover plate off the damping yoke, remove the spring and shims, and refit it. Refit the bolts, but only tighten them enough to hold the yoke firmly against the rack.

8   Turn the pinion through 180° either way to settle the rack.

9   Measure the gap between the cover plate and the rack housing. (See Fig.10.6).

10 Select shims to a thickness 0.002 to 0.005 in. (0.5 to 0.13 mm) more than the measured gap. (Shims are available 0.1 and 0.15 mm thick).

11 Remove the cover plate again, and refit the spring.

12 Smear each shim with soft setting gasket compound, and fit them and the cover plate.

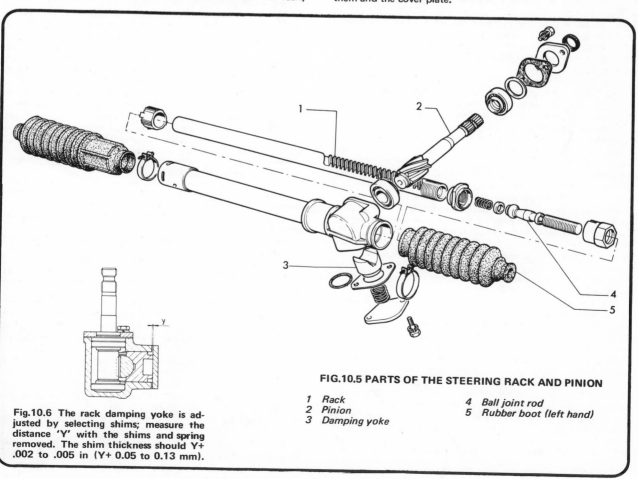

Fig.10.6 The rack damping yoke is adjusted by selecting shims; measure the distance 'Y' with the shims and spring removed. The shim thickness should Y+ .002 to 005 in (Y+ 0.05 to 0.13 mm).

FIG.10.5 PARTS OF THE STEERING RACK AND PINION

1   Rack
2   Pinion
3   Damping yoke
4   Ball joint rod
5   Rubber boot (left hand)

8 Steering rack lubrication

1   The steering rack and pinion is lubricated for 'life'. If it is dismantled, it must be reassembled with a new supply.

2   The lubricant is gear oil of SAE 90 EP, such as Castrol Hypoy B. The amount is 0.14 litre (0.24 imp pt, 0.3 US pt, 4¾ fl oz).

3   The oil is inserted into the rack at the pinion end, that is the driver's end. If this is being done on the bench before refitting the rack to the car, fit the rubber boot to the other end, pour in the oil at the pinion end, then fit that boot. Turn the rack to and fro to spread the oil and check the boots are not being blown out by excess oil.

4   If there has been a leak, and it is required to refill the rack on the car, undo the rubber boots, and allow any old oil left to drain out, so there will not be too much in it after refilling.

5   Refit the boot on the passenger's side. Jack up the car very high on the driver's side.

6   Pour the oil into the end of the rack and the boot, and quickly refit the boot to prevent any dribbling out.

7   Turn the rack from lock to lock to distribute the oil and check the rubber boots are relaxed, and showing no signs of the rack being over full.

8   Refit the clamping clips to the large ends of the rubber boots. (On current cars there are no clamps at the smaller, outer, ends). Position the tightening screws, if doing this on the bench, so their heads can be reached from below after the rack has been refitted to the car.

9 Front wheel toe-in

1   Garages have accurate gauges, so measure this readily. But even so there is possibility of error. Measuring at home is far less accurate, but time is at less of a premium, so it can be done often enough to get several consistant readings to know that the setting is correct.

2   If the car is old, and you have not set its steering yourself, the steering wheel and track rods may be off centre. It must be established that the steering rack is in the centre of its travel when the wheels are straight, and that then the steering wheel is straight too.

3   Turn the steering wheel from lock to lock, and find the rack's centre. Check the steering wheel is now straight. If not, unclamp the bottom of the steering column, removing the pinch bolt. Undo the clamps under the car holding the rack to the body.

Slide the column off the oinion shaft, and refit it straight. Now drive the car on the road, and see where the steering wheel is when travelling straight. This will tell you which track rod needs shortening, and which lengthening. Do this, altering each the same amount. This must be done accurately. Mark the track rods with chalk so the amount turned can be seen. Try only one turn at first. A little makes a lot of difference. The relative length of the two track rods can be measured too if the steering is a long way out; This is done by measuring the length of thread showing on the rod from track rod to track ball joint.

4   Now check the toe-in as follows. This is all that will normally be needed, once the foregoing setting has been done once and for all.

5   Check the tyre pressures. Then set up on level ground the measuring bars as shown in Fig.10.7.

6   The measuring bars must be very straight. Very useful ones are aluminium alloy strip, 1 in. by ¼ in. by 5 ft. On them put marks for the hub position 1 ft from the end. At the other end mark off a length twice the diameter of the wheel rim.

7   With the steering in the straight ahead position put the bars on blocks, or oil cans, or some such, so that they are at hub height. Arrange them to lie along the wheels, the marks for the hubs level with the hubs both vertically and horizontally. To make the bars firm, lean something against the bar opposite the hub so that it is pressed against the tyre on both sides.

8   Measure the distance across the gap between the two bars at their far end. Compare this with the distance apart at the nearer mark. The difference is twice the toe-in or toe-out. Make sure which it is you have got, toe-out is what is needed in the unladen condition.

9   Take another reading. It will probably vary from the first. If so take another to get an average. These subsequent readings must be after moving the car forward. Do not move the car back, as the wheels will push on the steering the wrong way. As the wheel will not be perfectly true, readings must be taken at various parts of the rims to get a fair sample.

10 If a correction is needed, adjust both track rods if the steering is accurately centralised. If it should be slightly off centre, adjust that one which will get it nearer straight. Mark the track rod with chalk so the amount turned can be seen. A quarter of a turn makes quite a difference. Then recheck.

11 Adjustment is made by screwing the rod of the ball joint on the end of the rack into or out of the track rod. Hold the track rod to prevent it turning, and undo the lock nut. Put a spanner on the rack ball joint rod, and turn that. If the rubber boot wrinkles up, turn this back to its original position. Carefully tighten the lock nut so the setting is not disturbed.

12 Mention has been made of ensuring the steering wheel is straight before adjusting the toe-in. It will probably prove impossible to get it quite straight. Also, different road cambers, or side winds, will affect the amount of steering applied. A careful note should be made of the steering wheel angle when driving on an absolutely straight and camber free road, without any wind. Then if a kerb is nudged, and the toe-in perhaps altered, the steering wheel angle can be checked to give a guide as whether there is any misalignment.

10 Camber and caster of front wheels

1   It is not practical for the owner to check front wheel camber. Camber is the amount the top of the wheel slopes out. It is not adjustable, and will normally only be upset by accident damage. Realignment of the body and suspension mounting points must then be done by a firm with the jigs, measuring equipment, and experience of such work.

2   Again, it is not practicable for the owner to do anything about caster. Caster is the arrangement whereby the ground contact point of the wheel is behind its centre of pivot for steering, so the wheel is self-centering. Caster is adjusted by shifting the lower mounting forward or back, in relation to the top mounting in the mudguard. This shift is achieved by altering the shims at the end of the anti-roll bar (or altering the tie-rod on Coupes). Such an adjustement is easily made. The difficulty with caster is the actual measurement of the angle. Small variations of caster are of minor consequence. The owner can limit these by always ensuring the same shims are kept on the end of the anti-roll bar. Again, after accident damage, the FIAT agent's skill and equipment should be used.

11 Steering wheel removal

1   Undo the two screws on the underside of the steering wheel. The horn button and cover should now be loose.

2   Unclip the cover from the button and then remove each, separately.

3   Remove the screws holding the steering column sleeves, and take these off.

4   Undo the nut at the centre of the steering wheel.

5   Pull the wheel off the column.

12 Upper steering column

1   The steering column is made in two Sections. The top part is mounted on two ball bearings. The lower part has a pair of universal joints, and connects the upper column to the steering pinion.

2   To remove the upper column, first disconnect a battery lead. Then remove the steering wheel as described in the previous Section.

3   Disconnect the electrical connections to the fittings on the column, at the connectors alongside.

4   Remove the switches from the column that are in the indicator switch group.

5   Remove the pinch bolt through the universal joint where the two parts of the column meet.

6 Remove the nuts holding the column supporting bracket, holding the upper column by hand.

7 Move the upper column away, and pull it off the lower column. Catch the spring and ring below the bottom bearing.

8 On the beach, take off the split ring at the top end of the upper column. Then push the column first one way then the other within the outer column, to get the bearings out.

9 Before reassembly, grease the bearings.

10 Ensure the wheels are in the straight ahead position, then engage the splines on the lower column with the wheel straight. If it is found difficult to reassemble due to the spring at the bottom end of the upper shaft, leave off the circlip at the top end until after the upper and lower columns are rejoined.

13 Lower steering column

1 Once the upper steering column has been removed, the lower

follows easily.

2 Take out the pinch bolt securing the bottom universal joint to the pinion shaft of the steering gear, then pull the shaft off.

14 Steering column lock

1 The ignition switch is combined with a steering lock.

2 If the lock jams, try turning the column gently, to take the load off the locking pawl, whilst working the key. Give the lock and column a squirt of oil from an aerosol of easing oil.

3 If the lock has to be changed, difficulty will be experienced getting out the screws, as these are 'burglar proof'. When the switch is fitted, the centre of three screws is tightened until its head shears off. To remove it, a hole must be drilled down the bolt, and then an 'Easiout' inserted, to screw it off. If no 'Easiout' is available, the old bolt must be completely drilled away.

FIG.10.8 UPPER STEERING COLUMN MOUNTINGS

1 *Nuts securing mounting bracket*
2 *Pinch bolt for top universal joint on lower column*
3 *Lower column*
4 *Electrical connections*
5 *Bearing spring*

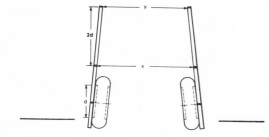

$$\frac{x - y}{2} = \text{Toe-in}$$

Fig.10.7 Toe-in measurement

9.11 When undoing the locknut at the inner end of the track rod, hold the rod with a spanner, so no stress is put on the ball joint pin at the outer end.

SECTION A-A

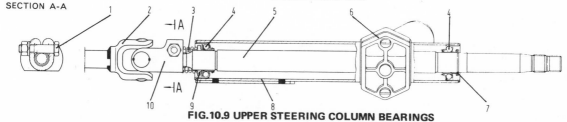

FIG.10.9 UPPER STEERING COLUMN BEARINGS

1 *Pinch bolt*
2 *Lower column*
3 *Bearing spring*
4 *Bearings*
5 *Upper column*
6 *Ignition switch/steering lock*
7 *Circlip*
8 *Outer column tube*
9 *Bearing ring*
10 *Universal joint*

15 Fault-finding

Before assuming that the steering mechanism is at fault when mishandling is experienced make sure that the trouble is not caused by:—

1 Binding brakes
2 Incorrect mix of radial and crossply tyres
3 Incorrect tyre pressures
4 Misalignment of the body and rear suspension

Symptom	Reason/s	Remedy
Steering wheel can be moved before any sign of movement of the wheels is apparent	Wear in the steering linkage, gear and column coupling	Check movement in all joints and steering gear and overhaul and renew as required.
Vehicle difficult to steer in a consistent straight line; wandering: unstable on corners	As above Wheel alignment incorrect (indicated by excessive or uneven tyre wear) Rear suspension toe-in camber wrong Front wheel hub bearings loose or worn Worn ball joints, track rods or suspension arms	As above Check toe-in. See Chapter 11. Adjust or renew as necessary. Renew as necessary.
Steering stiff and heavy	Incorrect wheel alignment (indicated by excessive or uneven tyre wear) Excessive wear or seizure in one or more of the joints in the steering linkage or suspension arm ball joints Excessive wear in the steering gear unit	Check wheel alignment. Renew as necessary. Dismantle, check, relubricate the rack and pinion.
Wheel wobble and vibration	Road wheels out of balance Road wheels buckled	Balance wheels. (See Chapter 11). Check for damage.
Excessive pitching and rolling on corners and during braking	Defective shock absorbers	Check and renew as necessary. (See Chapter 11).

Chapter 11 Front and rear suspension

Contents

Specifications

Front suspension ... ... Macpherson strut

Front spring length: saloon:—
- Free length about ... ... 16.8 in   (428 mm)
- Class A under load ... ... 270 - 290 kg more than 9.44 in   (240 mm)
- Class B under load ... ... 270 - 290 kg less than 9.44 in   (240 mm)
- Minimum load to achieve above length ... ... 255 kg

(For front toe-in etc. see Chapter 10).

Rear suspension ... ... Transverseleaf: independant
- Rear spring: saloon ... ... Two leaves with interleaf spaces
  - Camber under load of 330 kg ... ... 13 - 19 mm
- Rear spring: estate car ... ... Three leaves with interleaf spaces
  - Camber under load of 390 kg ... ... 10 - 16 mm

- Rear camber: loaded ... ... $- 2^o 40'$ to $- 3^o 20'$
  -       unloaded ... ... $- 30'$ to $+ 10'$
- Rear toe-in: loaded or unladen ... ... 1/8 to 1/4 inch   3 to 6.5 mm

Wheels ... ... Pressed disc 4½ J x 13 inch
- Tyres ... ... Radial ply   145 SR x 13
- Tyre pressures: saloon   Front ... ... 26 lb f./in^2 (1.8 kg/cm^2)
  -                 Rear ... ... 24 lb f./in^2 (1.7 kg/cm^2)
- Tyre pressures: estate   Front ... ... 27 lb f./in^2 (1.9 kg/cm^2)
  -                Rear ... ... 28 lb f./in^2 (2.0 kg/cm^2)

Maximum wheel out of true ... ... 0.06 in   (1.5 mm)

Estate car wheels: Thicker metal: marked by 5 mm hole one projection for fixing hub cap.

Tightening torques:

	lb f. ft	kg m
Wheel studs	51	7
Nuts; hubs to stub axle/drive shaft	101	14
Front suspension arm to body	18	2.5
Suspension arm to anti-roll bar	43	6
Anti-roll bar to body	22	3
Front strut mounting to body	7	1
Front strut mounting to knuckle	43	6
Brake caliper to knuckle	36	5
Shock absorber spindle top	18	2.5
Rear suspension arm to spring	22	3
Rear suspension arm to hub	58	8
Suspension arm pivot to body	36	5

Tightening torques continued						lb f. ft	kg m
Suspension arm pivot ends ...	...	...	...	...	...	32½	4.5
Brake back plate to hub ...	...	...	...	...	...	18	2.5
Rear hub to shock absorber	...	...	...	...	...	43½	6

1 General description

1 At a time when many cars use rubber or air as suspension, the FIAT is conventional in that the springs are steel. Nor are there refinements such as interconnection front to rear. However the spring rates chosen give a good ride. Because of the suspension's simplicity, it is easy to dismantle.

2 The suspension is independant all round. There is an anti-roll bar at the front, which on saloons and estate cars also acts as the fore and aft tie-rod for the suspension. Coupes have no anti-roll bar, so tie-rods are fitted instead. The front anti-roll bar on the Rally is stronger than on the normal saloon. The rear suspension uses one transverse leaf spring. This is not mounted at its centre, but in two clamps to each side. This gives an anti-roll action to the spring. The estate car rear spring is stronger than that on the saloon.

3 The rear suspension should seldom need attention. But when it does, the setting of the camber and toe-in is important, otherwise the steering effect of the rear wheels will affect the handling, and wear might be bad. Dismantling of the front suspension is sometimes needed, not because it wears, but to remove the drive shafts, or allow the transmission to be taken off the engine.

4 The handling of the car, and its reaction to road noises, have been specifically designed for the use of radial ply tyres. Tyres of other types should NOT be used.

2 Suspension inspection and checks

1 Checking the suspension is part of the 6,000 mile (10,000 km) task.

2 Inspect the outside of the shock absorbers for leaks, and check their operation by bouncing.

3 With the car parked on level ground check that it sits level from left to right, and does not appear to be drooping at one end, particularly down at the back.

4 Examine all the rubber bushes of the suspension arms and rear spring mountings. The rubber should be firm, not softened by oil or cracked by weathering. The pin pivotted in the bush should be held central, and not able to make metal to metal contact.

5 Check the outside of the springs. If rusting, they should be sprayed with oil.

6 Check the tightness of all nuts, particularly those holding the front suspension strut to the steering knuckle, and the rear shock absorber to the hub.

7 Grip the top of each wheel, in turn, and rock vigorously. Any looseness in the bearings, or the suspension can be felt, or failed rubber bushes giving metal to metal contact heard.

8 Free wheel slowly with the engine switched off, and listen for unusual noises.

3 Dismantling the front suspension

1 Sometimes the front suspension will need taking off to undo the drive shafts. In that case there is no need to remove the front suspension strut. At other times, the way work is tackled will depend on whether a steering ball joint removing tool is available. If it is the steering knuckle can be readily detached from the suspension arm. If not then it is going to prove easier to remove the arm from the car, then take the arm off the knuckle. Again, it is easier to take the anti-roll bar off the suspension arm if the arms are removed from both sides, and the anti-roll bar from the car, but this assumes both sides need attention. In

tackling a particular job, only go as far as is necessary, depending on the work needing doing, and the tools and space available.

2 Before jacking up, slacken the nuts on the outer ends of the drive shafts.

3 Jack the car up quite high, and support it firmly under the reinforced points behind the wheel arches, and the central jacking point at the front, and make sure definitely it is secure. Remove the front wheels.

4 If the front strut is to be removed without dismantling anything else, undo the two bolts at the bottom of the suspension strut, (photos) that hold it to the steering knuckle. Then undo the three nuts on the studs through the mudguard. Lift out the strut.

5 To completely dismantle the suspension leave the strut on until later.

6 Disconnect the steering ball joint on the outer end of the track rod from the steering arm. See Chapter 10/3 for methods of freeing these.

7 Take the brake caliper off. Either pull out the two spring clips and the wedges, or undo the two bolts holding the whole assembly to the knuckle. See Chapter 8 for details. Tie the caliper up with string so the flexible pipe will not get pulled.

8 Take out the bolt through the inner end pivot of the suspension arm, at the bracket on the body. (photo).

9 Undo the two bolts at the bottom of the suspension strut that hold it to the steering knuckle.

10 Detach the front suspension on the other side of the car in the same way.

11 Remove the two drive shafts from the hubs as described in Chapter 7. If leaving their inner ends in the transmission, tie them in. Then temporarily put back one bolt to hold the knuckle to the bottom of the suspension strut.

12 Undo the two brackets at the front of the car in which the anti-roll bar pivots. First take off the front shield, then take out the two bolts at each bracket. One bolt is threaded into the body; the other has a nut. On Coupe instead of taking off the anti-roll bar, take off the tie-rod at each side.

13 Take out the bolt temporarily put back either side, holding the knuckle to the struts, and lower the complete suspension to the ground. Undo the struts by taking off the three nuts from their fixing to the mudguard at their top.

14 Now the suspension arms can be taken off the anti-roll bar. Undo the nut on the end of the bar. Pull off the arm, noting the position of the washers, bushes, and the shims. The shims adjust the caster, and must not be moved. See Chapter 10.

15 Take the steering knuckle off the arm, again referring to Chapter 10/4.

16 Reassembly is the reverse process. Grease all bolts before fitting them, so they will be easier to strip next time. If any of the rubber bushes have been renewed, check the toe-in. (See Chapter 10). After road test, recheck all bolts for tightness.

17 When refitting the bolt at the inner end of the suspension arm, do not tighten it until the jack has been lowered, so the bush will be clamped in its relaxed position at the static height, so twist in it will be minimised.

4 Renewing front strut spring or shock absorber

1 The front suspension strut consists of a concentric spring and shock absorber. As an assembly the strut is simplicity itself to remove, as described in the last Section. Only the bolts at the bottom and the top have to be removed. But those at the top are for its mounting to the mudguard. When removed from the car, the shock absorber will be held at full extension by the spring.

2 To release the spring the load must be taken off the shock absorber, then the nut can be removed from the shock absorber's

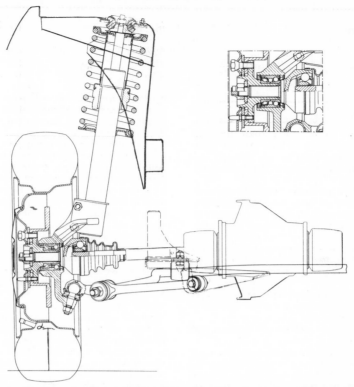

Fig.11.1 The left front wheel and suspension, for cars after 569417, with a hub bearing nut. Inset is the hub of earlier type, on which the bearings were held in the knuckle by a circlip

3.4a To remove the front strut it is only necessary to undo the two bolts at the bottom,

3.4b and the three nuts at the top. Do not undo the centre nut till the spring is in a special press/clamp.

3.8 The rest of the suspension is released by taking out the pivot bolt at the inner end of the suspension arm, and then dismounting the anti-roll bar.

3.9 Removing the bolts at the bottom of the strut last of all.

3.12 The Coupe has a simple tie-bar instead of an anti-roll bar.

central nut, and the spring allowed to expand. This must be done in a special spring compressor. Without the use of one of these, the nut must not be taken of the shock absorber rod, lest the spring fly out uncontrollably. Many makes of car have Macpherson strut suspension, so if a FIAT agent is not near where this can be done, some other should be able to release the spring.

3   The most common reason for needing to separate the two will be to replace the shock absorber, as this has a shorter life than the spring. Even so, the spring should be carefully examined when free, as should all the components of the bush at the top, and the spring seat at the bottom.

4   Springs come in two grades of length. It will usually be found that the one on the driver's side will have settled more than the other. This one alone could be replaced by a short one, class B, which will then match the old one on the passengers side better. The springs are marked with paint on the outside of the coils at their centre, yellow for class A, green for class B.

5   Renewing front suspension arm bushes

1   The rubber bushes at the inner end of the suspension control arm should be renewed if they perish or soften, which will show in the way they curl round at the ends, and the way the arm is not held centrally on the bolt.

2   The metal central tube and end washers are peened into position. (See Fig.11.4).

3   This peening is done in a powerful press with a load of 1 Ton. Unless this is done properly the bush as a whole will be too long, and it will prove difficult, or impossible, to get it into its mounting. The FIAT agent should therefore be given the job of putting in the new bushes.

4   However, if the rubber bushes need renewal, the condition of the ball joint at the outer end of the arm, for the steering

knuckle, must be suspect, and it may well be worth replacing that too. The complete assembly of arm, knuckle, with the rubber bushes pressed in properly, is serviced as a spare by FIAT. See Section 4 in the previous Chapter.

6   Overhauling the front hub bearings

1   Normally the front wheels should be silent, have neglible rim-rock, and turn smoothly. Incipient failure of the bearings will show by any of these signs. The bearings are sealed for life. They are a press fit in the hub, and need such force to extract them that this should only be done to replace them, as they will be overloaded by the stress.

2   The construction of the hub is shown in Fig.11.1.

3   First dismantle the suspension as described in Section 3 to remove the steering knuckle from the car.

4   Then take the brake disc off the hub by undoing the bolt and long-headed wheel aligning bolt.

5   Now the hub must be pressed out of the bearings. It is a tight fit, and may have rusted in. A good soak in penetrating oil will help. The steering knuckle must be well supported whilst the hub is pressed from the inside. The press mandrel must only rest on the hub, not the bearing inner race. Again, the help of a FIAT agent is recommended, as they have the special press tools.

6   Once the hub is out, the bearing locking collar on the outside can be reached. This is screwed in, and should have been staked in position with a punch. The staking should be cut away, and the nut undone. Early cars had a circlip. Again, a press is needed to get out the old bearings.

7   Clean and rub off all rust from the knuckle bearing housing, and the hub.

8   Press in the new bearings, only doing so on the outer race. Use a new bearing nut, and stake it in position.

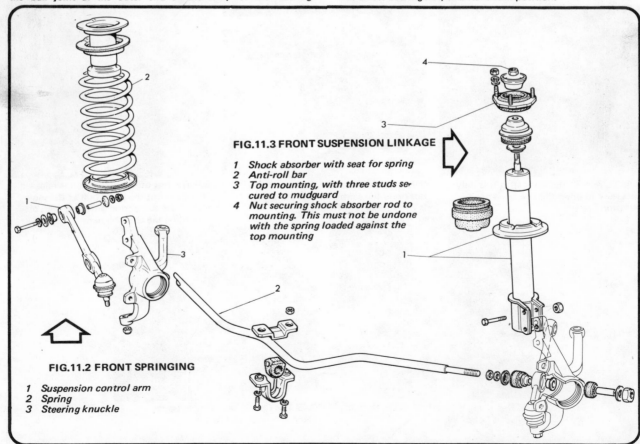

FIG.11.3 FRONT SUSPENSION LINKAGE

1   *Shock absorber with seat for spring*
2   *Anti-roll bar*
3   *Top mounting, with three studs secured to mudguard*
4   *Nut securing shock absorber rod to mounting. This must not be undone with the spring loaded against the top mounting*

FIG.11.2 FRONT SPRINGING

1   *Suspension control arm*
2   *Spring*
3   *Steering knuckle*

7 Removing the rear spring

1 The rear spring can be removed without disturbing the rest of the rear suspension.

2 Jack up, and block the body firmly on stands under the body strong points to support it safely so that work is comfortable underneath.

3 Disconnect the torsion bar for the rear brake regulator from the centre of the spring on early cars that have it actually connected to the spring. (Cars up to spares No 459,999). It is disconnected by taking out the split pin and taking the rod off the spring fitting.

4 Put a jack under the left end of the spring, and take it's weight so that no load is on the bracket under the suspension arm that normally holds the spring. (See Fig.11.5), (inset Section A-A).

5 Undo the two bolts that hold the spring bracket to the underside of the suspension arm, and take it off. (photos).

6 Repeat for the bracket on the other side of the car.

7 Take off the two inner brackets holding the spring to the body, and remove the spring, passing it over to the left to clear the exhaust.

8 The spring is refitted in reverse order, but ensure the spring is mounted centrally. (See Fig.11.7).

8 Overhauling the rear spring

1 The conditions of the spring leaves and the interleaf lining can be assessed with the spring still on the car. The height of the car when unladen is a good guide of the amount the leaves may have settled. With the weight off the wheels the leaves can be parted enough to assess their condition.

2 If a leaf is cracked or broken, this is easy to see, and the leaf must be replaced. If the leaves have lost their camber, it is possible to have them reset, and the heat treatment done again, by specialist blacksmith firms. Otherwise new leaves must be fitted.

3 New interleaf material will be needed after the car has run extended mileage, somewhat earlier than resetting of the leaves becomes really essential, and it is the need for these that will make the complete overhaul of the spring necessary on older cars. If it is not in good condition, the interleaf friction becomes high, and will vary between wet weather and dry. It will be prone to squeak when dry.

4 Having decided what needs to be done, get the parts, including new spring clips. These are likely to break whilst being taken off. Also get new rubbers for all the mountings. (See Fig.11.6).

5 Undo the spring clips, and part the leaves.

6 The spring leaves' rubbing surfaces should be smooth. If wear has made the leaves noticeably thin at any point.

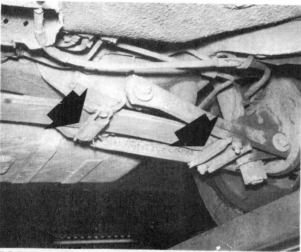

7.5 The rear spring is simply held by two clamps on either side.

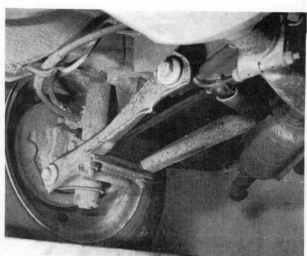

7.7 These can be removed when the load at the end is taken by a jack, and the spring threaded out over the exhaust.

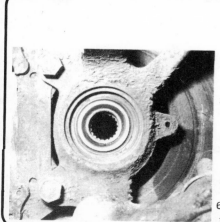

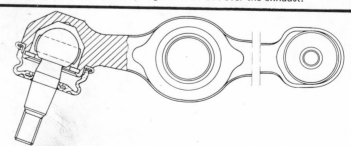

Fig.11.4 Sections of the front suspension control arm

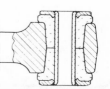

6.1 The front hub and bearings are pressed into place, and their renewal is difficult.

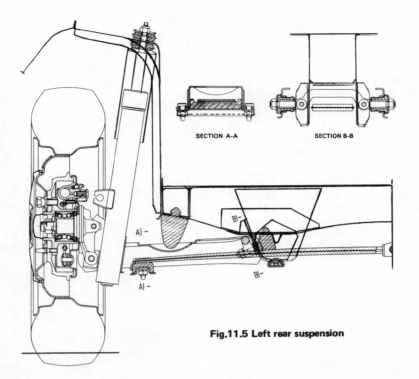

SECTION A-A   SECTION B-B

Fig.11.5 Left rear suspension

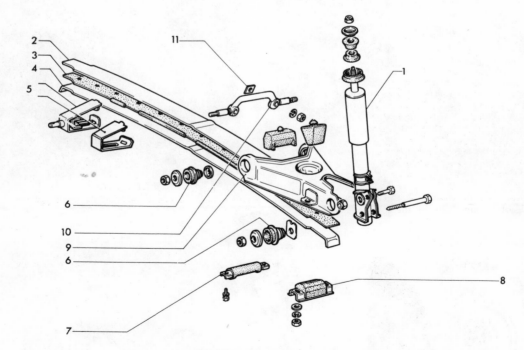

FIG.11.6 REAR SUSPENSION PARTS

1	Shock absorber	4	Main leaf	7	Spring securing brackets	10	Pivot for arm bushes
2	Spring top leaf	5	Spring clips	8	Spring securing brackets	11	Shims for adjusting toe-in
3	Interleaf lining	6	Arm bush	9	Suspension control arm		and camber

9 Removing rear suspension control arms and shock absorbers

1 Jack up the rear of the car, and support it on blocks under the body strong points.

2 Remove the wheel.

3 Disconnect the brake flexible pipe at the body end. Undo the end of the handbrake cable from the brakes. See Chapter 8 for details of this.

4 On cars after spares No. 460,000 disconnect the brake regulator torsion bar from its bracket on the left suspension arm taking out the spring pin.

5 Put a jack under the end of the spring, and take the load off the suspension.

6 Undo the two nuts holding the bracket under the spring to the suspension arm. Then lower the jack.

7 Inside the boot take the nut off the top of the shock absorber rod. An assistant will probably be needed outside to prevent the shock absorber from turning.

8 Remove the nuts on the top two studs that hold the suspension arm pivot shaft to the body. The assembly of arm, shock absorber and hub can now be lifted off. Secure the shims that are on the two studs on the body for the pivot: these control the rear wheel camber and toe-in. (photos).

9 Undo the two bolts that pass through the eyes on the rear hub knuckle. Take the suspension arm and the shock absorber off the knuckle. Secure the shims that were between the shock absorber and the bushes of the arm, noting which came from each side.

10 Overhauling the rear suspension arm

1 The rear suspension will normally be dismantled to allow new shock absorbers to be fitted. Such an opportunity should be taken to examine the rubber bushes at the inner and outer ends. Their condition can be assessed by the rubber showing at the edges. This should be firm: not perished by weathering, or softened by oil. The pin through the bush should be held centrally, and not allow metal to metal contact.

2 The bushes at the outer end can be removed individually, but will be quite firmly in position, and need pressing. To remove those at the inner end first press on the pivot to push out one bush from one end. Then press from the other direction to extract the second. The first one should only be partially extracted so it can still hold the pivot straight whilst the second is removed.

3 Inspect the arm for signs of distortion, or bad rusting. Paint it before assembly with a rust inhibiting paint.

4 Press in the new bushes. They need good support whilst being inserted, so they are not distorted. It may be wise to get your FIAT agent to do this unless you have the equipment that makes it easy. If the job is found difficult, then damage to the bushes is likely.

5 Once the bushes have been fitted, the shims must be selected to give the correct fit with the shock absorber at the outer end of the arm. (See Fig.11.8).

6 Measure the width of the gap between the bushes in the suspension arm. This = a: see Fig.11.9.

7 Measure the width of the shock absorber across its mounting lugs. This = b.

8 Shims must go either side. Their total thickness = s.

$$s = (a-b) + 0.118 \text{ inch } (3.0 \text{ mm}).$$

The thickness, s must be divided by two, so that the shims either side are the same thickness, to within 0.020 inch (0.5 mm).

9 Reassemble the new components to the car, but do not tighten the nuts on the ends of the pivot, or through the outer end of the arm, until the weight is on the suspension, so they are clamped up with the rubber relaxed at the static laden position, then the twist in the bush is minimised. Load the car with 80 lbs (40 kg) in the boot, with two people on the rear seats.

10 After reassembly, check the camber and toe-in as described in the next Section.

11 Rear camber and toe-in

1 As the rear suspension is independant, there is no axle to ensure the back wheels are held upright and straight.

2 The wheel must be at the correct angle, otherwise the handling of the car will be upset, and tyre wear unsatisfactory.

3 Adjustment is made by varying the number of shims between the pivot at the inner end of the suspension arm and the body. (photo). If more shims are inserted into both mounting points, then the bottom of the wheel is pushed out, so camber reduced (or made more negative). If shims are taken out of the front point and transferred to the rear, the camber stays the same, but the toe-in will be increased. (See Figs.11.7 and 11.8).

4 The total toe-in can be measured by the system shown in Chapter 10. It must be ensured that this toe-in is given equally be each wheel. This can be done by looking along the toe-in setting bars when they are laid along the wheel, and seeing where

9.6 To remove the suspension arm and shock absorber, undo the clamp at the outer end of the spring, taking the load with a jack.

9.8 Take the nuts off the pivot mountings and inside the boot, off the top of the shock absorber rod.

11.3 The rear wheel toe-in and camber is adjusted by varying the number of shims behind the pivot mountings.

the bars, if extended, would touch the front wheels. Of course, it is important the front wheels are set truly straight ahead too. It will take some care to ensure this is correctly done.

5 The camber is quoted in the specification for the laden and unladen condition. This load is four persons and 88 lb (40 kg) of baggage. This is difficult to organise; and people's weights vary. Anyway, the unladen camber is easier to measure. Zero camber is within the specification. The wheel can therefore be adjusted to be upright, and the only gauge needed to measure it is a builder's plumb. Even a nut hung on a piece of string will make a crude plumb line.

6 These two adjustements have been described separately. But toe-in and camber should be done concurrently so that the number of times the suspension has to be dismantled to insert shims is minimised.

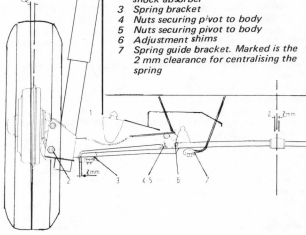

FIG.11.7 REAR SUSPENSION, SHOWING CAMBER ANGLE

1 *Bolt securing shock absorber to knuckle*
2 *Bolt securing arm to knuckle and shock absorber*
3 *Spring bracket*
4 *Nuts securing pivot to body*
5 *Nuts securing pivot to body*
6 *Adjustment shims*
7 *Spring guide bracket. Marked is the 2 mm clearance for centralising the spring*

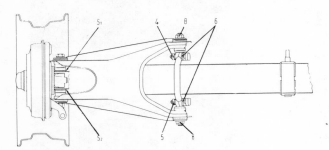

FIG.11.8   REAR   SUSPENSION ADJUSTMENT

S1 & S2 *Shims adjusting fit of shock absorber to arm*
4 & 5   *Nuts securing arm pivot to body*
6   *Shims adjusting camber and toe-in*
8   *Nuts clamping bushes on pivot*

Fig.11.9 Measurements 'a' and 'b' used in determining shims in mounting the shock absorber to the arm

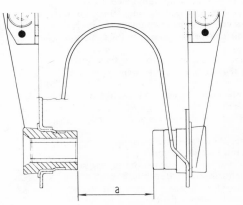

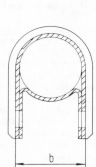

12 The rear hub

1   The rear hub bearings are sealed for life, and serviced as a complete assembly. The construction can be seen in Fig.11.5.

2   Failure of the bearings will be brought to notice by the test in Section 2. But it will also be convenient to remove the hubs when changing the rear brake shoes, as it makes the job much easier, particularly for someone who is not used to the job.

3   Jack up and remove the wheel.

4   Remove the brake drum by undoing the one bolt and the long headed wheel aligning bolt that hold it to the hub flange.

5   Prise and hammer off the bearing cap. This is soft and readily deformed if not removed carefully. It can be started by prising with a screwdriver between its flange and the hub. Make sure it is kept square, or it will jam. Hammer blows from the direction of the brake shoes can also help.

6   Undo the collared nut on the stub axle, and take off its washer. (photos).

7   Pull off the hub from the stub axle. A conventional hub puller may be needed.

8   The hub will have to be replaced if the bearings no longer move smoothly and silently, or if they have developed free play.

9   Before reassembly, smear a little grease on the stub axle. If the old hub is being reused, do not immerse it in cleaning fluid, as this will get past the bearing seals, but cannot be dried out, or new grease put in.

10 Put the hub onto the stub axle, and fit the washer, and a new collared nut.

11 Tighten the nut to a torque of 101 lbf ft (14 kg m) and lock it by staking it to the groove in the stub axle with a punch. (photo).

12 Smear a little grease over the bearing cap, and tap it gently and squarely into place. There is no need to drive it hard in to get it fully home, as long as it has gone on far enough to be secure.

13 Reassemble the drum and wheel. Then check the new hub turns freely, smoothly, and without rim rock.

13 Shock absorber checking

1   Failure comes on gradually, so sometimes loss of damping is not noticed in normal driving.

2   Leaks of fluid from the shock absorber are a sure sign of failure.

3   Loss of performance can be checked by bouncing the car.

4   Bounce vigorously on one end of the car, timing the bouncing to be in phase with the car's spring bounce. When a good movement has been set going, release the car: stop bouncing. It should go on once more only past the normal position; the next time stopping at the static height.

5   Do not replace single shock absorbers unless the failure is an unusual one after a short mileage. Replace them as pairs, front or rear.

6   To do the replacement, the suspension must be dismantled as described in Section 10 for the rear suspension.

7   The front suspension strut is very easily removed, as described in Section 3. But then the spring and shock absorber must be separated, as described in Section 4.

8   It is probable that the FIAT agent will stock the shock absorber in its outer casing. But the inside working parts are serviced as a sub-assembly. To extract them from the casing, the shock absorber should be extended. Then the gland fitting where the rod enters the casing should be unscrewed. Cleanliness is most important.

14 Wheels

1   Wheels can get damaged if a kerb is struck. During maintenance tasks spin them round and check they are not out of true by more than 1/16 in (1.5 mm).

12.5 The bearing cap must be carefully prised and tapped off to give access to the sealed bearings.

12.6 Remove the nuts and washer.

12.7 Then pull off the hub. This is replaced with its bearings as a unit.

12.11 After tightening the nut to the specified torque stake it to the indentation on the stub axle with a punch, to lock it.

2   Include in your car cleaning programme washing the backs of the wheels. These get caked with mud. Always do this before having them balanced.

3   The wheels require repainting occasionally, either after fitting new tyres, or after some two years use. Rusting is liable to start where the wheel rim is joined to the disc. If this becomes severe the wheel may fail.

4   The wheels for the estate car (wagon) are stronger than those on the saloon, being made of thicker metal. They can be recognised by a 5 mm hole on the projection to which the hub cap fixes. Estate car wheels can be used on saloons. But the saloon wheels must not be put on the estate, as this is equipped to carry a heavier load.

15 Tyres

1   The tyres are very important for safety. The tread should not be allowed to get so worn that it is near the legal limit. Not only is there fear of police action, but it is dangerous, particularly in the wet, or at speed. The recommended pressures must be used to ensure the tyres last, and to preserve the handling of the car.

2   The car has been designed for radial tyres (in fact special radial tyres at that). Use of cross ply tyres will give noise, and spoil the handling. They also last much shorter mileage. Mixing radial and cross ply tyres, even putting the cross ply on the front, should not be done on this car, as the handling will be upset.

3   Fitting tubeless tyres is best left to a tyre factor, because they have the equipment to force the tyre into position on the rim before inflating it.

4   Changing tyres round to even out wear is not recommended. Apart from the expenditure when all five tyres have to be replaced in one batch, it masks any aberrations of wear which might be happening on one wheel.

5   If the tyres nearest the kerb side, that is the left tyres in Great Britain, wear faster than the one on the opposite side, this indicates the wheels are toe-ing too much: and vice versa.

6   If the tread wear in the centre is worse than that at the edges it indicates over-inflation. And vice versa.

7   It will pay to have the wheels balanced. Wheel out-of-balance gives shaking, which is unpleasant, and causes much wear to the suspension and tyres. In bad cases it will spoil the road-holding.

8   Examine the tyres for cracks. Any cracks or bulges should be dealt with by a tyre repairer: though seldom can they be cured, as the carcase will have been damaged. Such tyres are dangerous: and illegal.

Chapter 12 Bodywork

Contents

1 General description

The body is fabricated from steel pressings welded together. At the rear the basic body shell is reinforced by boxed sections, but these are welded on, and not detachable.

2 Maintenance - bodywork exterior

1 The body is easy to keep clean due to its shape. The general condition of a car's bodywork is the one thing that significantly affects its value. Maintenance is easy but needs to be regular and particular. Neglect, particularly after minor damage, can lead quickly to further deterioration and costly repair bills. It is important also to keep watch on those parts of the car not immediately visible, for instance, the underside, inside all the wheel arches and the engine compartment.

2 The basic maintenance routine for the bodywork is washing - preferably with a lot of water from a hose. This will remove all the solids which may have stuck to the car. It is important to flush these off in such a way as to prevent grit from scratching the finish. The wheel arches and underbody need washing in the same way to remove any accumulated mud which will retain moisture and rust. Paradoxically the best time to clean the underbody and wheel arches is in wet weather when the mud is thoroughly wet and soft. In very wet weather the underbody is usually cleaned of large accumulations automatically and this is a good time for inspection.

3 Periodically it is a good idea to have the whole of the underside of the car steam cleaned, engine compartment included, so that a thorough inspection can be carried out to see what minor repairs and renovations are necessary. Steam cleaning is available at many garages and is necessary for removal of accumulations of oily grime which sometimes cakes thick in certain areas near the engine and transmission. The facilites are usually available at commercial vehicle garages but if not there are one or two excellent grease solvents available which can be brush applied. The dirt can then be hosed off.

4 After washing paintwork, wipe it with a chamois leather to give an unspotted clear finish. A coat of protective wax polish will give added protection against chemical pollutants in the air. If the paintwork sheen has dulled or oxidised, use a cleaner/polisher combination to restore the brilliance of the shine. Always check that door and ventilator opening drain holes and pipes are completely clear so that water can drain out.

5 Bright work should be treated the same way as paintwork. Windscreens can be kept clear of the smeary film which often appears if detergent is added to the water in the windscreen washer. Use a mild one such as washing up liquid. Never use any form of wax or chromium polish on glass.

3 Maintenance - body interior

1 Floor mats should be brushed or vacuum cleaned regularly to keep them free of grit. If they are badly stained remove them from the car for scrubbing or sponging and make quite sure they are dry before replacement. Seats and interior trim panels can be kept clean by a wipe over with a damp cloth. If they do become stained (which can be more apparent on light coloured upholstery) use a little liquid detergent and a soft nailbrush to scour the grime out of the grain of the material. Do not forget to keep the roof lining clean in the same way as the upholstery. When using liquid cleaners inside the car do not over-wet the surfaces being cleaned. Excessive damp could get into the seams and padded interior causing stains, offensive odours or even rot. If the inside of the car gets wet accidently, it is worthwhile taking some trouble to dry it out properly, particularly where carpets are involved. DO NOT leave oil or electric heaters inside the car for this purpose.

4 Minor body repairs

1 A car which does not suffer some minor damage to the bodywork from time to time is the exception rather than the rule. Even presuming the gatepost is never scraped or the door opened against a wall or high kerb, there is always the likelihood of gravel and grit being thrown up and chipping the surface, particularly at the lower edges of the doors and sills.

2 If the damage is merely a paint scrape which has not reached the metal base, delay is not critical, but where bare metal is exposed action must be taken immediately before rust sets in.

3 The average owner will normally keep the following 'first aid' materials available which can give a professional finish for minor jobs:

a) Matching paint in liquid form - often complete with brush attached to the lid inside. Aerosols are extravagant. Spraying from aerosols is generally less perfect than the makers would have one expect.

b) Thinners for the paint (for brush application) (like Belco).

c) Cellulose stopper (a filling compound for small paint chips).

d) Cellulose primer (a thickish grey coloured base which can be applied as an undercoat in several coats and rubbed down to give a perfect paint base).

e) Proprietary resin filler paste (for larger areas of in-filling).

f) Rust-inhibiting primer (a zinc based paint).

g) "Wet or dry" paper grade 220 and 400.

4 Where the damage is superficial (i.e. not down to the bare metal and not dented) fill the scratch or chip with stopper sufficient to smooth the area, rub down with paper and apply the matching paint.

5 Where the bodywork is scratched down to the metal, but not dented, clean the metal surface thoroughly and apply the primer (it does not need to be a rust-inhibitor if the metal is clean and dry), and then build up the scratched part to the level of the surrounding paintwork with the stopper. When the primer/stopper is hard it can be rubbed down with "wet or dry" paper. Keep applying primer and rubbing it down until no surface blemish can be felt. Then apply the colour, thinned if necessary. Apply as many coats and rub down as necessary.

6 Rub down each coat before applying the next. It is likely three coats of the colour paint will be needed to get enough thickness for polishing.

7 If the bodywork is dented, first beat out the dent as near as possible to conform with the original contour. Avoid using steel hammers - use hardwood mallets or similar and always support the back of the panel being beaten with a hardwood or metal 'dolly'. In areas where severe creasing and buckling has occurred it will be virtually impossible to reform the metal to the original shape. In such instances a decision should be made whether or not to cut out the damaged piece or attempt to re-contour over it with filler paste. In large areas where the metal panel is seriously damaged or rusted, the repair is to be considered major and it is often better to replace a panel or sill section with the appropriate part supplied as a spare. When using filler paste in largish quantities, make sure the directions are carefully followed. It is false economy to try and rush the job as the correct hardening time must be allowed between stages or before finishing. With thick application the filler usually has to be applied in layers - allowing time for each layer to harden.

8 Sometimes the original paint colour will have faded and it will be difficult to obtain an exact colour match. In such instances it is a good scheme to select a complete panel - such as a door, or boot lid, and paint the whole panel. Differences will

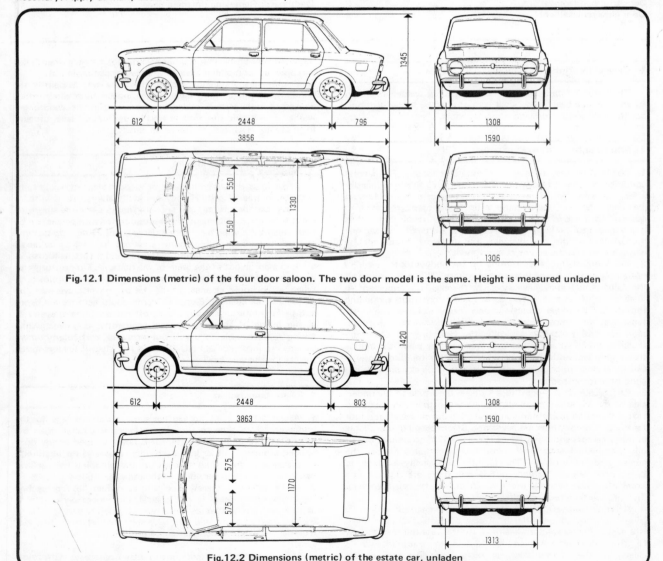

Fig.12.1 Dimensions (metric) of the four door saloon. The two door model is the same. Height is measured unladen

Fig.12.2 Dimensions (metric) of the estate car, unladen

be less apparent where there are obvious divisions between the original and repainted areas.

9 Do not expect to be able to prepare, fill, rub down and paint a section of damaged bodywork in one day and get good results. Give plenty of time for each successive application of filler and primers to harden before rubbing it down and applying the next coat.

10 Do not think that it is necessary, or even desirable to spray the paint on. To get a satisfactory result requires good equipment and experience. Yet a coachbuilder's finish is easily got by brush painting. The secret is the preparation and final polishing. All undercoats must be rubbed down with wet "wet or dry" paper of grade about 220, to remove all traces of the original paint, the edge of the filler, and the brush marks in the undercoat. Paint on a coat of top, the coloured paint, brushing it out with criss-cross brushing to get it even. Brushing type thinners must be used as paint prepared for spraying will dry too fast, and go tacky before it is brushed smoothly out. This coat of the top paint cannot be the final one as it cannot be put on thick enough without risk of weeping. Some areas will be so thin the undercoat will be visible immediately after painting. Anyway a good thickness of paint is needed for the polishing. So

allow this coat to harden for 24 hours. Then lightly rub it down with wet "wet or dry" of about 380 - 400 grade. It must be rubbed mat all over for the final coat to key in, and to get rid of brush marks. Extend the rubbing down into the surrounding original paint if patching part of a panel. Then put on the top coat. Do not take it beyond the area rubbed down. Brush the edges out thin to blend in well, leaving about 1/8 inch still mat. Take great care with this. Dry weather, without any wind to stir up dust is needed. Again, when hard after 24 hours, rub down very gently with grade 400 wet "wet or dry" just enough to take off the tops of the brush marks, and any blobs of dust. Then polish up with "rubbing compound", an abbrasive paste. Then give the paint a few days to really harden, and polish with car polish; a cleaner or restorer, not a wax. Silvo metal polish is excellent for this. Incidentally Silvo can often be used for polishing out minor scratches that have marked the paint but not got down to the undercoat.

11 If you do apply the paint by spraying, then the guidance for rubbing down is still the same. The "orange peel" effect of one coat must be removed before the next coat is applied. Also polishing will be needed after the final coat, preceded by the gentle rub to get off the top of its lumps.

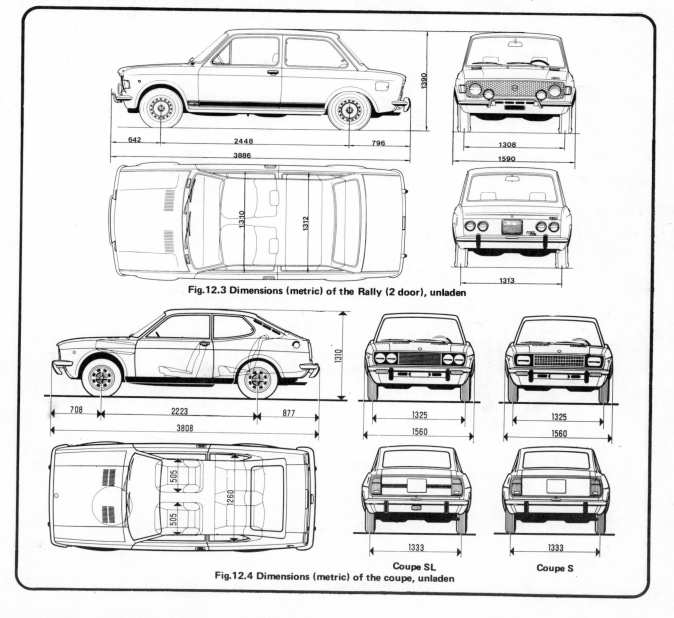

Fig.12.3 Dimensions (metric) of the Rally (2 door), unladen

Fig.12.4 Dimensions (metric) of the coupe, unladen

Coupe SL   Coupe S

5 Major body repairs

1 Where serious damage has occurred or large areas need renewal due to neglect, new sections or panels will need welding in and this is best left to professionals. If the damage is due to impact it will also be necessary to check the alignment of the body structure.

2 If a body is left misaligned it is first of all dangerous as the car will not handle properly - and secondly, uneven stresses will be imposed on the steering, engine and transmission, causing abnormal wear or complete failure. Tyre wear will also be excessive.

6 Body corrosion

1 The ultimate scrapping of a car is usually due to rust, rather than it becoming uneconomic to renew mechanical parts.

2 The rust grows from two origins: From the underneath unprotected after the paint was blasted off by the road grit: From inside, where damp has collected inside hollow body sections, without a chance to drain, and no rust protection to the metal.

3 The corrosion is particularly prone to start at welding joints in the body, as there are stresses left in after the heat of welding has cooled. These seams are also traps for the damp, and difficult to rustproof.

4 Salt on the roads in winter promotes this horror. It is hygroscopic; it attracts wet, so the car stays damp even in a garage. It is also an electrolyte when wet, so promotes violent corrosion. If the car has been used on salty roads it must be desalted as soon as possible. A couple of days rain after a thaw clears the roads, and then driving the car in the wet does this naturally. The damage is worse if a car is not used for some time after getting salty.

5 The 3,000 miles task includes the checking of the underneath for rust. It should be done just before the winter, so that the car is prepared for its ravages whilst dry and free of salt. Then it wants doing in the spring to remove the winter's damage.

6 The bodywork should be explored and all hollow sections found. Into these a rust inhibitor should be injected; aerosols like Supertrol 001, or Di-Nitrol 3B are good. Areas easier of access can be wetted by the inhibitor bought more cheaply as a liquid and applied by paint brush. An example are the insides of the doors, which can be reached by removing the panel linings. If hollow sections are sealed, it pays to drill a hole, spray in the aerosol, and then seal with the underneath paint smeared over the hole. Rust traps that need drain holes are the fixings for the front bolts for the anti-roll bar at the very front of the car.

7 The underneath needs painting, and where abraded by grit flung up by the wheels, this must be one of the special thick resilient paints. "Adup" bronze super seal is recommended. It is compatible with the Supertrol 001 and Di-Nitrol 33B inhibitors. So if these are put on first the two between them make a good job in getting into corners. The "Adup" underneath paint can be used as ordinary paint on sheltered areas. On those showered by grit from the wheels, thick layers need to be applied. At the mudguards the underneath paint wants to be brought nearly round the edges so that these are protected, the corners being particularly vulnerable.

7 Door rattles - tracing and rectification

Door rattles are due either to loose hinges, worn or maladjusted catches, or loose components inside the door. Loose hinges can be detected by opening the door and trying to lift it. Any play will be felt. Worn or badly adjusted catches can be found by pushing and pulling on the outside handle when the door is closed. Once again any play will be felt. To check the window mechanism open the door and shake it with the window first open and then closed.

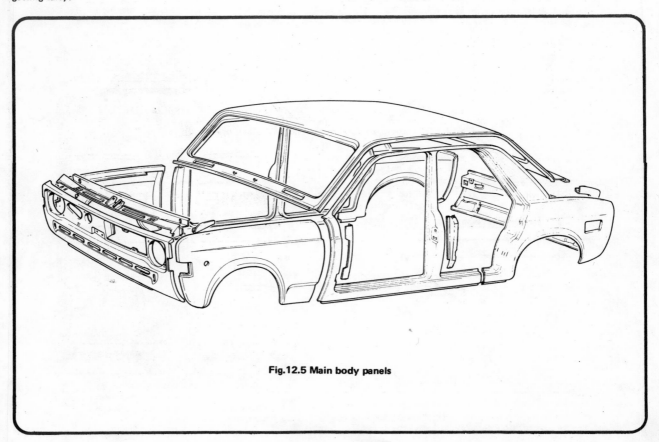

Fig.12.5 Main body panels

8 Door trim pad removal

1 Unscrew the two screws holding the door arm rest.
2 Prise off the escutcheon round the interior door handle. This is best done with two screwdrivers to get a straight pull. (photos).
3 Remove the window winder. With one hand push the winder surrounding escutcheon towards the door so the spring clip holding the handle to the shaft is visible. Insert a thin screwdriver to push out the clip. Normally the clip will have been inserted in such a way that this push must come from the axis of the handle.
4 Carefully prise out the trim pad from the door, starting at the bottom. Insert a screwdriver close to a clip. Then pull out the next clip.
5 When refitting everything, put the winder handle halfway on its shaft. Then put the spring clip in position, in as far as it will go. Then push the handle fully home onto its shaft, and the clip will spring into its groove.

9 Door glass replacement

1 Remove the trim pad as described in the previous Section.
2 Remove the waterproof plastic sheet over the openings in the door panel.
3 Wind the window to the 2/3 open position. Get an assistant to hold the glass.
4 Undo all the bolts holding the winder mechanism to the inside door panel, and the glass to the winder mechanism.
5 Thread the winder mechanism out of the door.
6 Lower the glass out of its channel, through the aperture at the bottom of the inside panel.
7 One cause of the window winding mechanism failing is that the bracket to the glass comes unglued. This type of glueing is covered in the next paragraphs on the vent windows.
8 The vent windows can be taken out complete with their mountings and frame. The trim around the window opening in the door must be removed first. Also the trim on the door must come off to give access to the window channel, Then undo the two screws that hold the vent frame to the front of door. Tilt the frame, and lift it out.
9 The vent glasses are serviced for spares with the pivots already glued on. But if any of the door glasses need re-glueing then the special adhesives must be obtained. A number of car makers use gluing, so some glue should be available locally, and the glue maker's instructions should be followed. FIAT's own instructions are as follows. Clean the bracket and the glass with petrol (gas) to remove all traces of old glue. Apply a layer of 'Locquic 312 NF' over the surfaces to be glued. Wait a few minutes, then spread 'Loctite Cat. 33' on the parts, and press together lightly. The window may be refitted after 10 minutes.
10 For the rear doors, the glass is then lowered into the door, turned edge uppermost, and thne lifted out through the window opening in the door.

10 Door locks

1 To gain access to the door locks, remove the trim panel as described in Section 8.
2 Wind the window up. The lock can then be reached through the access hole in the inner panel.
3 When any lock is removed, paint its hole, and use rust preventer, so the paint will not start to peel from the locks.
4 See the next Section for adjustment.

11 Door adjustment

1 The door position is adjustable at the hinges and the striker at the lock by the use of mounting points with large holes. The

8.1 Two screws hold the arm rest.

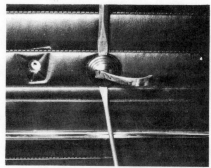

8.2 Prise off the escutcheon: the lever is not removed.

8.3 The spring clip can be pushed out with a long thin screwdriver.

8.4 Prise the trim close to the spring clips so it does not bend much.

9.6 After removing the winder mechanism the glass comes out of the bottom opening of the front door.

9.7 The winder bracket is glued to the glass.

10.2 With the trim off the door, and the window shut, the lock can be reached.

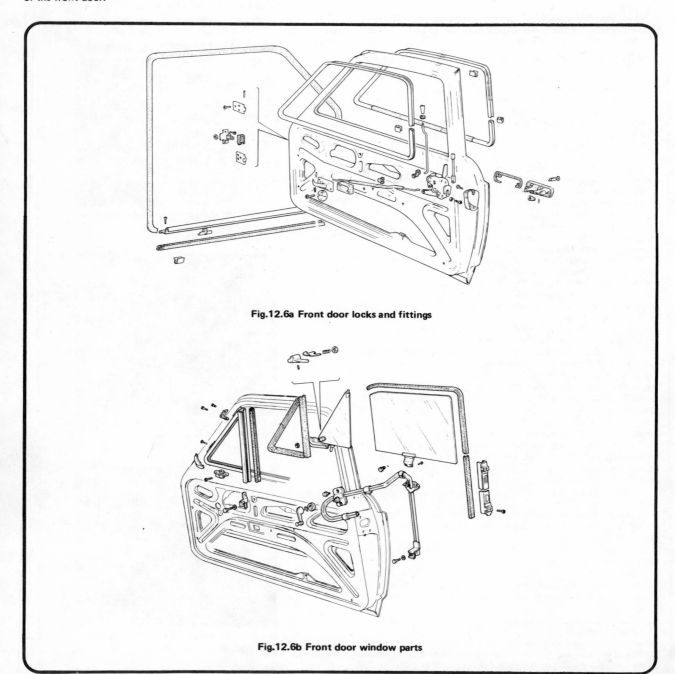

Fig.12.6a Front door locks and fittings

Fig.12.6b Front door window parts

hinge attachment points to the body have adjustment, as does the striker, achieved by slackening their fixing screws, moving them, and retightening.

2 Before making any adjustment mark round the edge of the striker, or hinge, with pencil, so that the original position and the amount moved can be seen.

3 It should not be necessary to move the hinge. The striker may need to be moved in, or up, to compensate for wear in the lock. After long periods, the hinges wear, so more weight is taken by the striker. This makes the door difficult to close. But the striker must not be lowered, or the bottom of the door will rub on the body.

4 The hinges should be oiled regularly. The key locks to the doors should also be oiled, particularly in winter to keep out the damp, and prevent them freezing.

12 Windscreen and rear window

1 The windscreen and rear window glasses are glued in place. Fitting them requires special sealing glue, it cannot be done quickly, and is liable to make a.mess of glass and the car's paint if not done properly.
2 Other makes of car have glued windscreens, so body builders locally will have glues and expertise, should it be impossible to get to a FIAT agent.
3 Most of these glues take 24 hours to cure, and the glass and window frame need lengthy preparation. If on a long journey a new screen cannot be put in quickly as can be done for one mounted in rubber. It is recommended an emergency plastic screen is carried if the car is fitted with a toughened glass screen. Whether the glass is toughened or laminated (it will be the latter in North America) can be discovered from the makers markings on the glass. Toughened will also show coloured rings when viewed from outside at an acute angle.

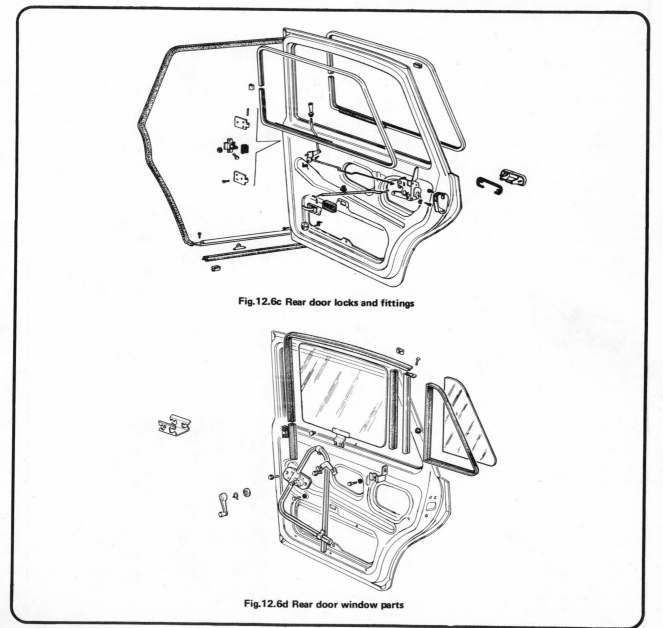

Fig.12.6c Rear door locks and fittings

Fig.12.6d Rear door window parts

13 Bonnet (hood) removal

1 Because the bonnet is hinged at the front, it gets in the way when working on the engine. Usually FIAT mechanics are so used to the cars, know their way about so well, and have the benefit of special tools, they do not remove the bonnet even when taking out the engine. However its removal is recommended for such jobs as taking off the cylinder head, or taking out the engine, as everything can be reached more easily, and seen better, so time is saved in the end.

2 On the Coupe, the hinges can only be reached from in front, so the front grille must be removed. First take out the screws holding the centre section, and take this off. Then unplug the wires to the back of the headlamps. Take out the screws holding the headlamp mounting plates, and remove the assemblies.

3 On the saloon or estate the hinges can be reached from in front after simply taking off the grille, or from behind, from the engine side. But the radiator obstructs the left hand one. (photo). If nothing else is being taken off, and only the bonnet needs to be removed for its own sake, then it is quickest to remove the front grille, by undoing its screws. In this case, unlike the Coupe, the headlamps need not be touched. However usually the bonnet will only be taken off when the engine is being dismantled, the coolant drained, and the radiator hoses disconnected. It then becomes more satisfactory to remove the radiator instead. By doing this the opportunity can be taken to give the latter a good clean out, to clean around its mountings, and it also gives more room in the engine compartment. The additional work after draining the coolant and undoing the radiator hoses at the thermostat end is as follows. Undo the pipe to the expansion tank at the radiator filler neck, and unclip it from the side of the radiator. Unplug the blue radiator wire from the relay under the battery tray, and undo the black earthing wire from its screwed terminal. Unplug the two wires from the sender unit for the fan relay from the bottom of the radiator. Take off the two bolts holding the radiator at the top, and lift it up out of its bottom rubber mounting.

4 Mark the fore and aft positions of the hinges on the body front panel, with pencil. Unclip the bonnet stay. Undo the hinge bolts.

5 Unclip the bonnet stay, on the saloon/estate pushing in the bottom ends of the clip.

6 Undo the hinge bolts whilst an assistant holds the bonnet.

7 Tip the top of the bonnet towards the windscreen, and lift it up, so the hinges can come clear of their mountings. Put the bonnet where it cannot get scratched.

8 Refitting the bonnet is the reverse. Be sure to get the hinges back in the same position so the bonnet lines up with the body. Close the bonnet gently, in case it is not straight, to check it fits properly into its opening. If necessary slacken the hinges and reposition it. If it is too far to the right, difficulty may be experienced with closing it, to get the catch to engage.

14 Emergency bonnet opening

1 If the bonnet release handle, cable, or the catch itself, should jam or break, the bonnet must be undone from outside.

2 On no account prise at the edge of the bonnet, or it will be damaged in a place very difficult to straighten again.

3 Take off the front grille. Undo the bonnet hinges as described in the previous Section.

4 Lift up the front of the bonnet a short way to free the hinges, and to allow a firm grip to be taken.

5 Pull the bonnet forwards hard. The catch is a pin that lies fore and aft in the bonnet lock, and it can be pulled straight out forwards.

13.2 On the Coupe the centre grille and then the headlamps in their mounts come off to undo the bonnet hinges.

13.3 On the Saloon the hinges can be reached either way: here the radiator is off.

16.4 Once the instrument panel is pulled forward enough to disconnect the speedometer cable.

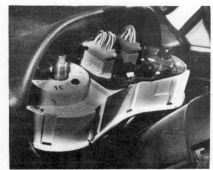

16.5 it can be turned over to get at the wiring plugs.

15 Emergency boot opening

1   If the boot lock fails or jams shut, access must be got to the inside to unbolt the catch.
2   Inside the car lift and pull the back rest of the rear seat, to release it from its fastenings. It is then possible to reach past the body reinforcing struts to the catch. Undoing the bolts will be easier if using a socket spanner on a long extension.

16 Dashboard: removing the instrument panel

1   The panel in front of the driver that carries the instruments is easily removed.
2   Remove the fixing screw just below the centre of the face of the panel.
3   Push the panel down slightly to disengage two little hooks at the top.
4   From the engine compartment push the speedometer cable, after releasing it from its clip, through the scuttle (fire wall) till inside the car the instruments panel can be pulled out far enough to reach behind, to undo the speedometer cable from the

instrument.
5   Turn the panel over, till the wiring at the back is uppermost. Unplug the wiring. (photo).
6   When refitting the panel make sure the speedometer cable is pulled gently from the engine compartment so that it adopts a fair curve.

17 Dashboard: removal of the main panel

1   This is a complex task, and should be avoided if possible.
2   Remove the instrument panel as described in the previous Section.
3   Remove the steering column side covers.
4   Take out its mounting screws and remove the parcel shelf below the dash.
5   Disconnect the pipes from the windscreen washer pump.
6   Remove the seven screws along the bottom edge of the dash.
7   In the engine compartment remove the nuts from the three studs from the dash through the scuttle, just below the bottom of the windscreen.
8   Disconnect the wires from the light switches on the dash.
9   Remove the dashboard complete.

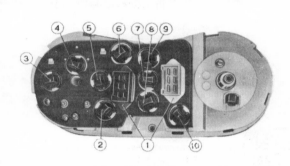

FIG.12.7a DETAILS OF THE REAR OF THE INSTRUMENT PANEL

1 Electric connectors	6 Instrument cluster light
2 Low fuel warning light	7 Parking light indicator
3 No-charge warning light	8 High beam indicator
4 Heat warning light	9 Direction signal repeater light
5 Low oil pressure warning light	10 Instrument panel light

FIG.12.7b DETAILS OF THE INSTRUMENT PANEL

1 Speedometer	(red)
2 Mileage recorder	7 Heat indicator (red)
3 Parking light indicator (green)	8 Screw, attaching instrument panel to dashboard
4 Direction signal repeater light (green)	9 Low fuel indicator (red)
5 High beam indicator (blue)	10 Fuel gauge
6 Low oil pressure indicator	11 No-charge indicator (red)

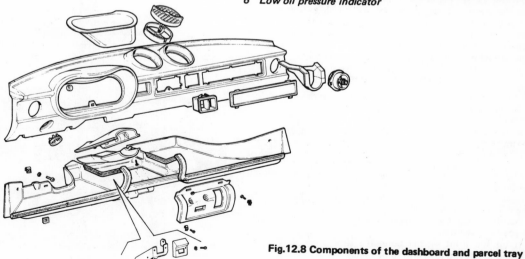

Fig.12.8 Components of the dashboard and parcel tray

FIG.12.9 SALOON/ESTATE CAR DASHBOARD (1971 EUROPEAN VERSION)

1   Adjustable outlets for air to car interior
2   Headlight selector switch
3   Direction signal switch
4   Instrument panel
5   Horn button
6   Windshield wiper switch, three-position
7   Outer lighting master switch
8   Instrument light switch
9   Front ash tray
10 Adjustable outlets for air admission into car or against windscreen
11 Choke control knob
12 Hand throttle control
13 Radio recess ornament cover
14 Utility shelf under instrument panel
15 Outside air shutter control lever
16 Control lever for hot water valve from engine to heater
17 Heater fan switch, three position
18 Air admission shutter to passenger compartment
19 Gear lever
20 Parking brake lever
21 Accelerator pedal
22 Brake pedal
23 Clutch pedal
24 Ignition and starting switch, also energizing warning lights circuits
25 Fuse box
26 Windscreen washer pump
27 Bonnet release lever

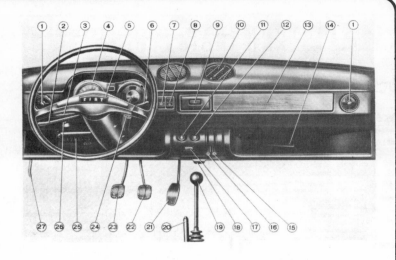

FIG.12.10 RALLY DASHBOARD (1972 EUROPEAN VERSION)

1   Swivel outlets
2   Headlight switch lever
3   Direction indicator control lever
4   Horn button
5   Instrument panel
6   Wiper control
7   Outside lighting switch
8   Instruments lighting switch
9   Swivel outlets
10 Water thermometer
11 Oil pressure gauge
12 Choke knob
13 Hand throttle knob
14 Hot air control lever
15 Fresh air control lever
16 Radio housing blanking panel
17 Utility shelf
18 Air outlet shutter
19 Gear lever
20 Front ash tray
21 Hand brake lever
22 Accelerator pedal
23 Three-position heater fan switch
24 Brake pedal
25 Clutch pedal
26 Ignition lock switch also activating warning and lights and starting circuits
27 Fusebox
28 Windscreen washer pump control
29 Parcel shelf
30 Hood catch release lever

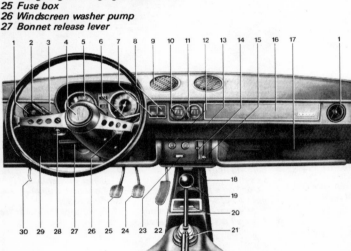

FIG.12.11 COUPE DASHBOARD (1972 EUROPEAN VERSION)

1   Water temperature gauge
2   Headlamp lever
3   Direction indicator lever
4   Instrument panel
5   Horn button
6   Ignition switch
7   Windscreen wiper lever
8   Fuel gauge and warning light
9   Choke knob
10 Hand throttle
11 Blower switch
12 Lighting switch
13 Panel light switch
14 Ashtray
15 Fascia vents
16 Courtesy light/switch
17 Ventilation control
18 Heating control
19 Top shelf
20 Radio recess cover
21 Bonnet release lever
22 Windscreen washer control
23 Fuse unit
24 Clutch pedal
25 Brake pedal
26 Accelerator pedal
27 Heater flap
28 Gear lever
29 Handbrake lever
30 Floor tray
31 Parcel shelf
32 Map pocket

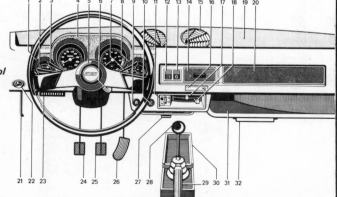

Fig.12.13 1973 North American sedan/wagon dashboard — note better labelling of controls

Fig.12.14 1973 European Rally dashboard

Fig.12.12 1973 European saloon/estate dashboard — note minor changes of steering wheel design

Fig.12.15 1973 European coupe SL dashboard

Fig.12.16 1973 North American coupe SL dashboard

Metric conversion tables

Inches	Decimals	Millimetres	Millimetres to Inches		Inches to Millimetres	
			mm	Inches	Inches	mm
1/64	0.015625	0.3969	0.01	0.00039	0.001	0.0254
1/32	0.03125	0.7937	0.02	0.00079	0.002	0.0508
3/64	0.046875	1.1906	0.03	0.00118	0.003	0.0762
1/16	0.0625	1.5875	0.04	0.00157	0.004	0.1016
5/64	0.078125	1.9844	0.05	0.00197	0.005	0.1270
3/32	0.09375	2.3812	0.06	0.00236	0.006	0.1524
7/64	0.109375	2.7781	0.07	0.00276	0.007	0.1778
1/8	0.125	3.1750	0.08	0.00315	0.008	0.2032
9/64	0.140625	3.5719	0.09	0.00354	0.009	0.2286
5/32	0.15625	3.9687	0.1	0.00394	0.01	0.254
11/64	0.171875	4.3656	0.2	0.00787	0.02	0.508
3/16	0.1875	4.7625	0.3	0.01181	0.03	0.762
13/64	0.203125	5.1594	0.4	0.01575	0.04	1.016
7/32	0.21875	5.5562	0.5	0.01969	0.05	1.270
15/64	0.234375	5.9531	0.6	0.02362	0.06	1.524
1/4	0.25	6.3500	0.7	0.02756	0.07	1.778
17/64	0.265625	6.7469	0.8	0.03150	0.08	2.032
9/32	0.28125	7.1437	0.9	0.03543	0.09	2.286
19/64	0.296875	7.5406	1	0.03937	0.1	2.54
5/16	0.3125	7.9375	2	0.07874	0.2	5.08
21/64	0.328125	8.3344	3	0.11811	0.3	7.62
11/32	0.34375	8.7312	4	0.15748	0.4	10.16
23/64	0.359375	9.1281	5	0.19685	0.5	12.70
3/8	0.375	9.5250	6	0.23622	0.6	15.24
25/64	0.390625	9.9219	7	0.27559	0.7	17.78
13/32	0.40625	10.3187	8	0.31496	0.8	20.32
27/64	0.421875	10.7156	9	0.35433	0.9	22.86
7/16	0.4375	11.1125	10	0.39370	1	25.4
29/64	0.453125	11.5094	11	0.43307	2	50.8
15/32	0.46875	11.9062	12	0.47244	3	76.2
31/64	0.484375	12.3031	13	0.51181	4	101.6
1/2	0.5	12.7000	14	0.55118	5	127.0
33/64	0.515625	13.0969	15	0.59055	6	152.4
17/32	0.53125	13.4937	16	0.62992	7	177.8
35/64	0.546875	13.8906	17	0.66929	8	203.2
9/16	0.5625	14.2875	18	0.70866	9	228.6
37/64	0.578125	14.6844	19	0.74803	10	254.0
19/32	0.59375	15.0812	20	0.78740	11	279.4
39/64	0.609375	15.4781	21	0.82677	12	304.8
5/8	0.625	15.8750	22	0.86614	13	330.2
41/64	0.640625	16.2719	23	0.90551	14	355.6
21/32	0.65625	16.6687	24	0.94488	15	381.0
43/64	0.671875	17.0656	25	0.98425	16	406.4
11/16	0.6875	17.4625	26	1.02362	17	431.8
45/64	0.703125	17.8594	27	1.06299	18	457.2
23/32	0.71875	18.2562	28	1.10236	19	482.6
47/64	0.734375	18.6531	29	1.14173	20	508.0
3/4	0.75	19.0500	30	1.18110	21	533.4
49/64	0.765625	19.4469	31	1.22047	22	558.8
25/32	0.78125	19.8437	32	1.25984	23	584.2
51/64	0.796875	20.2406	33	1.29921	24	609.6
13/16	0.8125	20.6375	34	1.33858	25	635.0
53/64	0.828125	21.0344	35	1.37795	26	660.4
27/32	0.84375	21.4312	36	1.41732	27	685.8
55/64	0.859375	21.8281	37	1.4567	28	711.2
7/8	0.875	22.2250	38	1.4961	29	736.6
57/64	0.890625	22.6219	39	1.5354	30	762.0
29/32	0.90625	23.0187	40	1.5748	31	787.4
59/64	0.921875	23.4156	41	1.6142	32	812.8
15/16	0.9375	23.8125	42	1.6535	33	838.2
61/64	0.953125	24.2094	43	1.6929	34	863.6
31/32	0.96875	24.6062	44	1.7323	35	889.0
63/64	0.984375	25.0031	45	1.7717	36	914.4

1   Imperial gallon = 8 Imp pints = 1.16 US gallons = 277.42 cu in = 4.5459 litres

1   US gallon = 4 US quarts = 0.862 Imp gallon = 231 cu in = 3.785 litres

1   Litre = 0.2199 Imp gallon = 0.2642 US gallon = 61.0253 cu in = 1000 cc

Miles to Kilometres		Kilometres to Miles	
1	1.61	1	0.62
2	3.22	2	1.24
3	4.83	3	1.86
4	6.44	4	2.49
5	8.05	5	3.11
6	9.66	6	3.73
7	11.27	7	4.35
8	12.88	8	4.97
9	14.48	9	5.59
10	16.09	10	6.21
20	32.19	20	12.43
30	48.28	30	18.64
40	64.37	40	24.85
50	80.47	50	31.07
60	96.56	60	37.28
70	112.65	70	43.50
80	128.75	80	49.71
90	144.84	90	55.92
100	160.93	100	62.14

lb f ft to Kg f m		Kg f m to lb f ft		lb f/in^2 : Kg f/cm^2		Kg f/cm^2 : lb f/in^2	
1	0.138	1	7.233	1	0.07	1	14.22
2	0.276	2	14.466	2	0.14	2	28.50
3	0.414	3	21.699	3	0.21	3	42.67
4	0.553	4	28.932	4	0.28	4	56.89
5	0.691	5	36.165	5	0.35	5	71.12
6	0.829	6	43.398	6	0.42	6	85.34
7	0.967	7	50.631	7	0.49	7	99.56
8	1.106	8	57.864	8	0.56	8	113.79
9	1.244	9	65.097	9	0.63	9	128.00
10	1.382	10	72.330	10	0.70	10	142.23
20	2.765	20	144.660	20	1.41	20	284.47
30	4.147	30	216.990	30	2.11	30	426.70

Index

Printed by
J. H. HAYNES & Co. Ltd
Sparkford Yeovil Somerset
ENGLAND